Zi Wang
The Discursive Construction of Hierarchy in Japanese Society

Contributions to the Sociology of Language

___

Edited by
Ofelia García
Francis M. Hult

Founding editor
Joshua A. Fishman

Volume 116

Zi Wang

The Discursive Construction of Hierarchy in Japanese Society

—

An Ethnographic Study of Secondary School Clubs

ISBN 978-1-5015-2731-9
e-ISBN (PDF) 978-1-5015-1487-6
e-ISBN (EPUB) 978-1-5015-1459-3
ISSN 1861-0676

Library of Congress Control Number: 2020937831

Bibliographic information published by the Deutsche Nationalbibliothek
The Deutsche Nationalbibliothek lists this publication in the Deutsche Nationalbibliografie; detailed bibliographic data are available on the Internet at http://dnb.dnb.de.

© 2022 Walter de Gruyter Inc., Boston/Berlin
This volume is text- and page-identical with the hardback published in 2020.
Cover image: sculpies/shutterstock
Typesetting: Integra Software Services Pvt. Ltd.
Printing and binding: CPI books GmbH, Leck

www.degruyter.com

To my grandmother, with love.

Contents

1	**Introduction: Contextualising *jouge kankei* —— 1**	
1.1	Getting to know the hierarchical social world —— 1	
1.1.1	Research on *jouge kankei* —— 3	
1.2	Studying *jouge kankei*: Linguistic and discursive constitution of hierarchy —— 6	
1.2.1	The phase-one study —— 6	
1.3	*Jouge kankei* in secondary school extra-curricular clubs: Socialisation in and through language and discourse —— 8	
1.3.1	Language socialisation —— 8	
1.3.2	From language to discourse and discursive practices —— 13	
1.3.3	Operationalisation of discourse —— 15	
1.3.4	An ethnographic study of extra-curricular clubs —— 18	
1.4	Organisation of the book —— 26	
2	**Studying the discursive construction of *jouge kankei* in secondary school clubs —— 29**	
2.1	The Japanese secondary education —— 29	
2.1.1	Types of secondary schools and the focus on schools with six-year programmes —— 32	
2.2	Club life and social life: Early-stage *jouge kankei* socialisation in and through discourse in secondary school clubs —— 34	
2.2.1	Type of clubs and the main focus of this study —— 42	
2.3	Introducing the two schools —— 45	
2.4	The three student clubs —— 47	
2.5	Social situations as focus of data collection —— 54	
2.6	Summary of chapter —— 55	
3	**Ideologies, power, text, and discourse: *Bukatsudou* as sites of learning and socialisation in language and discourse —— 57**	
3.1	First socially meaningful experience of *jouge kankei* —— 58	
3.2	How are actors socialised into *jouge kankei*? —— 61	
3.2.1	New members' first encounter with hierarchical orders: Interactions and rituals in clubs —— 61	
3.2.2	Texts as basis and building blocks of *jouge kankei*: The specific function of guidebooks/rule books and seniors' right to enforce rules —— 64	

3.2.3	Macro Discourses as new ways of thinking about the social world: Guidance sessions, meetings, and the "*senpai* know best" approach to create a "common-sense" knowledge —— 70	
3.2.4	Observing the environment: Who does what? —— 75	
3.2.5	Efforts, mistakes, reprimands, corrections —— 78	
3.3	Seniors' influence on the degree of manifestation of *jougei kankei* in a club and impact on juniors —— 81	
3.4	Summary of chapter: The textual constitution of *jouge kankei* and socialisation process —— 84	

4　Address terms, honorific word choices, and the construction of hierarchy —— 85

4.1	Terms of address (ToA): Cognition, legitimisation, and knowledge —— 85
4.1.1	Analysing ToA: Theoretical frameworks and previous studies —— 87
4.1.2	ToA in Japanese contexts —— 90
4.2	ToA in Japanese secondary school clubs —— 93
4.2.1	Seniors to juniors —— 95
4.2.2	Juniors to seniors —— 96
4.2.3	Between equals —— 100
4.3	Similarities and differences of ToA use in secondary school clubs: At the intersection of social roles and gender —— 101
4.3.1	Different in manifestation, similar in nature —— 102
4.4	When deviant cases occur: The impossibility of ToA transition in school clubs —— 104
4.5	Summary of chapter: ToA maintain, strengthen, and legitimise hierarchy —— 108

5　The linguistic constitution of *jouge kankei*: Ideology in micro-level discourse and epistemic orders —— 111

5.1	Ideology and language —— 112
5.1.1	Forming the language-ideology-power nexus in discourse: Power, power semantic, power in and behind discourse —— 114
5.2	Politeness, honorifics, and ideology: Theories and conceptual links —— 117
5.3	Ideology and honorifics: The cases of exalting words and "polite" forms of talk —— 123
5.3.1	Exalting words —— 123
5.3.2	"Polite" forms of talk —— 125

5.4		Plain and *desu/masu* forms of talk and their constitution of *senpai* and *kouhai* identities and interpersonal relations —— 127
5.4.1		Active identity construction with the addressee honorific *desu/masu* form —— 128
5.5		Language-ideology-power and the epistemic order in discourse —— 140
5.5.1		When age and length of service do not correspond —— 143
5.6		Deviation from the conventions —— 145
5.7		Summary of chapter —— 147
6		**Space, signs, symbols, and objects used in conjunction with discourse —— 151**
6.1		An analytical framework for the use of space —— 152
6.2		The allocation and use of space during lunchtime on Sundays —— 153
6.3		Encoding, experiencing, and appropriating meanings in space in daily behaviour —— 158
6.3.1		Entering and leaving the music room —— 158
6.3.2		Reserved territories for seniors —— 159
6.3.3		Learning process of juniors —— 160
6.4		Language and spatial segregation based on grades —— 162
6.5		The use of signs and symbols as discursive practice: The case of school uniforms —— 164
6.5.1		Tokyo Daiichi Girls' Junior and Senior High School uniform: Marked from head to toe —— 165
6.5.2		Tokyo Daini Boys' Junior and Senior High School uniform: More subtle and less-nuanced markings —— 167
6.5.3		Implications of such signs, symbols and objects —— 169
6.6		Summary of chapter —— 171
7		***Jouge kankei*: Discursive construction, characteristics, implications and future outlook —— 173**
7.1		Summary of findings and answers to research questions —— 173
7.2		Implications across time and space in secondary school *bukatsudou* —— 175
7.2.1		Further implications on the connection of *jouge kankei* between secondary school and adult contexts —— 178
7.3		Limitations, suggestions, and outlook —— 184

Appendix 1: Junior High School Curriculum Guidelines, Published by the Ministry of Education, Culture, Sports, Science and Technology (MEXT) —— 189

Appendix 2: Guidelines for codes of conduct in extra-curricular club —— 191

Appendix 3: On the Romanisation of Japanese —— 199

Appendix 4: Glossary of Japanese Terms —— 201

Appendix 5: List of Standard Abbreviations used according to the Leipzig Glossing Rules —— 203

References —— 205

Index —— 213

1 Introduction: Contextualising *jouge kankei*

1.1 Getting to know the hierarchical social world

On a clear afternoon in May 2016, a group of 50 new junior high students in Tokyo Daiichi Junior and Senior High School's Choir joined in for their first ever practice upon entering secondary school. The seniors in the choir prepared an orientation session at the beginning to facilitate their integration into the daily choir life. The group of new juniors seemed overwhelmed by the sheer size of the music room (able to accommodate up to 150 people) and did not know how to organise themselves. Yamazawa,[1] the acting president, shouted at the group and asked them to form a neat circle around the three senior members, with their bags neatly placed in front of their feet, and standing in attention. The juniors followed this instruction and started to shuffle while mumbling to each other, at which point Yamazawa and the seniors showed dissatisfaction and shouted "*koko wa mou shougakkou jyanai*, mazu wa *akarui henji 'hai' wo shite kudasai*"[2] (this is no longer primary school, please first give us a loud and clear response with '*hai*'). Puzzled, the juniors looked at each other and started talking among themselves. It was only when Yamazawa repeated her words sternly again that the junior new members stopped talking and attempted a not-so-unified *hai* to Yamazawa's order. The seniors then proceeded to explaining the daily routines and what is expected of them: since these new members just joined the choir, they should start and conclude each practice session with preparing and cleaning up the music room. During practice, juniors should not talk to each other, go to the restroom, or drink water unless permission is granted by a senior, and juniors should behave properly in the presence of seniors by politely greeting them, replying them when addressed, and obeying what they say. When the brief session was over, Yamazawa told the new members to pack up, leave the room, and follow her to an empty classroom to complete some administrative forms. Just as they turned around and were about to leave, the group of three seniors reminded them that it is an important etiquette that juniors hold the doors and let seniors

---

[1] All names are aliased.
[2] Throughout this book, a modified version of the Hepburn system is used in the romanisation of Japanese. It is for this reason that some terms are Romanised slightly differently in this work as compared to elsewhere. Refer to appendix 3.

https://doi.org/10.1515/9781501514876-001

leave first. At this point, the juniors figured that this was another order that they simply have to obey, and so they did.[3]

In the above scene observed in the choir of a secondary school in Tokyo, a group of new junior high school students were trying to come to terms with something unanticipated during their first choir practice at the beginning of their secondary school stint. Rather than focussing on music and singing, senior students in the choir first taught them specific ways to behave (always reply and greet seniors, only leave the room after seniors) and obligations to fulfil (replying promptly to seniors, cleaning duties). Yamazawa's words reminded them that, since the new members were no longer in primary school, they ought to learn to make sense of this hitherto unfamiliar social world of roles, duties, and obligations. Why, then, does a biological difference in age carry identity and behavioural consequences that define who they are and posit what they ought to do in a group activity? In effect, the afore-mentioned new students were stepping into the world of hierarchy, known as *jouge kankei* (literally higher-lower relations, see sub-section 1.1.1) that defines social relations in Japanese group dynamics. Despite the ubiquitous presence of *jouge kankei* in almost every domain of social life, extant literature has taken its existence largely for granted. As a result, current scholarship only reveals the existence of this hierarchy and the basic rule of thumb for acceptable behaviour: a *kouhai* (subordinate) ought to respect and obey her/his *senpai* (superior). This book engages the topic of *jouge kankei* in Japanese society with a critical empirical examination of its constituent nature, as well as ways in which members of the Japanese social world acquire comprehensive knowledge of it. In what follows, I define this unique hierarchy in Japanese social organisation and review key works that mentioned it. Next, I show the ways in which *jouge kankei* could be approached as an object of inquiry, taking into consideration the goals of this volume. I present my multi-stage empirical research and demonstrate how initial findings of the first fieldwork phase shaped the focus and methodology of my research and how this work fits in the broader language socialisation scholarship. As I review the state of the art in language socialisation research (both in general and in Japan), I explicate contributions of this book to the existing body of literature, from the vantage point of discourse analysis. In addition, the appropriate research site (secondary schools) and methods (a range of qualitative methods) to achieve the aims of this work will also be presented.

---

[3] Vignette 1.1. Scenes of new junior high students' (12–13 years old) first session in a secondary school choir practice. Observed on 16.05.2016.

1.1.1 Research on *jouge kankei*

Jouge kankei is a compound term that is made up of two constitutive elements: *jouge* (up-down) and *kankei* (relationship). According to the Digital Online Dictionary of the Japanese Language, *jouge kankei* means "the relationship between persons of higher and lower positions based on rank, status, age, etc."[4] This was first brought to the attention of global scholarship through a series of essayistic works on Japanese social organisation, beginning with Nakane Chie, who affirmed that the seniority-based *jouge kankei* is the central tenet of a vertically organised hierarchy in Japanese society (Nakane 1970). This is manifested in the form of interpersonal relations that constitute a group, and within a group, "one-to-one relationship between two individuals of unequal ranks, i.e., superior and subordinate" (Nakane 1972: 575). Contrasting this to social organisations in other societies, Nakane highlighted the particularity of the Japanese social organisation by arguing that:

> [T]he position of the individual in relation to his immediate superior and inferior is fixed on his entry into the group. Although in the formal organization of an institution individuals may be shifted from one section to another, so that combinations of particular individuals may change, in the informal order who is ahead and who is behind is clearly perceived by those concerned. (Nakane 1972: 575)

Nakane posits that the core of interpersonal relations and the most characteristic feature of Japanese social organisation is a vertical principle of one-to-one relationship between two individuals of unequal ranks, that is, a superior and a subordinate. This higher-lower relationship forms not only the basis of Japanese social structure, but is also persistent across time and context (Nakane 1970). Along the hierarchical orders of *jouge kankei*, a Japanese person's world, according to Nakane, is divided into the three categories of *senpai*, *kouhai*, and *douryou* ("colleagues"), and the corresponding position of an individual along this hierarchical ladder is in turn fixed upon the individual's entry into the group or organisation (Nakane 1970). In other words, these "persistent modes of interpersonal relationship" (Nakane 1972: 575) that defy changing social circumstances make Japanese social organisation peculiar. In the afore-mentioned choir scene, the type of relationship between the new members (*kouhai*, subordinates) and the group led by Yamazawa (*senpai*, superiors) was clearly defined by their respective point of entry into the group (in this case also inextricably linked to age), just as what Nakane (1970) described. As its name suggests, the *senpai* in a *jouge*

---

4 Taken from the Digital Japanese Dictionary: http://dictionary.goo.ne.jp. All translations are mine unless otherwise stated.

kankei takes the position of a superior/senior, as someone who is in front (*sen*) and leads, whereas a *kouhai* occupies the position of a subordinate/junior, as someone who is behind (*kou*) and who follows (Rohlen 1983).

Since Nakane's revelatory writing on Japanese social organisation in 1970, numerous works on various aspects of the vertical hierarchy in Japanese society have been published (Hendry 1995; Kevenhörster, Pascha and Shire 2010; Mendenhall and Oddou 1986; Nishiyama 2009; Sugimoto 2014). However, the vast majority have either taken the very topic of hierarchy for granted or simply mentioned its existence in passing. In one work that sought to translate and define it, Bestor (1989) used "higher-lower relationship" and offered the following description:

> Relationships between kohai and senpai – between a subordinate and a superior, based on seniority within an educational institution or a bureaucratic organization – characterize Japanese social life in many domains: higher education, companies, government bureaucracies, political parties, and artistic groups, among others. Typically a kohai may rely on his or her senpai for advice and aid; in turn a senpai should be able to count on the kohai's loyalty and respect. (Bestor 1989: 220)

In this light, *jouge kankei* is hierarchy, for "it relates people and it defines social relationships" on unequal terms (Diefenbach 2013: 37). At the same time, *jouge kankei* is also unique due to its high degree of rigidity, for "[t]here is only one ranking order for a given set of persons, regardless of variety of situation. No individual member of this set (not even the man who ranks highest) can make even a partial change [to the fixed hierarchical order]" (Nakane 1970: 29). Furthermore, this type of hierarchy can be observed whenever group dynamics are present in Japan. In addition to its presence in the mainstream society, as suggested by Bestor (1989), it has also been observed in subcultural groups in Japan, such as free-climbing and surfing clubs (Manzenreiter 2013). Its ubiquitous and enduring nature is moreover manifested by the fact that "[a] superior in one's place of work is always one's superior wherever he is met, at a restaurant, at home, in the street" (Nakane 1970: 33). This type of hierarchical relationship comprising *senpai* and *kouhai* contributes to building entire webs of hierarchical social relationships in Japan (Enyo 2013; 2015; Nakane 1970). Hence, it would be difficult to fully grasp the mechanisms of social life in Japanese society without a thorough understanding of *jouge kankei*.

The pervasiveness of *jouge kankei* in Japanese society notwithstanding, there is a dearth of scholarship devoted to this topic. Most studies on various aspects of Japanese social life, such as those cited thus far, mention the presence of this hierarchical order, but only as a given fact, rather than an object of inquiry. While works by Bestor (1989), Hebert (2012), Rohlen (1983), and Sugimoto (2010) attempt to describe and translate *jouge kankei*, their cursory treatment of this issue leaves the impression that *jouge kankei* is just an objective reality existing "out there" in Japanese society. To date, scant attention has been paid to the analysis of the nature and constituent elements of this hierarchical social order.[5] Thus far, the most influential and comprehensive work remains Nakane's (1970) dated book *Japanese Society*, who, as mentioned earlier, argued that such a social organisation based on *jouge kankei* is the key to understanding Japanese society. Despite the revelatory nature of her work at explaining the dynamics of Japanese society, it should be noted that her work does not go beyond a *description* of the existence of such a set of hierarchical relationships in Japanese group dynamics.[6] As a result of the scarcity of empirical evidence on all aspects of *jouge kankei* at present, we know little about it other than its existence and the basic principles guiding people in it, as described by Bestor (1989). Such sparse and essayistic attention paid to *jouge kankei* leaves important questions regarding the nature of this hierarchy as well as individuals' socialisation and adaptation process into it unanswered. The goal of this volume is to provide answers to some of the fundamental questions relating to *jouge kankei* in Japanese group dynamics:

- When, where, and how do individuals growing up in Japan first come into contact with *jouge kankei*?
- Why do people behave in the ways they do in such hierarchical relations?
- What constitutes *jouge kankei*?
- How is knowledge of *jouge kankei* transmitted from one generation to the next?

In what follows, I present the approach of this book and the direction towards which my empirical research takes. I explain why this work fits in the scholarship on language socialisation and explicate the ways in which this book fills current lacunae. I then introduce the empirical research methodology I devised, and methods utilised.

---

5 The few exceptions are Nakane (1970) and Enyo (2013; 2015), both are discussed in this chapter.
6 An exception in extant scholarship are works by Enyo (2013; 2015), who does examine the *senpai-kouhai* relationship, an important aspect of *jouge kankei*, from an empirical perspective: how specific language use could enact certain superior/subordinate identities in certain contexts. See section 1.3.1.

1.2 Studying *jouge kankei*: Linguistic and discursive constitution of hierarchy

Revelatory as current scholarship on the social organisation of Japanese society is, most studies lead us back to the same set of unanswered questions mentioned above. This is because they only explicate actors' behaviours, but not when, where, and how such behaviours are acquired, as well as the ways in which the knowledge of *jouge kankei* takes shape in the collective Japanese psyche. Such fundamental questions on Japanese social relations provided the rationale for this book, as well as motivated my data collection in Japan, which consisted of two phases, lasting a total of ten months. The first phase of my multi-stage fieldwork is dedicated to the exploration of how *jouge kankei* functions in actual inter-personal relations. The following sub-section presents this first-phase study, and how findings helped sharpen the analytical focus of the study. It also contributed to the development of appropriate theoretical and methodological approaches, as well as further data collection methods.

1.2.1 The phase-one study

The lack of extant literature detailing the mechanisms by which *jouge kankei* functions led me to devote the first phase of my field research, from September to October 2015, to gaining an understanding of some basic issues. Specifically, at this stage, I hoped to answer the following questions:
1. When and where do individuals growing up in Japan first come into meaningful contact with *jouge kankei*?
2. What constitutes *jouge kankei*?

This phase of the fieldwork consisted of seven one-to-one in-depth interviews with respondents aged between 18 and 30 from all walks of life. It showed that an overwhelming majority referred to their experiences in junior and senior high schools, notably participation in extra-curricular club activities, as a watershed moment. This is because, during this stage of their lives, they became conscious of *jouge kankei* in daily inter-personal relations and were taught proper behavioural etiquette in *senpai-kouhai* interactions. Table 1.1 below presents a summary of what they thought were the defining characteristics of their first meaningful encounter with *jouge kankei*.

Table 1.1: Defining characteristics of *jouge kankei* as revealed by respondents of the initial phase of fieldwork.

Constituting elements of *jouge kankei*	Sub-elements	Partial Extracts of Data
1. Norms and conventions on language use	1.1 Terms of address	"Well if a *kouhai* specifically wants to come up to me and ask me something, she'll come and say "*sumimasen, surname+senpai*" [excuse me, surname+*senpai*] first, in order to get my attention."
	1.2 Honorifics	"[S]ubordinates always had to use the *desu/masu* form[7] of talk, and honorifics as much as we can."
	1.3 Guidance	"I remember that when I first joined my junior high school club, like during the first week of official practice for us new members, the seniors organised a meeting and told us all about it. Like, they told us the importance to speak properly to them."
2. Age-based seniority	2.1 Senior's power to hold office	"Every year the out-going senior third graders choose the new leaders from the senior second graders who are about to become the most senior members. Students from other younger grades are not eligible to be considered anyway."
	2.2 Senior's power of decision-making	
	2.3 Senior's right to use objects/space and junior's duties	"[Before being told by the seniors] We really didn't know anything, not even that it was our duty to set up the room and our seniors' instruments before each session and clean up at the end, while seniors chilled in the school cafeteria or lounge."
3. Codes of conduct on bodily behaviour in interaction with seniors		"[W]henever juniors spot seniors in school or in the neighbourhood, I mean outside of club hours, they are supposed to run to seniors, bow deeply, and salute them."

---

7 In Japanese, the different forms of talk (*desu/masu*, plain) express different social meanings, and the usage of which depends on contexts and indexical relations among interlocutors. Refer to chapter five.

The information on *jouge kankei* as presented in Table 1.1 above consists of new data that have not been revealed by the current state of the art. The results above highlight that "norms and conventions on language use", "age-based seniority", and "codes of conduct on bodily behaviour in interaction with seniors" form the core initial experience of *jouge kankei* by the informants, and that junior and senior high school years represent an important stage in *jouge kankei* exposure. In particular, the context of extra-curricular club activities (*bukatsudou*), where students of all age cohorts interact (hence the formation of seniority-based hierarchy) was accorded importance. Results of this first phase study hence highlighted: (1) the importance of language in constituting *jouge kankei*, (2) knowledge of behavioural norms in *jouge kankei* is not innate but learned, and (3) secondary schools might prove to be one of the critical junctures in this learning and socialisation process. Such conclusions steered this work towards the language socialisation scholarship, in particular in educational contexts. In what follows, I present an appraisal of extant literature on language socialisation and what this strand of research has achieved. On the basis of an initial understanding of the constituent elements of *jouge kankei* and the theoretical underpinnings of language socialisation scholarship, I show how, by adopting a broader operationalisation of language (in terms of "Discourse/discourse") in the socialisation of individuals into *jouge kankei*, a full empirical study was developed to address the research questions mentioned in section 1.1.

1.3 *Jouge kankei* in secondary school extra-curricular clubs: Socialisation in and through language and discourse

Results of the initial phase of my field study reveal the central role of language in bringing into existence the *jouge kankei* in the Japanese social world: if different aspects of language constitute an important element of this hierarchy, then individuals growing up in Japan must, at some point in time, acquire such knowledge and be socialised into the cultural system of a social order replete with *jouge kankei*. In this vein, this book adopts the *language socialisation* framework which incorporates both linguistic and para-linguistic practices (together called discourse, see following section) as the theoretical perspective to analyse micro and macro level enactment of *jouge kankei*.

1.3.1 Language socialisation

I aim to show, throughout this work, that language and other discursive practices (see following section) constitute and enact *jouge kankei*. It is therefore befitting to situate this book in the *language socialisation* scholarship. Language socialisation is broadly understood as the "process by which people are socialized both to use the language of their community and to become members of that community" (Guardado, 2018: 34). Underlying this is the key assumption that yet-to-be members of a particular community/group/society, in most cases children, acquire language *in tandem* with the acquisition of social knowledge. This is due to the intrinsic connection between language and culture, and the fact that language itself not only communicates, but also codifies social and cultural elements such as hierarchical relations (Guardado 2018; Schieffelin and Ochs 1986). Language socialisation as a paradigm evolved in the late 1970s and early 1980s with the publication of several seminal anthropological works. Shirley Heath's (1983) *Ways with words: language, life, and work in communities and classrooms* represents a classic in the ethnography of communication (with a total of nine years of qualitative fieldwork) that examines young children's language socialisation at home and literacy skills in two communities. Both located in the Piedmont region in the United States, the two communities are culturally apart despite their geographical proximity: the white-working class community of Roadville and the black-working class community of Trackton. Her work not only highlighted literacy practices and cultural differences between the two groups (in the case of a new born, people generally talked *to* the baby in Roadville, whereas talking *about* the baby was the norm in Trackton), but also differences in such practices between both communities and those who subscribed to "mainstream" middle-class values (Heath 1983). In the same linguistic anthropological tradition, the publication of Elinor Ochs' (1988) *Culture and Language Development: Language Acquisition and Language Socialization in a Samoan Village*, and Bambi Schieffelin's (1990) *The give and take of everyday life: language socialization of Kaluli children* further consolidated the basis of this strand of scholarship and established language socialisation as a research paradigm in its own right. Focussing on issues of language acquisition among Kaluli children in Papua New Guinea and children in Samoa, their ethnographic fieldwork consisted of analyses of children's naturally-occurring speech patterns and revealed the fact that in the process of acquiring language skills, children in these communities also learned specific ways of thinking and socially acceptable comportment, hence re-affirming that learning a community's language on the part of children means that they also become members of that community and are able to speak and behave in socio-culturally acceptable ways (Ochs 1988; Schieffelin 1990).

1.3.1.1 Language socialisation research in Japanese contexts

This sub-section discusses language socialisation in the context of learning to recognise hierarchy in inter-personal relations through speech in Japan. I first show the state of the art, which covers language socialisation in various life stages. I then show that extant scholarship has hitherto paid little attention to language socialisation during a critical stage of growing up: the adolescent years in secondary school. I argue that, by identifying the appropriate milieu during this stage of life (the non-formal extra-curricular clubs), we find new evidence and gain an enhanced understanding of how Japanese students are socialised into the *jouge kankei* style of communication. This volume hence contributes to existing literature by focussing the data collection and analysis on adolescents in secondary schools.

As discussed in 1.3.1., the main theoretical premise of language socialisation steers the research focus of this scholarship first and foremost to children, especially processes of language and cultural knowledge acquisition in early stages of life (Guardado 2018). To date, most research on the socialisation of children into competent members of adult society has focussed on family and early educational contexts (from pre-school to elementary school) (Guardado 2018). Insofar as Japan is concerned, extant literature in first-language contexts (L1 contexts) focussed on issues such as (i) socialisation of affect, (ii) politeness and honorifics, (iii) gendered speech, (iv) connections between narrative and literacy, and (v) participation in primary school classroom interactions (Cook 2008: 315). More often than not, Japanese L1 language socialisation research has dealt with linguistic and cultural contexts at home and in school (overwhelmingly primary schools). Insofar as children's socialisation in and through language into indexical social orders and hierarchical inter-personal relations are concerned, our focus here is on language socialisation regarding politeness and honorifics. This is manifested in the fact that politeness and honorifics in the Japanese language encode social status and hierarchy, hence learning to use such a language means not only to speak, but also to recognise the system of *jouge kankei* and situate oneself in the hierarchical order (Mühlhäusler and Harré 1990; Miwa 2000). Some of the seminal works that studied young children's acquisition of knowledge of their social world in and through language examined the ways in which children familiarised themselves with social values. These include otherness, group orientation through politeness routines such as giving appreciation, offering apologies, as well as making requests (Burdelski 2010). In the specific area of learning to use honorifics in interactions (thereby recognising indexical social relations), Burdelski (2013) examined how caregivers utilised referent and addressee honorifics to children in pre-schools during role-play sessions to highlight various social personae linked to the public self, as well as the use of addressee honorifics in ordinary conversations to show affective stances such as expressing directives and objections. In addition,

Cook (1999) analysed the ways in which teachers train primary school pupils to be attentive listeners. Since the "Japanese classroom interactional pattern requires students to learn to a great degree from peer students and to relate their opinions to their peers" (Cook 1999: 1443), transmitting such cultural skills of attentive listening formed a main goal of teachers' classroom interactions. This primarily included interactions in which teachers repeatedly required pupils to listen attentively, respond appropriately (both in terms of timing and content), and in general, to respond to others when addressed (Cook 1999).

Despite prior studies on language socialisation in Japan, when it comes to socialising the young into the non-kinship-based *jouge kankei* hierarchical order, whose sets of status-based rules, norms, and constraints are prevalent in Japanese group dynamics, the key questions of when and how does this socialisation take place remain unaddressed in existing scholarship mentioned above. Focussing on the home and early school contexts might not reveal much, since morphologically complex honorifics do not usually occur in such milieux and children/primary school pupils "do not develop competence in appropriate use of the referent honorifics till much later in life" (Cook 2008: 316). This implies that the main process of individuals' acquisition of language and culture of *jouge kankei* through interactions occur beyond the stages of early care and primary education. Among existing studies that examined other life stages, Enyo (2015) has analysed the linguistic constitution of age-based seniority among university students. Notably, her work reveals that participants in an extra-curricular club in a university use non-reciprocal speech styles to construct hierarchical identities among them under certain contexts. In particular, during off-stage talks when students' club-related roles (as discussion leader, participant, etc) take backstage, the use of the addressee honorific *masu* form from a subordinate (*kouhai*) to a superior (*senpai*) and the latter's non-reciprocal plain form replies (see detailed analysis on this form of talk in chapter five) constitute the *jouge kankei* between them (Enyo 2015). A revelatory and rare work on language and *jouge kankei* notwithstanding, the question that comes to mind is that, in Enyo's study, the participants involved – university students – were already familiar with the language and culture of *jouge kankei*, as well as how and when to use what types of speech styles naturally. This manifests that they were not in the initial learning and socialisation stage. Hence, a life stage that is in between primary and tertiary education, namely the adolescent years of secondary schooling, warrants our attention.

In effect, the question of how interactional routines in various contexts of junior and senior high schools (what I collectively call "secondary educational phase" in this book) socialise students and prepare them to become competent adults have already been identified as directions for future language socialisation research (Cook 2008: 323). This in fact echoes the two questions I had in mind as I embarked on the first phase of my field study, and points to the linguistic constitution of hierarchy and the important milieu of secondary school clubs as the main learning environment. Indeed, this book shows that the socio-cultural structures and relations into which individuals will be socialised from junior high school onwards (in *bukatsudou* contexts) differ from those of previous stages of language socialisation. More than just being socially competent through language and being able to recognise status and power, individuals are expected to accept and conform to institutional status and power which carry consequences in daily behaviour and constrain actions, the likes of which students have hitherto not experienced in family and pre-junior high school language socialisation settings. As later chapters of this volume show, a case in point is how secondary school club *senpai* go to great lengths at teaching, disciplining, and correcting *kuohai*'s deviant linguistic comportment and social behaviours. The regulations on behaviour for members implicated in *jouge kankei* is furthermore impersonalised and do not spare even siblings who are categorised as *senpai* and *kouhai* in the same *bukatsudou*, as interview extracts and participant observation vignettes in this book show.

This volume therefore focusses on a hitherto neglected life stage in language socialisation literature on Japan: secondary school non-formal *bukatsudou* settings. Such a focus is important in two main ways. Firstly, crucial differences in socialisation and hierarchy exist between the phase of secondary education and prior stages of life. To be sure, children are exposed to non-kinship-based socialisation and hierarchical structures in pre- and elementary schools: with teachers, while sharing playgrounds with others, and so on. However, as this volume shows, *jouge kankei* from secondary school onwards is governed by much stricter rules, and failure to comply with them, or attempts to challenge them, carry consequences (punishments). This aspect by and large does not exist in earlier life phases. Secondly, secondary school-aged adolescents are in a critical stage of growing up and what they experience here follows them a long way into adult life (Heinrich and Galan 2018). Scholars in education science recognise that adolescents in secondary schools experience a crucial stage of learning as they become more conscious than primary school children of social status, ranks, roles, and relationships (Fukuzawa and LeTendre 2001; LeTendre 2000). However, they do not yet possess the same extent of knowledge of social norms and behavioural conventions as compared to university students and working adults (see Cook 2018; Dunn 2011; Enyo 2015). Since "individuals are crucially and forever shaped by experiences of their youth" (Heinrich and Galan 2018: 8), examining how individuals learn to function in *jouge kankei* during these formative years of their growing up serves to solve an important piece in the larger puzzle of different phases and nature of socialisation in an individual's life course. What is more, the kind of socialisation in and through language, as well as the discursive construction of *jouge kankei* hierarchy as examined in this book is novel and has not been studied in-depth.

The research milieu of *bukatsudou* in secondary schools therefore contributes to the state of the art by showing evidence of *jouge kankei* socialisation on a *well-organised* and *collective scale* in the adolescent years of growing up in Japan. This complements the established body of literature on this topic focussing on the early stages as well as adult life.

1.3.2 From language to discourse and discursive practices

The established literature in language socialisation shows that language occupies a central role in the socialisation of actors into social and cultural systems. As I argued in the previous sub-section, this applies to the *jouge kankei* hierarchical order as well, hence I situate this book in the language socialisation scholarship. However, as I show in this work, more than just linguistic elements alone, it is a whole ensemble of "discursive practices" that together constitute this hierarchical social world in junior and senior high school *bukatsudou*, into which student members are socialised. In this sub-section and the next, I present an approach of discourse analysis that is compatible with empirical language socialisation research on *jouge kankei*.

Following the "cultural" and "discursive turn" in human and social sciences, "discourses" are seen in social constructionist research as "ways of referring to or constructing knowledge about a particular topic of practice: a cluster (or formation) of ideas, images and practices, which provide ways of talking about, forms of knowledge, and conduct associated with, a particular topic, social activity or institutional site in society" (Hall 1997: 6). The general notion of "discourse" is more encompassing than "language", since the former can be taken to include not only spoken and written language, but also images, signs, symbols, and how these, taken together, communicate meaning (Hall et al. 2011). In the following sub-sections, I provide a concise overview of discourse analysis in various fields of social sciences research. I then show ways of operationalising "discourse" and "discursive practice" in the analysis of institutional hierarchy in this volume.

Discourse is an analytical framework employed in a plethora of disciplines, such as in sociology, linguistics, psychology, anthropology, and literature (Hall et al. 2011). Due to this multi-disciplinary presence of discourse, there are also a wide variety of research aims, methods, theories and concepts, which vary according to the discipline. For empirical social science research in general, conducting "discourse analysis" often means "the practice of exploring what kinds of speaking, writing and images are treated as 'normal' (and 'abnormal') in real situations, and the proportions, combinations and purposes of discourse that are conveniently acceptable (or not) in these situations" (Hall et al. 2011: 76). To be sure, the ways in which discourse analysis is to be conducted differ according to how discourse is conceptualised in diverse fields and approaches. One can often distinguish two broad traditions, each with a subset of approaches, theories and methods to conduct discourse analysis (though not all elements are mutually exclusive):

i. Linguistic/psycholinguistic tradition: research in this tradition often aims to describe contextualised language use, and examine how discourse (language and images) is processed in the human mind (Hall et al. 2011). To researchers following this tradition, "language provides the components of discourse and the mind is the ultimate seat of language" (Hall et al. 2011: 76).
ii. Sociological/critical/sociolinguistic tradition: research in this tradition often explores the ways in which discourse (language and images) both reflects and creates objects (social facts), events (social situations), and people (identities) (Pennycook 1994). To researchers following this tradition, "mind, people and cultures are the product of discourse, not its source" (Hall et al. 2011: 76).

Since I adopt a constructionist approach (informed by the sociology of knowledge, as I will show below) to understand the ways in which discourse brings into existence the institution of *jouge kankei*, my discourse analytic approach anchors mainly in the sociological/critical/sociolinguistic tradition.

Berger and Luckmann's (1966) work on the sociology of knowledge has served as one of the main intellectual foundations for the various present-day approaches to discourse analysis in the sociological tradition – including both the theoretical and methodological aspects – of studying linguistic and textual constructions of social facts. If we return to the opening vignette of this chapter, we see that the starting point is the "physico-biological fact" that new club members and senior club members are four to five years apart in terms of age. In the context of a secondary school *bukatsudou*, however, besides being members, there is now the added dimension of an accepted and objectified social fact that younger new members are *kouhai* and the older senior members are *senpai*, with rules, obligations, and entitlements attached. The processes in which a physico-biological fact (a question of age) becomes a social fact (a question of status and attached obligations), as well as how this social fact "transforms" from being a fact "out there" to an objective fact accepted by all, and finally to an internalised, taken-for-granted knowledge, deserve our attention. Berger and Luckmann (1966) affirm, in their work, the crucial role language plays in *constructing* social facts. Notably, they highlight how language in the form of daily routines (conversations) constructs a shared social reality and how "simple language" (everyday vocabulary and use) facilitates the legitimisation of institutionalised social relationships (such as *jouge kankei*). They furthermore attest the importance of language in *transmitting* and *legitimising* such social reality from one generation to the next (Berger and Luckmann 1966). This makes newcomers to the social world (of *jouge kankei*) perceive it as an objective, given and unalterable social world.

One important common feature shared by Berger and Luckmann's sociology of knowledge approach to the study of language and institutions in society, and that of discourse analysts hailing from various schools,[8] concerns the nature of linguistic *construction* of social knowledge on the epistemological level: that they are (partial) constructivists, or weak realists (Reisigl 2013). That is to say, while social facts are constructed and represented by discourse (more encompassing than "language", as I argue below), once brought into existence, such social facts also shape and restrain the discourse. Such is the stance of this book as regards *jouge kankei*. As I show in subsequent chapters, while discourse is needed to bring into existence the very social roles and hierarchical structure, such social roles and facts also become stable and in turn shapes language and discursive behaviours of actors involved.

1.3.3 Operationalisation of discourse

In the previous sub-section, I demonstrated the feasibility of studying the institution of *jouge kankei* from a discourse analytic approach based on a social constructionist perspective that puts an emphasis on the role of language and paralinguistic features, as well as how they enact institutional hierarchy. I now turn to the operationalisation of this approach. For that, I focus on discussing "discourse" and "discursive practices" rather than just "language" and "language use", because, as it will transpire in later empirical chapters, a focus on the discursive level entails the possibility of considering paralinguistic features that accompany language use, but are themselves not language *stricto sensu*. Here is also where my approach diverges from that of Enyo's (2015). Enyo

---

[8] Discourse analysis is normally classified into several broad approaches, see Jorgensen and Phillips (2002) for an example. At times, each approach is also further sub-divided into different schools, see Reisigl (2013) for an example of how the approach of "critical discourse analysis" is further categorised. Note, however, that such classifications are by no means "standard", and the list is not exhaustive.

used two aspects of Japanese language – the plain/"*masu* polite" form endings and address/referent terms – to study hierarchy. Though innovative in showing the linguistic construction of hierarchy, I argue that this approach needs to be expanded from a purely linguistic approach to what I call a *broader and multi-level discursive approach*. This is to capture, in a holistic way, the dynamism of *jouge kankei* and its constituting discursive elements.

Contrary to Enyo (2015)'s research context in a university, there would be a socialisation process in which members are taught proper conduct in my research context in secondary schools, as results of the first stage of my fieldwork revealed. The teaching that goes on, whether explicit or implicit, is crucial. An important part of my research process is dedicated to finding out who does the teaching, the ways in which teaching is done, the contents being taught, as well as any correction of mistakes. To capture this purposeful imparting of knowledge, or in Berger and Luckmann's sociology of knowledge tradition; the portrayal of an objective social world to incoming members, it is necessary that I adopt a more pragmatic definition of discourse. Such a definition should furthermore traverse narrow and disparate disciplinary perspectives: one that incorporates not just language, but also related paralinguistic features used in conjunction with language. Therefore, I propose a two-pronged approach to examine discourse.

Firstly, I suggest looking at the macro-level social behaviour (of which language use is a part) on the part of students. Certain discourse analysts consider this as "Discourse" with a capital "D", which also serves as the first part of an operationalised definition of "discourse":

> [People] enact identities and activities not just through language, but by *using language together with other "stuff" that isn't language*. I use the term "Discourse", with a capital "D", for ways of combining and integrating language, actions, interactions, ways of thinking, believing, valuing, and using various symbols, tools, and objects to enact a particular sort of socially recognizable identity . . . You can't just "talk the talk", you have to "*walk the walk*" as well. (Gee 2014: 222, emphases added)

In short, "Discourse" (with a big D) in this study encompasses "ways of thinking, believing, valuing, and using various symbols, tools, and objects to enact a particular sort of socially recognizable identity" (Gee 2014: 222), such as that of *senpai* and *kouhai* in *jouge kankei* hierarchy. In essence, what I believe needs to be examined at the macro-level are the modes of communication (language and any supplementary materials used) and ways of thinking (in the world of hierarchy) by certain existing members imposed onto new members to instil in them a common-sense knowledge and ideology of the hierarchical order. In addition, the ways in which members with different roles and of different statuses in *jouge kankei* make use of symbols, objects, and bodily movements (that is, how they "walk the walk") to enact their identities will also be considered under "Discourse", for such actions always involve concomitant ways of language use stipulated by conventions, as my research will show.

Secondly, and complementing the analysis of this macro-level Discourse, I adopt the analysis of micro-level language use as "text" (both spoken and written). This is commonly found in conversations among members and will be referred to as "discourse" with a small "d" (Gee 2014) – the second part of the operationalised definition of "discourse". In this context, the discourse with a small "d" consists of various aspects of Japanese language use (refer to empirical chapters) – *masu/* plain forms, honorifics, greetings and routines – by actors (*bukatsudou* members) in their daily interactions. For this, I examine, just like Enyo (2015), meanings and contexts in which various address and referent terms are used, as well as the diverse functions of the plain and *desu/masu* forms of talk in spoken Japanese. However, unlike Enyo (2015), I do not simply limit my analytical focus to indexicality and on- and off-stage talk (refer to chapter five). Instead, I also focus on instances of "epistemic orders" manifested in interactions between seniors and juniors (Heritage 2008). In addition, I also examine how the very idea of having to use specific micro-level discourse when talking to or *about* one's seniors is often sufficient to create a hierarchical order in club members' daily routines. As I will demonstrate in the empirical chapters of the book, this two-pronged Discourse-discourse operationalisation enables the analysis of how discursive practices, be it the use of linguistic aspects of Japanese or the use of signs and symbols by *senpai* and *kouhai* in tandem with language, constitute *jouge kankei*.

Therefore, in my empirical inquiry, "discursive practices" refer to a combination of macro-level Discourse and micro-level discourse in the daily social interactions in club settings. Furthermore, four major analytical categories will be used in my analyses:

i. Written institutional texts and spoken macro-level Discourses; such as "tall tales", "lores" (Meyer and Rowan 2006) (macro-level Discourse)
ii. Address terms, as well as honorific registers (micro-level discourse)
iii. Plain form and *desu/masu* form endings (micro-level discourse)
iv. Space, signs, symbols and objects used in daily routines (macro-level Discourse)

For instance, (i) and (iv) focusses on the ways in which club seniors and teachers impart knowledge of *jouge kankei* to new junior members via the explanation of "tall tales" (that is, grand narratives and new ways of making sense of their social world; refer to chapter three) and the communication with signs, objects and space (chapter six); while (ii) and (iii) allow us to examine the ways in which actors implicated in the hierarchical system in clubs "talk the talk" (chapters four and five), that is, interact on a daily basis.

In line with most discursive approaches informed by a certain degree of social constructionism, my principal concern is not only how language, signs, symbols, and objects produce meaning in this institutional arena of *jouge kankei*, but also the ways in which such discursively produced social facts relate to and shape power, regulate comportment, construct identities, and define perspectives (Hall 1997: 6). Moreover, by adopting such an approach, this study does not take the existence of *jouge kankei* for granted and consider it part of a natural order of things in Japanese social organisation. Instead of assuming it is innate to a "Japanese personality", this book shows how *jouge kankei* emerges, where it comes from, and how it is propagated.

Such a methodological approach is compatible with the premise of language socialisation research, for in language socialisation we "investigate the microlinguistic processes [discourse with a small d] and broader socio-cultural-ideological factors [Discourse with a big D] implicated in how individuals become competent members of their communities" (Guardado 2018: 36). Scientific inquiries informed by this perspective and methodological approach have long been influenced by ethnography (Duff 1995; Guardado 2018). In the following sub-section, I introduce the second stage of my fieldwork, an ethnographic study, which allowed for data collection and the further examination of the processes by which each generation of (young) individuals learn to speak and behave appropriately in the broad social order of *jouge kankei*, as well as the formation of identities ("self" vis-à-vis "other") and the acquisition of a particular worldview (of *senpai* and *kouhai*).

1.3.4 An ethnographic study of extra-curricular clubs

In the previous sub-section, I presented my discourse analytic approach and explained its suitability in the empirical inquiry of the discursive construction of *jouge kankei* in Japanese secondary school club contexts. With the aforementioned operationalisation of discourse in mind, and contributing to existing language socialisation research on Japan, field data was gathered in an ethnographic fieldwork.

With results of the first phase of my fieldwork highlighting the constituent elements of *jouge kankei* and helping to locate a research site (secondary school *bukatsudou*), I proceeded to the second stage of fieldwork – seven months of ethnographic study in secondary school clubs (November 2015 to May 2016) – with the following questions in mind:

1. How are individuals socialised into *jouge kankei* in the selected sites?
2. How, or if, the dynamics of *jouge kankei* social order in school clubs change following leadership renewal (i.e. when a new group of *senpai* assume the most senior status)?

Since I had the aim of analysing the ways in which discursive practices constitute the hierarchy in school clubs, a qualitative research methodology that permits the exploration of day-to-day language and discursive practices in social interactions, as well as interpersonal relations of club members through the perspective of *jouge kankei* is desired. In this light, the qualitative research methods I will present here not only serve to supplement or affirm existing studies that show the existence of honorific practices in *jouge kankei* relations (Cook 2008; Enyo 2015; Miwa 2000; Mühlhäusler and Harré 1990; NINJAL 2002), but more importantly, provide the hitherto missing insights on *how* such discursive practices construct *jouge kankei* through interactions in secondary school clubs in Japan.

To this end, research methods that take into account social interactions of actors focussing on their language use (and the broader discursive practices) in diverse contexts are needed. This means that, not only do we need to know the kind of language used as part of behaviour in *jouge kankei*, but also how actors "walk the walk" while they "talk the talk" (Gee 2014: 222). Coalescing discourse analysis with ethnography implies my presence on site for real-time observations and recordings, in order to grasp the complexities of the process of construction and maintenance of *jouge kankei* and actions of all those who are involved in the hierarchical order.

In fact, there has been a recent but burgeoning practice in qualitative social science research to integrate discourse analytic and ethnographic approaches (Macgilchrist and Van Hout 2011). Such techniques of combining participant observation (as an aspect of ethnographic fieldwork) in the study of discursive practices in daily interactions and routines prove useful in capturing and explicating actions that seem normal and natural to the informants, but have considerable significance in helping researchers better comprehend the generated social orders. Quantitative surveys with an extended period of data collection, such as NINJAL (2002), revealed that, insofar as the persistence of honorifics in *jouge kankei* relations in secondary school clubs is concerned, little has changed in the space of 25 or so years. This has implications which extend beyond the confines of secondary school clubs, because, given the formative role a secondary school club fulfils (see chapter two), it also implies that there has been similarly little change in social expectations of what constitutes a competent social actor in the adult corporate world (including a calibrated way of speaking, as well as the mastery of honorifics and related etiquette) in Japan. However, this does not always mean that everyone is willingly socialised into the system. By employing ethnographic approaches, notably extended participant observations, this current study is able to reveal that there are individuals who attempt to "revolt", only to be "suppressed", as well as some other nuances in behaviour that constitute *jouge kankei*. These have thus far not been captured by existing large-scale quantitative surveys such as NINJAL (2002).

1.3.4.1 Main methods of data collection and analysis

During this fieldwork period, data collection and analysis pertained mainly to the use of Discourse/discourse in daily situations in clubs. As far as language use is concerned, I analysed spoken interactions to examine the social order of club members and the ways in which their daily lives in clubs are coordinated in speech. As regards discourse incorporating both linguistic and paralinguistic features, such as the use of images, signs, and symbols, I utilised discourse analysis to examine relationships between texts, talk, and identities. Notably, this approach proved useful in highlighting certain identities and ideologies which underpin language use, as well as asymmetrical power relations between speakers. These afore-mentioned social approaches to discourse analysis were complemented by observations of further language/non-language discursive practices in daily lives, for instance, specific rules on the use of terms of address, the use of images, objects, and space in communicating status differences, as well as the acts of seniors reprimanding juniors.

Besides observation vignettes based on fieldnotes as the primary source of data, my data archive also comprised of speeches made during important events (some of these were tape recorded), conversations among selected group members,[9] as well as tape recorded student interviews and selected group conversations. Such data facilitate the understanding of club members' everyday discursive practices on both the macro and micro levels, as well as their thoughts on and experiences of being implicated in the *jouge kankei* hierarchy (refer to the end of this section).

In transcribing the recorded interactions, a series of conventions were followed. Each conversational turn was treated in three steps (see chapter five for illustration). The first step was romanisation: the process of transliterating Japanese *kana* and *kanji* (Chinese characters) into the Latin alphabet. Romanisation in my work follows the "modified Hepburn" system when transliterating Japanese into the Latin alphabet. For an overview of different systems of transliteration and their usage, refer to the article on "Japanese Romanization" prepared by the University

---

9 Conversation also means my own conversations with students during daily interactions, but these were, due to practical reasons, not tape recorded.

of Hawai'i at Manoa Libraries.[10] The second step was transcription: a media change of the recordings from oral to visual data. This step also dealt with word for word translation of utterances following the Japanese word order, plus grammatical functions. Finally, the third step involved the translation of the utterances into English with the appropriate syntax. In addition, abbreviations denoting grammatical glosses are also attached to transcriptions of the naturally occurring utterances. I adopted a musical score format in which multiple lines of data represented the above-mentioned steps. In presenting such data, I have followed the Leipzig glossing rules.[11] All recordings obtained prior approval from the schools' management boards, the respective *bukatsudou*'s teachers, as well as all individuals partaking in the interactions. The recordings were made with a digital audio-only recorder, visible to everyone throughout each session, and in my presence. The entire procedure remained anonymised and the audio files were securely stored offline. Within a few hours after each recording session, I personally transcribed the conversational data following the afore-mentioned conventions. The transcriptions were then rectified by two native Japanese speakers to ensure accuracy.

Taken together, all these portray the ways in which discursive practices constitute the institution of *jouge kankei* in secondary school club activities in Japan. This is achieved by combining ethnographic methods such as participant observations of club activities and in-depth interviews with student/graduate/teacher informants and a series of discourse analytic methods of naturally occurring conversations and text/image analysis. Through these, the present work analyses how *jouge kankei* are enacted, legitimised, transmitted, and reified, by social actors through language use and paralinguistic discursive practices. It also looks at how established rules could be challenged, or the possibility of slight alterations to their enforcement following "leadership renewal" (with a new group of *senpai* assuming top seniority status). The combination of the afore-mentioned theoretical and methodological approaches enables this book to reveal the discursive origins and characteristics of *jouge kankei* at work during the formative stage of adolescent years.

---

10 The article can be accessed here: http://www.hawaii.edu/asiaref/japan/online/rom_hist.htm.
11 Information on the Leipzig Glossing Rules can be found here: https://www.eva.mpg.de/lingua/resources/glossing-rules.php. This is used for transcription of conversations for analysis in chapter five sections 5.4 and 5.5.

1.3.4.2 Negotiating researcher identity: From a "foreign researcher" to a "half-foreign *oniisan*" to a "member of the club"

This sub-section discusses the issue of researcher positionality and reflexivity in ethnographic studies. Ethnographic research having a rich tradition notwithstanding, questions of researcher identity and the relations between the researcher and the researched have not been a prominent feature in discussions on methodology and data collection. Much of this could be traced back to the realist assumption of what constituted the "proper" scientific method and its implications on ethnographic practices (Alcadipani et al. 2014). This understanding persisted until a reflexive turn in anthropology towards the late 1970s that led to fundamental changes in thinking about ethnography (Alcadipani et al. 2014). This meant a shift towards a more conscious attention on relationships between the researcher and the researched, and an acknowledgement that ethnographic participant observation involves working on identity construction and reflection both on the part of the researched and the researcher (Coffey 1999).

My research follows such a reflexive approach. As Davies (1999) suggested on reflexivity:

> Reflexivity, broadly defined, means a turning back on oneself, a process of self-reference. In the context of social research, reflexivity at its most immediately obvious level refers to the ways in which the products of research are affected by the personnel and process of doing research. These effects are to be found in all phases of the research process from initial selection of topic to final reporting of results. While relevant for social research in general, issues of reflexivity are particularly salient for ethnographic research in which the involvement of the researcher in the society and culture of those being studied is particularly close.
>
> (Davies 1999: 4)

Given the heavy reliance on ethnographic fieldwork methods in my data collection, the issue of reflexivity is of relevance. In effect, one of the first and most significant instances of reflexivity came about as I realised the extent to which my identity in participant observation sessions was co-constructed by people in the fieldwork sites. Throughout my fieldwork, I remained conscious about my "self" that had been portrayed in front of and co-constructed by my informants, not least because my researcher identity remained fluid, evolving and context-dependent. Furthermore, this had an impact on not only the possible level of involvement and the degree of participation on my part as the researcher, but also my access to information in different social situations. I sketch in Figure 1.1 below the evolution and fluid nature of my researcher identity throughout my fieldwork:

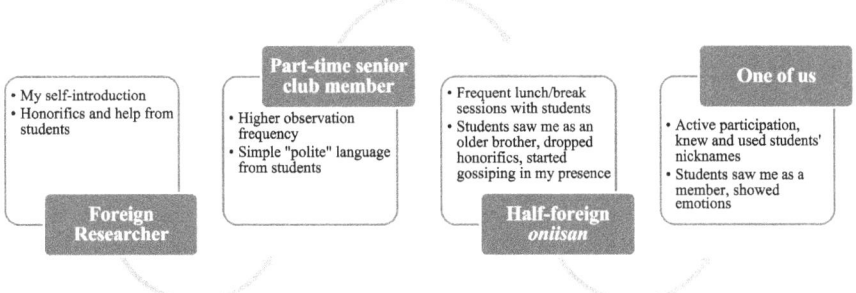

Figure 1.1: Fluid and context-dependent researcher identity.

Texts in bold in Figure 1.1 above show different researcher identities and the texts in bullet points refer to actions that I and the student members in clubs performed in accordance with these identities. For instance, at the beginning of my fieldwork, the teachers in charge in the clubs first introduced me to the students, followed by my self-introduction when I explained to them my presence and the research I hoped to conduct. At this moment, I was considered a **foreign researcher**, an outside guest whom students treated with utmost respect, including the use of honorifics and their constant offers to help me (carrying my bag, bringing me a chair, etc). As time went by in the initial weeks and months, I increased the frequency of my participant observation sessions with each club (and within each club, with specific groups), avoided taking fieldnotes in their presence, and started interacting with members on club-related matters (discussion on playing techniques, instruments, music they were playing/I played in my own school days). I was able to act as a **part-time senior club member** and most students used only the simple addressee honorifics of *desu/masu* endings, while dropping much of the referent honorifics when interacting with me (refer to chapter five on the discussion of honorifics and implications of their usage in *senpai-kouhai* relations). As I broadened the scope of observation to activities outside the normal, routine practice schedule, the level of my participation increased. I started having lunch together with senior second year students almost every Sunday during their lunch break, as well as spending break sessions and chatting with diverse groups of members in all clubs under study (see chapter two). This was also the period when I had the opportunity to participate in external events with the clubs. One such event at the Tokyo Daiichi School was the annual open day, held at the end of November 2015 to showcase the school's programmes to primary school children who aspire to study at Tokyo Daiichi. As part of the programme, each club also welcomed interested students, and I was with the orchestra helping members to explain how to play certain instruments to the interested primary school visitors. There was a moment when a fifth grade primary school girl came up to try out the euphonium, and the senior second year player was sitting next to her to coach her. The primary school girl seemed talented, and very determined to enrol in Tokyo Daiichi for her secondary education. The senior second year euphonium player called over one of her close friends, a senior second year alto saxophone player, and the two of them started talking to the primary school girl about daily school life in Tokyo Daiichi: how fun and exciting it was to study in the school. The primary school girl was worried that she could not follow English classes in junior high school, and at this juncture, both the senior second year orchestra members pointed to me and reassured the little girl that she would get help along the way, and that in Tokyo Daiichi, above all in the orchestra, there was even "*eigo ga perapera no oniisan*[12] *mo iru*" (there is even an elder brother who is good at English), and that they themselves get to practice their English because of this (my presence). They then proceeded to talk about other stuff like how students create a mess in their class and annoy the teachers, the primary school girl looked at me anxiously again, and once more the two senior second year members assured her "*sensei dewanai, daijoubu*" (he is not a teacher, don't worry). This marks a clear instance in which members considered me as an **English-speaking elder brother on their side,**[13] for they could talk about things with me, things that they would not mention in the presence of their teachers or even the orchestra's alumni members. In addition, fewer and fewer people used honorifics when having conversations with or about me. Towards March 2016, I had the occasion of engaging in active participations with the students, especially in the context of their imminent annual concerts. Frequent meetings, rehearsals, and stage planning sessions were held, to which I was invited to participate. The active participation in meetings and stage management sessions allowed me the chance to memorise most

---

12 Such informal fictive kinships and the corresponding use of kinship terms are abundant in Japan, above all among young people. Although used almost exclusively to address and refer to persons older than the speaker, a certain degree of intimacy and acquaintance is needed for the use of kinship terms denoting elder siblings. For more information refer to Norbeck and Befu (1958). The use of *oniisan* by certain informants to address or refer to me during my fieldwork is yet another indicator of my **partial insider status** in their eyes, at least in certain situations.

13 A similar moment in which I attained the identity of a "elder brother who could teach" occurred in Tokyo Daini Boys' Orchestra. The orchestra had been planning for a study cum performance trip to Germany as I started my fieldwork with them. As we got closer, some of the members took the initiative to approach me to learn some conversational German. One boy even asked me to correct his speech to be made in German. The fact that they did not talk to me in the way they would to their seniors suggested an "elder brother" rather than *senpai* identity.

of the senior first and second year members' names, hobbies, and instruments by heart, which on one occasion I recounted openly. This led to members repeatedly claiming that I had become "*buin no hitori*" (**member of the club, one of them**).

Note, however, that the above-mentioned development of my researcher identity does not suggest a strictly linear process of identity evolution. In particular, after the first two months or so of participant observation, my identity switched from one to the other depending on social situations (refer to chapter two). Even towards the end of my stay when a very close relationship existed between me and my main informants, I was not regarded as one of them all the time (for example, not during their actual practice/performance where my role went back to being a passive observer).

Given that two out of the three clubs were located in Tokyo Daiichi Girls' Junior and Senior High School, the **question of gender** also has to be considered. Reflexive ethnographic studies calls for the constant need to examine the presence of the "gendered ethnographer", and how this changes the tone of the "naturally occurring" interactions and events in fieldwork sites (Dewalt and Dewalt 2002). Current works with rich ethnographic accounts of Japanese school students' adolescent life (LeTendre 2000) and student club activities in secondary schools and universities (Blackwood 2016; Cave 2004; 2016; Hebert 2012; McDonald and Hallinan 2005) have not discussed the gender of the ethnographer(s) and its possible implications for data collection and the relationship between the researcher and the researched. This is perplexing, not least because most of the afore-mentioned works were conducted by white, male, and middle-aged researchers.

As I began my participant observations, I had the perception that there were certain "weaknesses" that made me "unnecessarily foreign" (a foreigner of Asian heritage), and my gender (male researcher) in Tokyo Daiichi was one of these issues. I feared that this could hinder the development of an "acceptable identity" in the eyes of my informants. However, as the quantity and quality of my involvement increased over time, I realised that my initial "weakness" actually worked out in the end to serve my data collection purpose. The students understood that I was someone from the "outside" and my purpose there was not to judge or patronise them. On the contrary, I was eager to learn from them and hear their experiences in clubs and interpersonal relations. Specifically, the "foreign elder brother" image (involving both my gender and nationality) further facilitated my communicating with the young informants. Seen in this light, I was not considered as an adult member of *their* society. In their eyes, I did not represent their social institutions and relationships, which in turn made it easier for informants to recount their stories. This had a profound impact, especially on junior students, since their institutionalised role as juniors who were either not supposed to know anything or to express what they know (see chapter five) was reversed whenever they interacted with me, because they realised that they could actually teach me something.

Towards the end of January 2016, there were some clear signs showing that club members in all clubs, at least the senior first and second year students, have not only gotten used to my existence, but also accepted my presence in their group: I would help clean up their music rooms and re-arrange chairs after practice, and they started to joke and chat with me as we did those chores together, just like among friends. Also, the student leaders in these clubs started taking the initiative to tell me about the upcoming events and invited me to join them. Hence, the "outsider/foreigner" identity that I at times assumed helped me to build better rapport with my main informants. In addition, such an identity allowed a better access to information, such as how juniors disagreed with their seniors' leadership style and disliked the strict hierarchy in their clubs, but how they remained powerless so long as they were junior members. As far as research with and on adolescents is concerned, such sensitive information would not have been easily revealed by informants if the researcher were not someone from the outside: not implicated in their social world and institutions (White 2003). Furthermore, it permitted a constant reflexive take on what I observed as it allowed me to bring in "global perspectives", partly stemming from the six years of experience in my own school's/country's junior and senior high schools' orchestras, to question practices and beliefs (regarding *jouge kankei* and discursive practices) that are usually taken for granted in Japan. Lastly, my half foreign/outsider identity (due to age, gender, cultural background) throughout my fieldwork ensured necessary distances with the informants and served as a reminder of my aim to draw up a series of explanations of a social reality (*jouge kankei* in secondary school clubs) that was not only external to me as the researcher (lest I became "over involved" in my research context), but also explanations that could be applied beyond the boundaries of my fieldwork sites.

All in all, such an extensive period of fieldwork in Tokyo and my presence onsite from 2015 to 2016 allowed ample opportunities to collect, analyse, reflect upon the data, which form the backbone of this book: the first monograph-length empirical work on *jouge kankei*.

1.4 Organisation of the book

Chapter two begins with a concise overview of the Japanese pre-tertiary education landscape, affirming that this is a comparatively centralised education system which accommodates slight variations in different domains across regions and types of schools. The chapter proceeds to explain the rationale for site selection with regard to the topic of this book, and introduces the clubs and informants under study. This chapter argues that the basic set of organisational principles of *bukatsudou* applies rather uniformly across the board. With the high levels of both school and club participation rates up until the end of pre-tertiary education (i.e. end of senior high school), as well as the amount of time students spend in *bukatsudou*, I show that, for secondary school students, club life is an essential aspect of their social life. Hence, the education and socialisation processes in clubs deserve detailed analysis. In addition, I introduce some key elements of my main ethnographic study before presenting empirical results in the next few chapters.

In chapter three, the first empirical chapter, I show how specific discursive and language practices (with accompanying ideologies regarding hierarchy) are produced and communicated to new junior high school club members at the beginning of every school year. This chapter attests that group thinking and a hierarchically-oriented mentality are far from being innate in a "Japanese personality", as new junior high school club members repeatedly "fail" to grasp what their seniors demand. Hence, multiple teaching and training sessions by *senpai* are needed, during which detailed club documents and rule/etiquette books are used. Data reveal that such internal school club documents and methods of teaching rules and norms concerning hierarchy analysed here are a common feature in Japan, but they have not been featured in previous studies. I therefore present a new type of data and analysis based on it. Later chapters show that the practice of using such teaching materials in organisations extends from school clubs to companies, hence underscoring the socialisation link between school clubs and adult working life.

Chapter four then highlights the ways in which common and ostensibly trivial features of everyday speech sustain unequal relationships between superiors and subordinates in *bukatsudou*. Sample case studies include the ways in which students from different age cohorts (hence seniority level) in the three student clubs in Tokyo are expected to address each other (part of the discursive etiquette).

Chapter five continues the previous chapter's analysis of micro-conversational features of discursive practice by showing how *masu* and plain forms in Japanese are used in specific ways in junior and senior high school club contexts, so that such usage reifies hierarchy. Discourse analysis of recorded interactions will feature here too. Participant observation vignettes of instances in the three clubs in Tokyo, as well as interview data with students and graduates of other schools across Japan reveal the extent to which a *senpai* could go at reprimanding and correcting a *kouhai*'s deviant behaviour, even in cases when they are siblings/childhood friends. This therefore distinguishes once again the nature and extent of *jouge kankei* socialisation in secondary school *bukatsudou* from socialisations in previous stages (e.g. family, nursery, and primary school).

The key focus of chapter six switches to non-verbal practices which, together with the afore-mentioned discursive behaviour, construct hierarchical interpersonal relations. This is the first instance in existing literature where students' use of space, objects (blackboard) and symbols (colour coding on school uniforms) in constructing and maintaining hierarchy is analysed.

Finally, chapter seven concludes the entire study and offers a glimpse of the prevalent hierarchical interpersonal relations in Japanese social life. Notably, I present the main characteristics of *jouge kankei* in Japanese group dynamics, and answers to the main research questions: how does it take shape, what is its constitutive nature, as well as how is it transmitted from one age cohort to the next in the context of secondary school club activities. I reiterate this book's contribution to our enhanced understanding of the socialisation in and through discursive practices of youths into *jouge kankei*, as well as the fact that language socialisation into *jouge kankei* extends beyond the confines of secondary schools into the adult world. I furthermore argue that, although the degree of *jouge kankei* manifestation varies across time and space in different school and club contexts, its basic nature and ideology remain rather constant. Lastly, I point out to the enduring nature of *jouge kankei* in Japanese group dynamics, as well as implications of this volume's findings on future research on Japanese social life.

2 Studying the discursive construction of *jouge kankei* in secondary school clubs

This chapter begins with a concise overview of the Japanese pre-tertiary education landscape, affirming that this is a comparatively centralised education system which accommodates slight variations in different domains across regions/types of schools. The chapter proceeds to explain the rationale for site selection with regard to the topic of this book, and introduces the schools, clubs and informants under study. Firstly, I argue that schools and clubs providing a six-year "integrated programme" combining junior and senior high education under one roof provide a conducive environment in which to examine the language socialisation processes of individuals into *jouge kankei*. Next, I justify the type of schools and clubs I select, and how we can gain an enhanced understanding of the seniority-based hierarchy by doing research in these settings. Then, I present a detailed overview of the schools and clubs selected as fieldwork sites in this study, especially the clubs' organisational structure and manifestations of student governance. A review of secondary literature shows that many characteristics of the selected clubs in my study are both similar to most other schools across (urban) Japan, and bear resemblance to organisational structures and institutional contexts in the adult corporate world. I conclude this chapter by presenting the series of social situations in these clubs in which I conducted my ethnographic research and gathered data. With the high levels of both school and club participation rates up until the end of senior high school, as well as the amount of time students spend in such "extra"-curricular activities, club life represents an essential aspect of social life for a great majority of secondary school students in Japan. *Bukatsudou* is, therefore, an important factor contributing to the socialisation of Japanese students into *jouge kankei*. This is not to say that hierarchy and socialisation do not exist prior to this stage of life. However, the extent to which *jouge kankei* regulates behaviour from secondary schools onwards, and negative consequences for not following rules, mean that *bukatsudou* is both an important context for language socialisation, and provides a conducive environment in which to analyse it.

2.1 The Japanese secondary education

Since the advent of modern nation-states, education systems, in particular, schools, have played a major educating and socialising function in preparing youths for the economic and socio-cultural needs of adult society (Perez-Agote 2010). Notably, primary and secondary education have been considered by sociologists such as

Bourdieu as the "mechanism through which the values and relations that make up the social space are passed on from one generation to the next" (Webb et al. 2002: 105). This in turn implies that, by examining the context of pre-tertiary schools, we could also have a glimpse into the socio-political and economic mechanisms and practices of a society. In Japan, this is no exception, since secondary schools take on the duty of moulding today's youths into tomorrow's competent adults. On the international stage, the Japanese pre-tertiary education system enjoys considerable reputation as Japan's population is consistently ranked as one of the most literate and competent in the world. This is most evidently manifested in Japan's high performance in international academic assessments such as the Programme for International Student Assessment (PISA) by the Organization for Economic Co-operation and Development (OECD[14]), as well as the World Bank's Human Capital Index.[15] Equipping today's adolescents with the necessary knowledge stock is but one aspect of how schools train competent adults. Besides such academic achievements, Japanese schools also play a crucial role in creating order and shaping people's fundamental concept of the self and how it relates to others in society. This happens predominantly outside the classroom, in extra-curricular club activities (*bukatsudou*). Although officially classified as "extra-curricular", such activities command high participation rates and represent a common experience during the most formative years of youths' growing up in Japan (Blackwood 2016). Furthermore, *bukatsudou* are widely recognised by teachers, students, parents, and employers as an essential component of a holistic education, i.e. an integral part of school and social life for adolescents (Blackwood 2016; Cave 2004; Ono and Shoji 2015). Being perceived as both successful and unique, various aspects of Japan's school system have been extensively researched. However, as results of the first phase of my study revealed, little attention has been paid to the functions of and mechanisms by which *bukatsudou* create, maintain, as well as transmit a sense of social order and seniority-based hierarchy (*jouge kankei*) from one generation of students to the next, both within and beyond the confines of school club activities. By situating my main research context in secondary school clubs, and on the basis of 10 months of ethnographic fieldwork in 2015 and 2016, I show the language socialisation process of students into *jouge kankei* in and through discourse in the context of

---

[14] OECD PISA Country Report for Japan 2015: http://www.compareyourcountry.org/pisa/country/jpn?lg=en, in which both Japanese students' individual competencies in science, mathematics, and reading as well as the ability to work in groups for problem-solving were among the top ranked. Last accessed on 13.11.2018.
[15] World Bank Human Capital Index 2018: http://www.worldbank.org/en/publication/human-capital. Last accessed on 13.11.2018.

bukatsudou. Before we delve deeper into the main focus on school clubs, however, I first present a brief overview of the secondary educational landscape in Japan, the backdrop against which my fieldwork and data collection sites are situated.

In this book, I employ the term "secondary schools" to refer to junior and (academic) senior high schools in the Japanese "6 – 3 – 3" educational structure. This structure comprises six years of primary school education, three years of junior high and three years of senior high education, as shown in Table 2.1 below:

Table 2.1: The Japanese "6 – 3 – 3" school system and corresponding age group.

Age	6–7	8	9	10	11	12	13	14	15	16	17	18
Grade	1	2	3	4	5	6	1	2	3	1	2	3
Educational Level	Primary						Secondary (focus of my research)					
School Level	Primary						Junior High			Senior High		
Compulsory Education	Yes									No*		

* Note that even though the stage of senior high school is no longer part of compulsory education, an overwhelming majority, or close to 97 percent, of junior high school graduates continue to pursue their studies in senior high schools (Deutsche Industrie- und Handelskammer in Japan, 2017; Hendry 1995; Rohlen 1983; Sugimoto 2014).

From the information above, readers will notice that my focus is on students with ages of between 12/13 years old to 17/18 years old.[16] Following the common practice in Japan, I refer to students' educational levels as junior high (J) first/second/third grade, and high school (H) first/second/third grade in this book (contrary to many European/North American systems in which grades seven to 12/13 are used).

Among the educational goals starting at the outset of the junior high level, schools place a strong emphasis on students' ability to decide on collective goals, to foster group identification, and to live as group members (Cave 2016). This is taught in both formal, classroom education, as evidenced by the fact that curriculum guidelines stipulate that teachers should actively inculcate skills of appropriate "interpersonal relations", good "social life" and "group living" in students (Cave

---

[16] As later chapters show, the non-kinship-based hierarchical system becomes *institutionalised* at the stage of junior high school (12/13 years old), with established conventions, norms, and rules regulating behaviours in much stricter and consequential ways as have been experienced by actors prior to junior high school.

2016, also refer to appendix 1); as well as informal education, such as activities in student clubs, where educators take on a more passive, supervisory role. Inasmuch as our goal of gaining a comprehensive understanding of *jouge kankei* is concerned, we focus on the informal educational aspect of extra-curricular club activities in secondary schools. This is because, only in club settings do, and must, students from different age cohorts come together to take part in designated activities, hence the necessary existence of social interactions and interpersonal relations based on age (and as I show, status) differences.

2.1.1 Types of secondary schools and the focus on schools with six-year programmes

In secondary education in Japan, two common routes are possible. One could attend a three-year junior high education, at the end of which a high school entrance examination is taken, and then proceed to a three-year senior high education based on the examination results. Alternatively, one could attend a school which offers both junior and senior high education in an integrated approach, that is, allowing students to stay in the same school (and importantly, club) for all six years of secondary schooling.[17]

As students attending separate three-year programmes in different junior and senior high schools take a comprehensive examination at the end of junior high third grade, most students in such schools quit their club activities at the beginning of junior third grade, or in the summer of their third year at the latest. This is to prepare for their examinations by attending extra classes either in school or in external tuition centres/cram schools. The result is that, most of the time, only junior first and second year members are actively present in club activities. However, with an age difference of only one year, the interactional and behavioural dynamics for actors implicated in *jouge kankei* would be less observable. According to the common logic of how the higher-lower relationships would function, the junior second year students would, in this case, be in charge of running the club and responsible for the junior first year new members. However, because junior second year students have only close to one year of club experience (and correspondingly, one year of language socialisation experience into *jouge kankei*) under their belt, they, too, are in the very learning and socialisation process into *jouge kankei*. But, if the junior third graders are

---

17 Refer to LeTendre (2000) and Rohlen (1983) for an overview of the system and different pathways.

no longer present, no one would have a constant oversight of the junior second year students, should they become unclear or "ignorant" of conventions and rules. Yet, as interviewees in the first phase of my field study pointed out (and as later chapters of this volume will show), junior second graders, or rather, the new members' immediate seniors (*ikkoue no senpai*), are themselves still in the socialisation process (albeit more advanced). If members of higher ranks were present, they would readily intervene by teaching junior second graders appropriate manners of speaking and doing things. These are some of the occasions where one could observe the manifestation of seniority-based hierarchies in explicit ways. In schools with three-year programmes, such interactional dynamics are no doubt less rich, as most of the time two to three grades of students interact.

The situation is different, however, in schools that offer a six-year integrated programme from junior first grade to senior third grade. This is because such settings allow students to skip the examination at the end of their junior third year. As a result, students could stay in the same school and club and be active for at least five years, hence giving clubs in these schools an age range of five to six years: with members from 12–13 to 17–18 years of age. Besides staying longer, such settings also mean higher participation rates: one of the schools where I did my fieldwork boasts a participation rate of 97% for its junior high section and an overall club participation rate of more than 90%. At any one time, students from at least five grades interact, providing much richer dynamics of interpersonal relations.

Another advantage of researching in this type of school setting is that since students stay in the same school for six years, this offers a realistic opportunity for people to change their club activities in the middle, for instance, upon entering the senior high section. Getting to know these students' experiences proved to be valuable in helping to compare hierarchical relationships in various clubs, and the unique intersection of age and experience in a club in the constitution of senior-junior identities. This in turn presents an unique opportunity to examine the dynamics of *jouge kankei* and inter-personal relations should biological age and organisational experience not correspond, an aspect that is also present in the adult corporate world. This aspect of schools with six-year programmes as an added advantage became increasingly clear in the course of my fieldwork.

To be sure, such a selection, as with any site selection in empirical research, implies limitations. For instance, most secondary schools offering a six-year integrated programme combining junior and senior high education are single-sex schools. The two schools where the bulk of the data in this book were gathered were no exception: being an all-girls' and an all-boys' school respectively. This implies that language socialisation into *jouge kankei* in mixed-gender environments were not observed.[18] Equally beyond the scope of this book is the difference in language socialisation experiences between students in three-year and six-year programmes. Nevertheless, I argue, and as I show throughout this volume, that such a site selection did not hinder the achievement of the main goal of this book project – to provide a comprehensive understanding of *jouge kankei* and the processes by which individuals are discursively socialised into it in the hitherto neglected setting of secondary school clubs. Hence, insofar as the aims of this research are concerned, schools with six-year programmes that accommodate interactions with a larger age range serve as a more conducive setting in which to analyse interactions, socialisations, and the discursive constitution of hierarchy. In the concluding chapter, I highlight several questions towards which future research could orientate, building on the basis of this book's findings and making up for its limitations.

2.2 Club life and social life: Early-stage *jouge kankei* socialisation in and through discourse in secondary school clubs

Sociologists and discourse analysts agree that schools and educational settings in contemporary society serve as "sites for studying not only the micro-dimensions of classroom talk but also the ways in which social structures are reproduced at macro-levels" (Rogers 2011: 3). Indeed, much of the recent literature in discourse analysis in educational settings focusses on classroom talk.[19] As I have already justified in chapter one, and will repeatedly illustrate throughout this book, extra-curricular club activities represent the most suitable milieu in which to study various aspects of language socialisation of individuals into *jouge kankei*. After having explained the choice of the type of schools, I explicate in this section some unique characteristics of club activities in Japanese schools.

While extra-curricular activities represent a common feature of informal education in many countries, such clubs in Japanese schools possess certain peculiarities that set them apart. Firstly, participation in a club activity is compulsory in almost every junior and senior high school in the country. Although there are no uniform guidelines from the central government, schools usually make such

---

18 It is equally noteworthy to mention that a mixed-gender research site would not automatically and necessarily allow for the collection of substantial interactional data between the genders, as adolescents at this stage in the *bukatsudou* context usually tend to interact with people of the same gender. See Hebert (2012).
19 See for example works by Adger and Wright (2005) and Kumaravadivelu (1999).

participation obligatory for most students (senior grades preparing for entrance examinations may be exempted). This translates into an exceptionally high participation rate in club activities of between 70 to 90 percent across Japan. This is observed by the Benesse Educational Research and Development Center (Benesse 2008), as well as independent scholars (Blackwood 2016), as Figure 2.1 documents:

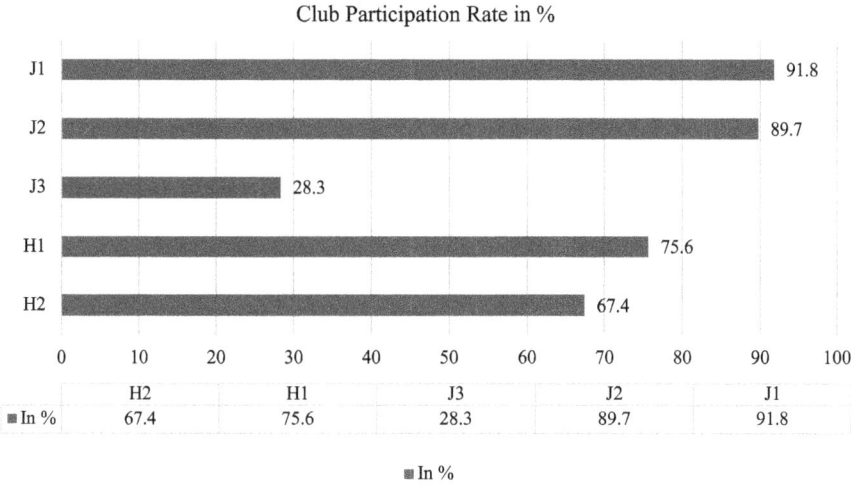

Figure 2.1: Club participation rate of secondary school students in Japan, taken from the Benesse Survey on Children's Time Management and Life After School (2008: 14).

As Figure 2.1 illustrates, save for students in their junior third year (J3), many of whom must prepare for the high school entrance examinations, and those in their final year of high school (not shown in Figure 2.1), who must prepare for the university entrance examinations, the national average participation rate in club activities reaches as high as 90 percent for junior high students (for J1 and J2 students) and 70 percent for senior high students (H1 and H2). Furthermore, a pertinent point to note is that, in Japan, the identity of a student who does *not* join a club is decidedly marked. This is manifested by the fact that such a person is often labelled as a "member" of *kitakubu* (literally "going home club", from *kitaku* – the act of going home, and *bu* – club). Such an identity ascribed to the minority of students who lack club membership highlights not only the group mentality of having to "belong" to a community in such a system, but also the fact that extra-curricular club life is deemed by many as an essential part of growing up in Japan; in other words, anything but "extra".

Secondly, although students can freely choose to join any club they like in the beginning, they are expected to stay with the same club throughout their school career, and not encouraged to try out diverse types of activity to explore one's interest and forte (Cave 2004; Rohlen 1983). To change a club is not only difficult, but most often also frowned upon (LeTendre 2000). This is due to Japanese secondary education's emphasis on perseverance, discipline, as well as the fostering of collective responsibility taking, decision-making, and a sense of belonging with one and the same group (Iwama 1995). Inculcating such values has been an important educational aspect of extra-curricular clubs in preparing their members for the adult world. As Iwama notes, "[a]ll through the Japanese company, teamwork, cooperation, consensus, equalization, human relationships, consciousness of belonging, and devotion to the company are observed" (Iwama 1995: 75). Since the same values have been highly regarded in corporate Japan, the uniqueness of extra-curricular clubs and the socialisation of student members into the *jouge kankei* social order in such contexts serve a direct socialisation linking school and work.

In addition to the high participation and low turnover rates, students spend a significant amount of time in club activities (Blackwood 2016). This is corroborated by a 2008 Benesse study which reported that junior high students spent 100 minutes and senior high students spent 120 minutes on average per day in club activities (Benesse 2008: 14). For many students, however, the amount of time spent in clubs could be much higher, especially if their clubs are active in competitions, performances and neighbourhood events. Furthermore, the Benesse survey did not take into account the amount of time students spent on club activities *outside* of the officially allocated after-school hours for club activities, which could include anything from midday meetings during lunch time, early morning practice sessions before classes, and extra sessions after the officially allocated hours.[20] In extreme cases, students devote so much of their time to club activities that the only other activity to which they devote more time is sleep (Hebert 2012).

So what kind of socialisation goes on in secondary school *bukatsudou* that is peculiar to Japan? Insofar as honorifics and general language etiquettes (*kotobazukai*) and the recognition of indexical relations in tandem with such language use is concerned (see 1.2.1), it is revealing that both realms of formal classroom and informal *bukatsudou* education are responsible for cultivating students' speech and the ability to recognise social relations. This is corroborated by results from the 2005

---

20 Refer to later chapters for empirical descriptions. In the course of my fieldwork, I have seen active members, that is, those not preparing for entrance examination, being asked to devote anywhere from two (weekdays) to eight (Sundays) hours per day.

nation-wide survey of the Agency for Cultural Affairs on the general public's consciousness of honorific speech (see Figures 2.2 and 2.3 below). When asked on the top five occasions in the past in which they learned honorifics, the age group of 16 to 19-year olds (senior high school equivalent) replied as follows:

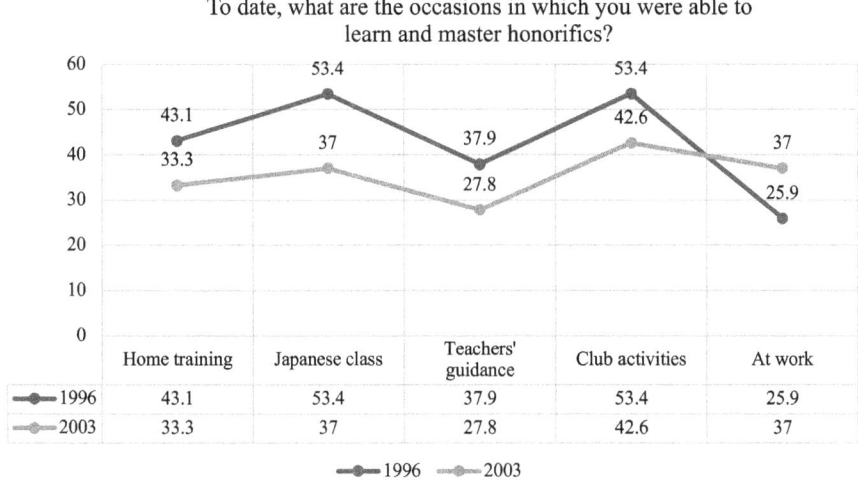

Figure 2.2: Top five occasions to learn polite language (multiple responses allowed) for boys aged 16–19, 1996 and 2003 comparison (Agency for Cultural Affairs 2005).

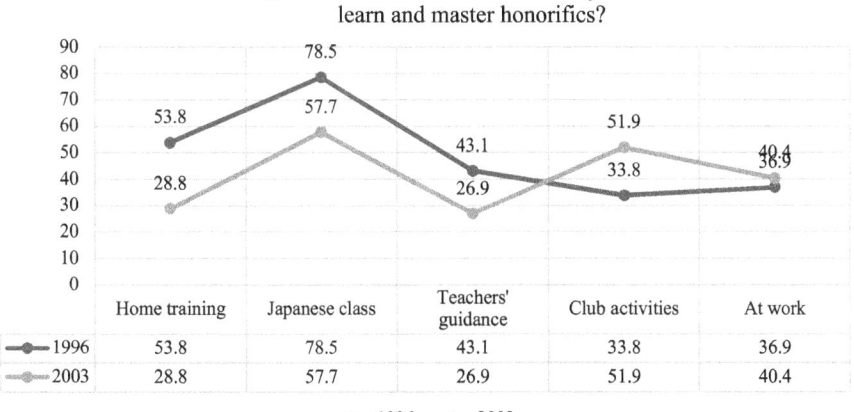

Figure 2.3: Top five occasions to learn polite language (multiple responses allowed) for girls aged 16–19, 1996 and 2003 comparison (Agency for Cultural Affairs 2005).

In general terms, we could observe in both figures that, by 2003, the "domestic" factor of home training has diminished in significance in an individual's acquisition of honorifics. In addition, both figures above reveal that school (as an "external" factor) is the most important context in Japan in which honorifics are learned and (speaking) manners cultivated. This underpins the significance of schools' socialising function in preparing students for the needs of adult society. The strength of the school to work linkage is again evidenced by the representation of important and prestigious economic and financial organisations, such as the Japanese Federation of Employers' Associations, the Japanese Committee for Economic Development, and the Japan Chamber of Commerce and Industry, on various state advisory councils including that of the Ministry of Education (McVeigh 2002). If the rationalisation of the *kokugo* is regarded as a necessary tool in building an economically powerful nation-state (Gottlieb 1996; McVeigh 2002), it will only be natural that there is an important link between the language socialisation in honorifics, in particular in extra-curricular clubs, and the needs of the economy. As shown in Figure 2.2 above, for most boys, club activities have been an important setting for learning and mastering honorifics; the perceived importance of club activities in the learning of honorifics grew from 1996, where club activities and Japanese classes were viewed as equally important, to 2003, where club activities stood as the single most important setting, ahead of Japanese classes and part-time work (*arubaito*). The situation for girls in the same age group was not drastically different, as Figure 2.3 reveals. For girls aged 16 to 19, Japanese classes in schools were, in both phases of the survey, the most important occasion to learn and master honorifics. However, if we observe the drastic change between 1996 and 2003 for girls, a noteworthy trend emerges. While club activities represented one of the least important settings to learn and master honorifics in 1996, they became the second most important setting in 2003, only several percentage points shy of Japanese language classes, and even ahead of home training (family education and discipline).

However, it should be noted that students' experiences and contact with honorifics and related language/social etiquettes regarding *jouge kankei* in the classroom and in clubs are qualitatively different. A look at the junior high school curriculum guidelines on teaching goals of Japanese language classes (*kokugo*) issued by the Ministry of Education, Culture, Sports, Science and Technology (MEXT), in Table 2.2, makes the point clear:

Table 2.2 reveals that, in formal classroom educational contexts, junior high students are only expected to *understand* the functions and logics behind honorifics by the end of their second year, and are expected to *use* honorifics (which in this case implies the ability to recognise indexical relations and self-identification) by the end of their third year. However, findings from the initial stage of my field study reveal (and later chapters show) that students are

Table 2.2: Junior high school curriculum guidelines, published by the Ministry of Education, Culture, Sports, Science and Technology (MEXT 2008). Emphasis added. All translations are mine.

Subject	Junior High Grade	Section	Guidelines
Japanese	2	Traditional aspects and special characteristics of the national language	– On matters related to rules and characteristics of the language – Students should *understand* the difference between spoken and written language, the roles fulfilled by the common language and dialects, and the functions of honorifics
	3	Teaching contents	– On nurturing students' speaking and listening abilities – To use honorifics appropriately according to interaction situations and the state of interlocutors
		Traditional aspects and special characteristics of the national language	– On matters related to rules and characteristics of the language – Together with the understanding of diachronic changes of language and the differences across generations, students should *appropriately use* honorifics in their social life

required to learn and apply a whole range of "polite" ways of speaking to seniors and recognise their place in the hierarchy as soon as they enter a club in junior first grade. It can be suggested, therefore, that in terms of the language socialisation and teaching of honorifics and the appropriate contexts for their application, the informal educational aspect of club activities far precedes the formal educational aspect of classroom Japanese teaching, at times by one to two years. In addition, whereas classrooms focus on theoretical and abstract learning, the school club context requires the real-world *application* of honorifics in practical settings, among individuals of different age-statuses.

In effect, a separate large-scale national empirical survey on honorifics in schools conducted by the National Institute for Japanese Language and Linguistics (NINJAL 2002) further attests to the extent of students' learning of honorifics through club activities (NINJAL 2002). Results of this survey as reproduced in

Figures 2.4 and 2.5 below demonstrate that secondary school students are most careful in taking care of their ways of speaking when interacting with seniors in club contexts, behind only interactions with external visitors and teachers in staffroom:

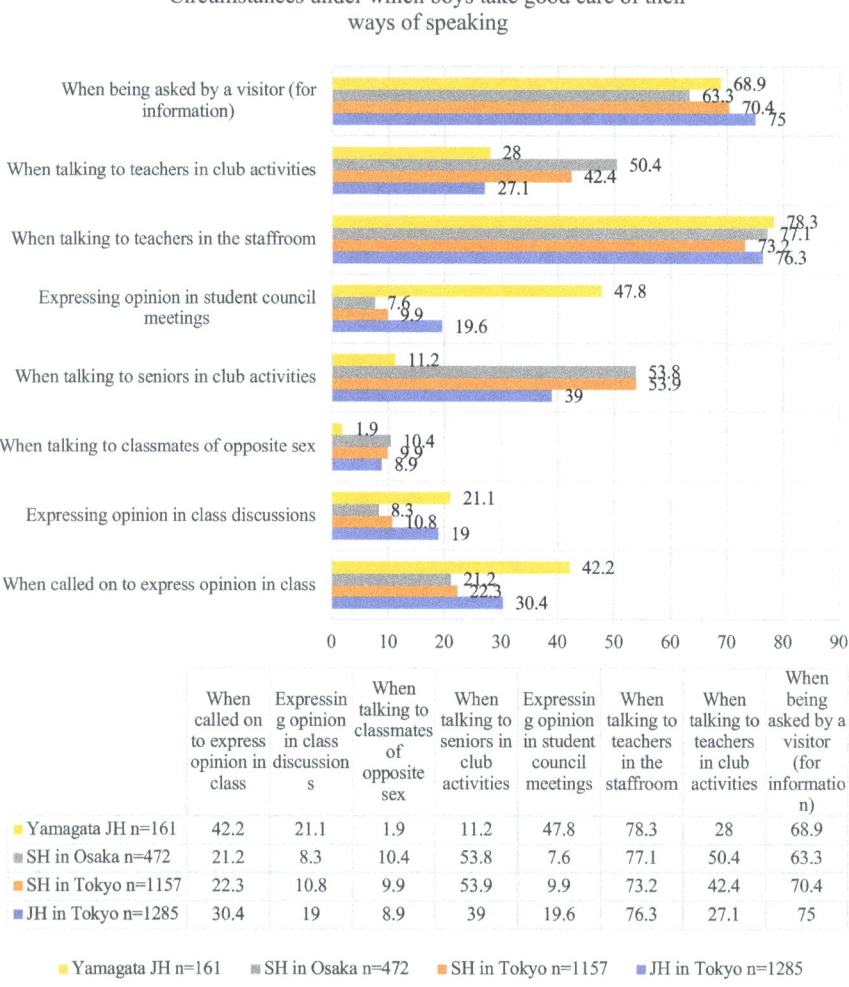

Figure 2.4: Circumstances under which boys take good care of their ways of speaking. Source: NINJAL (2002) Honorifics in Japanese Schools I: Results from Questionnaires (pages 144, 168, 170). Note: JH denotes junior high schools, SH denotes senior high schools, n denotes the total number of respondents, and only one school in Yamagata took part in the survey.

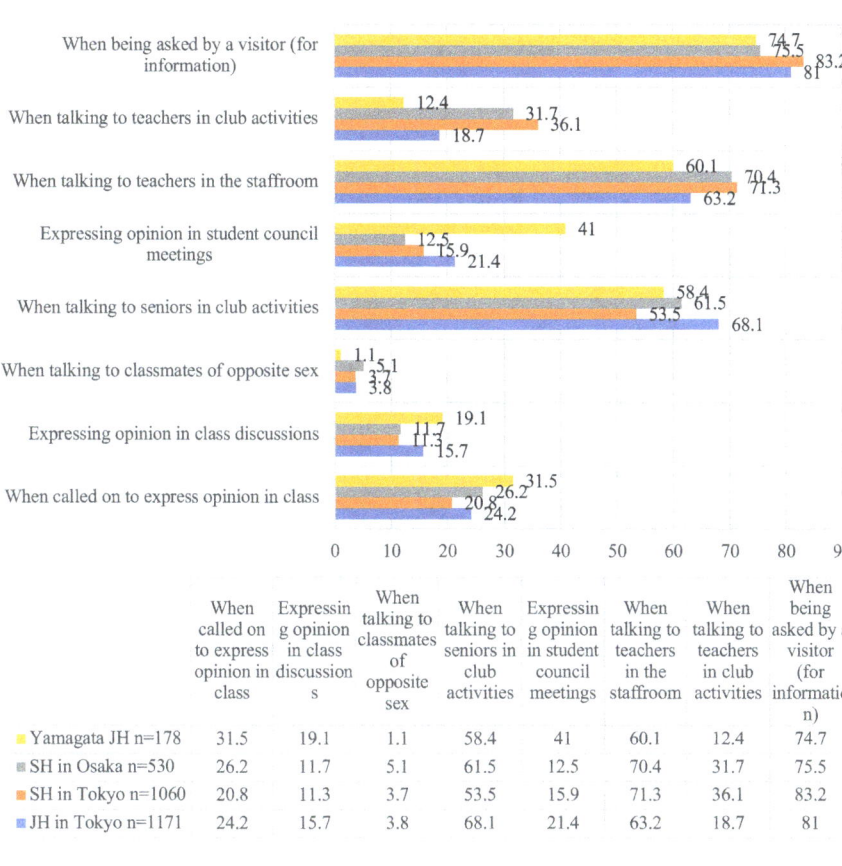

Figure 2.5: Circumstances under which girls take good care of their ways of speaking. Source: NINJAL (2002) Honorifics in Japanese Schools I: Results from Questionnaires (pages 144, 168, 170). Note: JH denotes junior high schools, SH denotes senior high schools, n denotes the total number of respondents, and only one school in Yamagata took part in the survey.

The results of the survey show the same trend for both (Figure 2.4) boys and girls (Figure 2.5). If we focus on interactional situations within the school context among actors in school, we see that talking to one's seniors in club activities is, on the whole, the second most important situation in which one should mind her/his language, just below talking to teachers in the staffroom (NINJAL 2002). What is revealing is that, within the setting of club activities, significantly more students think that they should be careful of the way they speak to seniors, as compared even to teachers.[21]

As a matter of fact, in today's Japanese society, individuals might be *learning* most of their honorifics in junior and senior high school Japanese lessons, but the setting in which they (are forced to) put the knowledge into practice, *apply* and *reinforce* what they have learned is primarily the club activities in junior and senior high schools. However, it would be a mistake to conclude that using honorifics and appropriate ways of speaking is simply a matter of uttering words. It is well established that the Japanese social hierarchical system is well encoded in the language, be it in the grammar of forms of address or in the use of honorifics, so that it is virtually impossible to utter a socially neutral sentence (Cook 2008; Mühlhäusler and Harré 1990). Therefore, to use appropriate and honorific language in the right context is to perform a social act, recognise fine-tuned social relationships, and put oneself and one's interlocutors in different social identities, roles, and statuses (Miwa 2000).

Results of my phase-one study, corroborated by survey findings from the Agency for Cultural Affairs (2005) and NINJAL (2002), thus show that club activities in secondary schools in Japan are important repositories of *jouge kankei*. In addition, *bukatsudou* represents an arena in which language norms and conventions interact intensively with the hierarchical system, and into which actors (student members) are socialised from the beginning. Therefore, "norms and conventions on language use", the "age-based seniority system", as well as "bodily comportment" represent the *defining* and central *constitutive* elements of this hierarchical system. In the following section, I introduce the world of *bukatsudou* in Japanese schools.

2.2.1 Type of clubs and the main focus of this study

Extra-curricular clubs in Japanese schools can be subdivided into either sports or cultural clubs. The former category usually consists of clubs such as baseball, football, rugby, basketball, tennis and kendo, whereas the latter category includes clubs such as wind orchestra, choir, pop music band, chess, art, science, broadcasting and foreign language societies/study groups. Though the exact offering of extra-curricular activities may vary from one school to the other (for example, not

---

[21] This shows, and is corroborated by my observations during fieldwork, that teachers play a secondary role in managing and organising clubs in schools, as these are settings where senior members assume primary responsibility and authority. Hence, teachers are not part of the *jouge kankei* of students. Refer to section 2.3.2.

every school has a sumo wrestling club), differences are kept at a minimum across cities and regions (LeTendre 2000). Most existing literature on Japanese schools and clubs have almost exclusively targeted sports clubs (see for example Blackwood 2015; 2016; Cave 2004; and Light 2008), with Hebert's (2012) ethnography of a Tokyo junior high school wind orchestra being the first to examine a cultural club in-depth. In this section, I explain the reasons for which I chose cultural clubs as main sites in the two selected schools. This overwhelming focus on sports groups is based on the conventional belief that sports clubs constitute an important element of spiritual and moral education in Japanese schools (Blackwood 2016; Cave 2004). In fact, as far back as the 1960s and 1970s, Nakane (1970) made the following observations as regards sports clubs in Japanese schools:

> The young Japanese, moreover, is never free of the seniority system. In schools there is a very distinct senior-junior ranking among students, which is observed particularly strictly among those who form sports clubs. In a student mountaineering club, for example, it is the students of a junior class who carry a heavier load while climbing, pitch the tent and prepare the evening meal under the surveillance of the senior students, who may sit smoking. When the preparations are over it is the senior students who take the meal first, served by the junior students. (Nakane 1970: 32)

What students experience and learn in these kinds of sports clubs are in fact subservience and manners that have been deemed necessary to function competently in the adult society, especially in corporate life. Recent research has also shown that students think that clubs can equip them with the right etiquette and character to be successful in the future (Blackwood 2016). However, does such educational experience, and by extension the language socialisation into *jouge kankei* occur only, or mainly in sports clubs? Do sports clubs in Japanese schools always have far stricter rules regulating behaviour and clearer manifestations of status than cultural clubs? Scholars who have studied clubs or mentioned them in passing have acknowledged that there are exceptions, notably with school orchestras, but so far none has taken to examine higher-lower relationships in musical groups.[22] During my initial fieldwork phase, interviewees (students and graduates) from different club backgrounds (sports and cultural) revealed that, in essence, if different clubs displayed different levels of strictness as regards interpersonal relations, the difference depended more on

---

[22] Recent studies on school clubs and schools in Japan include the experience and institutionalisation of adolescence (LeTendre 2000), functions of sports clubs in education (Cave 2004), and a general ethnography of a junior high school wind orchestra (Hebert 2012). Though Hebert's (2012) work represents the first major attempt to study a school musical club, it is more general and socio-historical in nature, and did not explore interpersonal relations in-depth.

a whole range of other factors – club history, ambitions,[23] number of members, personalities of leaders, amongst others – than the nature of activity per se. Musical groups could be highly demanding in terms of how members with different status should behave, just as there would be sports groups that tend to be more relaxed. With special regard to *jouge kankei*, it is telling to observe the general tendency that certain musical groups, most notably the orchestra, but also the choir, could be as demanding as, or even more so than most sports groups. This is exemplified by the empirical survey on the use of honorifics (*keigo*) in Japanese junior high schools (NINJAL 2002). For instance, on whether students in different types of clubs use the suffix "*senpai*" (which means senior) as a term of address to acknowledge the addressee's seniority, the survey, which included approximately 5000 junior and senior high school students from over 50 schools in Tokyo, Osaka, and Yamagata, found that girls in music and cultural clubs were as likely to use "*senpai*" to show respect and good linguistic mannerism to seniors as girls in sports clubs (NINJAL 2002: 115–116). As for boys, while boys in sports clubs showed a slightly higher tendency to use "*senpai*" than those in cultural clubs, the one exception came from boys who were in orchestra: with 71 percent of orchestra members reported using "*senpai*" to their seniors. This figure is quite a margin higher than most sports clubs including those in baseball (67 percent), basketball (65 percent), and football (54 percent) (NINJAL 2002: 115–116). Hence, it could be said that the same *nature* of hierarchy exists wherever there are groups, what varies, then, is the *degree* of manifestation of hierarchical order, which does not necessarily go along the lines of the types of activities. While the functioning and dynamics of sports clubs are well documented, it is not so much the case in musical groups, let alone in-depth analyses of interpersonal relations and hierarchical orders. This lack of research is despite the fact that wind orchestras represent the most popular extra-curricular club for girls in Japanese schools (Hebert 2012). The only one recent ethnographic work by Hebert (2012) comprised of a general description of the organisation and functioning of a junior high school wind orchestra, rather than a detailed examination of the discursive constitution of *jouge kankei*.

Furthermore, a unique aspect of certain musical groups, such as the orchestra and choir, is that they tend to be larger than most other cultural and sports groups, that is, usually with a membership of more than 50 students. Such large clubs in the context of schools offering a six-year programme means that their size, coupled with the fact that students from at least five different age-cohorts

---

[23] For instance, if a particular club is aiming for a prize in a regional/national sports/music/dance competition.

interact, rich interactional dynamics and language socialisation processes are present. Furthermore, these clubs have a highly developed organisational structure. For instance, besides the usual positions of president (*buchou*), vice-president (*fukubuchou*), and grade leaders (*gakunenchou*), the composition of orchestras means that there are at least seven to eight sub-divisions according to instruments, each headed by a 'part leader' (*paato riidaa*) and an acting/vice leader, plus at least one student conductor. Orchestras and choirs can afford to have such a refined organisational structure that bears resemblance to most organisations in adult society (such as enterprises, political parties, bureaucracies, etc) mainly thanks to their large membership (refer to section 2.4 for an overview of the organisational structures of the three selected clubs).

2.3 Introducing the two schools

As mentioned earlier, my fieldwork sites are two single-sex schools located in Tokyo, and both offer six-year programmes from junior high first grade to senior high third grade. The girls' school,[24] Tokyo Daiichi Girls' Junior and Senior High School (hereinafter Tokyo Daiichi), and the boys' school, Tokyo Daini Boys' Junior and Senior High School (hereinafter Tokyo Daini), are both located in the same ward, and are one metro station away from each other. They are each affiliated to a university and are *not* related to each other. Though both are academic secondary schools[25] and a majority of their graduates proceed to tertiary education, there is a considerable gap in academic reputation based on the universities to which each is affiliated. Some basic information on these two schools can be found in Table 2.3 below:

The fact that so many students in Tokyo Daini went on to the affiliated university could be explained by the good reputation of the affiliated university. On several occasions throughout my research stay, students and teachers of this school explained to me that as long as one maintained decent passing grades throughout the senior high school years, admission to the affiliated university was all but guaranteed (though one might not get into his most desired department). On the contrary, most students in Tokyo Daiichi did not want to proceed

---

[24] One of the commitments accompanying my research on and with minors was that strict anonymity was to be observed. Thus, whenever names of the schools or of informants from these schools are mentioned from now on, only pseudonyms are utilised.

[25] For a discussion on different types of junior and senior high schools in Japan (such as academic, technical, vocational, commercial, correspondence, and so on), see Dierkes (2009) and Rohlen (1983).

Table 2.3: Basic information on the two schools as my fieldwork sites. Information is taken from the schools' websites.

School	Tokyo Daiichi Girls' Junior & Senior High	Tokyo Daini Boys' Junior & Senior High
Type	Urban, girls', academic, 6-year programme	Urban, boys', academic, 6-year programme
Enrolment (approximate)	1500	2000
% of graduates proceeding to the affiliated university*	17.8	72.8
% of graduates proceeding to other 4-year universities	66.5	19.5
% total in university	84.3	92.3
% of graduates proceeding to 2-year junior colleges	2.4	0.2
Rounin+	13.3	7.5

* All figures are from the graduating class of 2014. +*Rounin* in this case refers to a high school graduate who has finished her/his studies and is preparing to take university entrance examinations (again); usually those who failed (to gain admission to her/his preferred university/programme) in the first attempt.

to the affiliated university due to its poor reputation. Those who could, would aim for admission elsewhere. Hence it was more common in Tokyo Daiichi than in Tokyo Daini to see students quit clubs early, that is, upon entering their last year in senior high school, in order to attend cram schools and prepare intensively during the year prior to their entrance examinations.

In terms of the immediate neighbourhood and environment surrounding the two schools, it can be said that both were located in densely-populated urban, middle-class areas. Tokyo Daiichi's campus is a 15-minute walk from the nearest metro station. Along the way are some shopping arcades lined with shops specialising in electronic products, alternative cafes and pubs. The school compound is not extensive, but attractive, with imposing new buildings (which are among the tallest and newest in the district, visible from afar with the school name inscribed) in maroon brick colour right beside the main street, and some older buildings in greyish concrete style at the back, surrounding a sports field, rounded off with high translucent fences. The main entrance and new buildings face the main street, whereas the older buildings and the field are surrounded by quiet but densely-packed residential areas with 2 or 3-storey houses next to each other. Like most other schools in urban areas in Japan, Tokyo Daiichi's main gate is always half closed, and there is at least one elderly guard on standby, even on Sundays, guiding visitors and vehicles in and out.

The district in which Tokyo Daini is located is slightly quieter and more affluent. It is a 10-minute walk from the nearest metro station, mostly along a narrow street with some bakeries, Western dining restaurants, and a stylish-looking hair saloon on one side, and rows of tracks on the other, with passing trains providing the only noise pollution. Also situated in the middle of a residential area, the school compound had been undergoing large-scale renovation and expansion works when I began my fieldwork in November 2015. The gates are equally guarded and the guards perform the same duties as observed in Tokyo Daiichi.

2.4 The three student clubs

Table 2.4 below provides an overview of the three student clubs where extensive data collection took place:

Table 2.4: Basic information on the three student clubs in the two schools.

Clubs	Tokyo Daiichi Orchestra	Tokyo Daiichi Choir	Tokyo Daini Orchestra
Strength of active members	80	150	100
No. of practice sessions/week*	6	6	6
Profile of main teachers in charge	A math and a science teacher	Two music teachers (pianist and vocal)	Two music teachers

* This represents the number of days per week when they have practice. Duration of each practice session varies: usually from 16:00 to 18:00 on weekdays, from 13:00 to 18:00 on Saturdays, and from 09:00 to 16:00 on Sundays. During school holidays and especially before important events such as annual concerts and competitions, all three groups will have a schedule of 09:00 to 18:00 seven days a week.

Being such big groups with people from diverse grades, how are social roles and statuses divided and occupied? In Japanese school club parlance, everyone involved in a club is a *buin* (club member). Among all the members, there exist two general statuses: one is either a *senpai* (senior) or a *kouhai* (junior), depending on one's age cohort in relation to others. The relationship between a *senpai* and a *kouhai* is the defining characteristic of *jouge kankei* and the main topic of our inquiry. Being a junior to someone else in a club does not simply mean acknowledging the fact that one is younger in terms of age, but such a status comes with sets of obligations, duties, and certain entitlements. As results of my first-stage field study and subsequent empirical chapters demonstrate, some of these include the regulated behaviour of using honorifics, taking care of one's bodily movements in the presence of seniors, as well as running errands for seniors and doing "dirty jobs". Conversely, being seniors imply having vast powers, privileges, and obligations vis-à-vis juniors. An understanding of the mechanisms in *senpai-kouhai* relations is paramount to the understanding of the construction and maintenance of hierarchy in Japanese school clubs.

Though each club remains unique in certain aspects, they all share some common features in their organisational structures (as with most extra-curricular clubs, at least in medium to large sized urban schools). I list below some common roles and ranks fulfilled by actors involved in the three selected clubs.[26] One important point to bear in mind is that, many of the following ranks and roles are often more administrative than interpersonal. In other words, they are designed principally to facilitate the smooth running of the clubs rather than regulating individual behaviours in the same way as in *senpai-kouhai* relations. It is nonetheless important to reiterate that, more often than not, the age-based seniority system, rather than individual capabilities, is decisive in assigning the following roles and functions to individual members[27] (see also 1.2.1). It should be useful for readers who are unfamiliar with extra-curricular activities and youth groups in Japan to have a clear grip on the basic organisational structure of the clubs below, as I will be referring to some of these roles and ranks throughout this book:

- *Kouchi* (coach): All three clubs employ external instructors who are professional musicians active in the music scene across the nation. They usually come once or twice a week during the final months leading up to the annual competitions and concerts. Such instructors are rarely, if at all, involved in the daily running and management of the clubs, for they only come for rehearsals and provide expert opinions to improve the musicality of the student performers. Hence, they are not involved in the social relations of *jouge kankei* in the clubs.

---

26 Although the description pertains specifically to the three selected clubs in my study, a comparison with others who had studied school clubs, such as Hebert (2012), shows that such roles and ranks are common across Japan.
27 This alone represents an important aspect of the raison d'être of extra-curricular clubs: to make individual adolescents adapt to the adult world which is also replete with hierarchy.

- *Komon sensei* (teachers in charge): Each club has at least one teacher in charge who is also a member of the school's teaching staff. Teachers in charge may or may not be music teachers, as manifested by the fact that none of the teachers in charge of Tokyo Daiichi Orchestra teaches music. In Japanese junior and senior high schools, it is usually part of a teacher's responsibilities to supervise an extra-curricular club, and though teachers may indicate a preference, it is ultimately decided by the school administration. In school clubs across the country, such teachers in charge play a predominantly supporting role, since students assume "virtually total responsibility for the diverse program of school clubs" (Iwama 1995: 77). The job of teachers, then, include making sure that club members have enough rooms to carry out their practice, printing out practice schedules (decided by senior students) for every member, and acting as adult liaison persons between the student clubs and external agencies such as concert halls and competition committees. They, too, fall outside the *jouge kankei* in the clubs.
- OG/OB[28] ("old girl"/"old boy"): This status is automatically acquired once members graduate from their respective high schools and become part of the clubs' alumni. Alumni members do not appear in daily practices, but they do show up from time to time, especially before and during important events such as concerts and competitions, either to coach their juniors or to help with stage set-up or other miscellaneous tasks. Their seniority is recognised by current members of the clubs, even if they do not personally know the alumni members, and members are taught to treat OG/OB with utmost respect, hence the application of *jouge kankei* here.
- *Buchou*[29] (president): This is the highest *administrative* position for student members in a club, and is always occupied by someone from the most senior grade present. The president runs, together with the rest of the administrative team, the club: from selecting outside competitions in which to participate to organising summer camps. The club president is also responsible for daily internal communications, that is, communicating important notices to members of the other grades and teachers/external instructors

---

28 Hierarchy among alumni members also exists according to the year in which one graduated.
29 It is also a common practice in many clubs to appoint one junior position each for the post of president, vice president, and student conductors. In this case, they will be occupied by the most senior students of the junior high section, that is, the junior third graders. Their duties are almost identical to those of the senior leadership, except that their administrative responsibility is limited only to junior high students. Such positions are often regarded by juniors as learning opportunities before assuming heavier responsibilities in senior high school, although being a junior leader does not guarantee senior leadership positions in the future.

via LINE group messaging, telephone, and/or emails. The president is also a representative of the club and speaks on behalf of the club during concerts and events. Another important function of the president is to shout out orders for various social activities (see chapter three) before, during, and after practice, as well as to encourage the active performance of greetings by junior members to their seniors.
- *Fukubuchou* (vice president): The post of vice president is also occupied by someone from the most senior grade in all three clubs. Besides the general role of supporting the club president, the vice president will usually be responsible for compiling contact information for the entire club, attendance-taking (this includes issuing warning to juniors with poor attendance records), and acting as secretary during meetings.
- *Gakusei shikisha* (student conductor): Student conductors in all three clubs are chosen by the outgoing cohort of most senior members based on their perception of potential new student conductors' musical ability. Although this is the only instance where ability is a factor for consideration, it ultimately follows the same logic that only members from the senior second grade could be chosen by outgoing senior third graders to succeed them.[30] The most important tasks of student conductors are to plan for monthly practice schedules and to conduct their respective orchestras/choirs in the absence of external instructors or teachers in charge. They also actively communicate with external instructors with regard to ways of improving the musicality of the student members.
- *Paato rida* (section leader): A section leader is a person who takes charge of an instrumental or vocal section (for example, a trombone section leader or a soprano section leader). This position is always assumed by a member from the most senior cohort in each section. Section leaders conduct sectional practices and are mainly responsible for teaching junior new members how to play their instruments. They also have the duty of attendance-taking within their sections and they should know the whereabouts of all their section members.
- *Gakunen rida* (grade leader): In the three clubs, each grade also has a grade leader, chosen by the most senior outgoing cohort. The grade leaders act as liaison persons between their grades and the clubs' senior management.

---

30 Hence ruling out the possibility that a younger student with a higher level of musicianship conducting her/his seniors.

In all three clubs, administrative posts, as well as positions of power and responsibility, are designated according to the age-based seniority principle, as is common practice throughout the country. The clubs' leadership organisational structures are re-created in the following three Figures 2.6, 2.7, and 2.8:

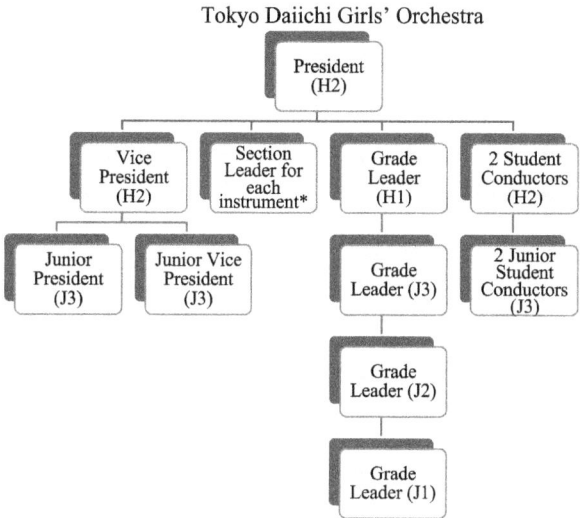

Figure 2.6: Organisational structure in Tokyo Daiichi Girls' Orchestra. The codes in parentheses denote the grade of students occupying a particular position (J1–J3 represent junior first to third graders respectively, while H1 and H2 represent senior high first and second grades).
*Note that not all section leaders are from senior high second grade because not every section has a senior second grader.

Figure 2.6 above shows the organisational structure of Tokyo Daiichi Orchestra. The club policy stipulates that once a member reaches senior third year (H3), she will have to "retire" (*intai*) so as to be able to fully concentrate on university entrance examinations. This explains the fact that senior second year students are de facto the most senior in the orchestra and occupy, consequently, available administrative positions. It should be pointed out that, in all clubs, the administrative arrangement for the various positions (such as the president and the student conductors) within one age cohort refers only to the scope of allocated duties and does not translate into social hierarchy in daily club life. In other words, all members of the senior second grade ought to be respected by members of junior grades in the same manner, regardless of the positions held. In addition, even though the senior third graders no longer hold executive positions, when they appear in the music room or when junior members come across them in school, they are still treated with the highest level of respect. Within each grade, a flat hierarchy dominates interpersonal relations, regardless of whether or not one occupies an administrative role.

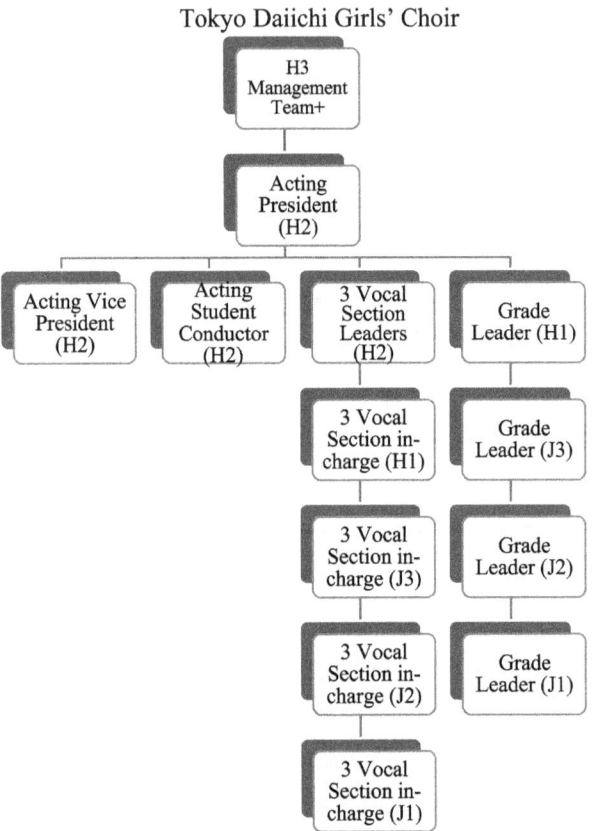

Figure 2.7: Organisational structure in Tokyo Daiichi Girls' Choir. The senior third year management team does not participate in club activities for the entire year.

Figure 2.7 above shows the organisational structure of Tokyo Daiichi Choir. There exists no strict rules as to when a member should retire from club activities to concentrate on her studies. What the teachers in charge encourage, according to one of them, is that members should decide for themselves what is important and prioritise what they want to do in their final year of studies. The usual practice, however, is that the entire cohort of senior third year students would stay on for at least six to eight months into their final year in high school, so as to form the backbone of the competitive choir that regularly aims to get into the All-Japan School Choir Competition's national finals. This means that, in any given academic year (from April to March), there will be times where the most senior grade present are the senior third year students, and at times the senior second graders. Hence the senior third graders hold both de jure power as well as de facto leadership when they are present. When they are absent, the senior second year members take over de facto leadership. The other organisational features and age-based hierarchical mechanisms work very much in the same way as Tokyo Daiichi's Orchestra.

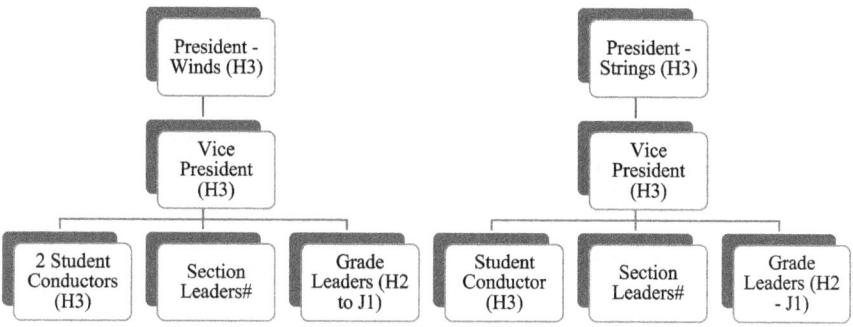

Figure 2.8: Organisational structure in Tokyo Daini Boys' Orchestra.
#Note that section leaders are those that occupy the oldest age cohort.

Tokyo Daini Boys' Orchestra is a symphony orchestra divided into strings and winds sections, as shown in the above Figure 2.8. Most of the time, these two groups practice separately and in each section, there is hence an independent organisational structure as shown above. A peculiarity in Tokyo Daini Boys' School is that, since the vast majority of the students proceed to the affiliated university, they do not have to worry about preparations for university entrance examinations. As a consequence, with the exception of a brief one-month period for the senior high third year final examinations, senior third graders continue to participate actively in club life until their graduation. This gives clubs in Tokyo Daini the largest possible age range of members from 12/13 (J1) to 17/18 years old (H3). In addition, although the orchestra club is divided into two sections in most of their daily activities, they remain members of the same club and hence hierarchical relations apply to both sections; for example, a junior second grader in the winds section is expected to acknowledge a senior third grader in the strings section in the same way as he would acknowledge a senior in his winds section. Compared to the two clubs in Tokyo Daiichi School, this orchestra's leadership structure and ranks appear to be less refined. For instance, there is no junior high leadership team.

It is apparent, by now, that all three clubs follow the same logic of organisational structures and the rule of thumb that forms the social organisation of clubs: age-based seniority system. In effect, the commonality of such organisational principles has been corroborated by interviewees throughout my fieldwork (when I asked them to describe organisational structures of other clubs in their schools).

2.5 Social situations as focus of data collection

In each of the three selected fieldwork sites, six social situations were the main foci of my data collection and analysis. In ethnographic parlance, a social situation is understood as "the stream of behavior (activities) carried out by people (actors) in a particular location (place)" (Spradley 1980: 86). Ethnographers are directly exposed to social situations and it is in social situations where participant observations are done (Spradley 1980). Any given social situation is comprised of:
- **Place**: a physical setting where actors gather to perform activities.
- **Actors**: particular kinds of people involved.

Throughout my fieldwork, I performed participant observations in and gathered data from the following social situations consisting of diverse locations, kinds of actors and activities:
- **Social situation 1: Annual concerts (*teikiensoukai*)**
    - Place: Public concert halls
    - Actors: Full club strength plus all teachers in charge, external instructors, alumni, and parents
- **Social situation 2: Combined rehearsals (*gassou*)**
    - Place: Music rooms (each of the three clubs possesses a large music room enough to hold all members plus instruments)
    - Actors: Full club strength plus teachers in charge and external instructors
- **Social situation 3: Small group practices (*paato renshuu*)**
    - Place: Designated classrooms in respective schools
    - Actors: Members of the same instrumental/vocal section

- **Social situation 4: Breaks (*kyuukei*)**
    - Place: Music rooms or classrooms
    - Actors: Members of the same grade[31]
- **Social situation 5: Weekend lunch breaks (*ohiru*)**
    - Place: Designated place according to grades
    - Actors: Members of the same grade[32]
- **Social situation 6: Cleaning up (*souji*)**
    - Place: Music rooms and classrooms
    - Actors: Both lower grade junior high students (cleaning) and higher grade senior students (supervision)

The six social situations outlined above covered altogether a wide spectrum of lived experiences by club members. These ranged from the daily life of club members (situations 2 to 6) to important annual events (situation 1). Moreover, these social situations covered the lived experiences of all members, irrespective of seniority. In addition, for each social activity, places were usually easily identifiable as they were fixed and designated locations.[33] From the next chapter onwards, I present empirical data gathered from the afore-mentioned social situations and analyse the ways in which language socialisation in and through discourse takes place in secondary school clubs to help student members become competent members of society.

2.6 Summary of chapter

This chapter provided an overview of the Japanese secondary education, and showed peculiarities of *bukatsudou* in Japanese secondary schools. It revealed how clubs serve as repositories of *jouge kankei* and represent an important milieu in which language socialisation occurs. Moreover, arguments for the selection of the specific types of schools and clubs to achieve the goals of the inquiry were

---

[31] Note that for breaks during full rehearsals or small group practices, there was always a presence of members of other grades. However, to be in a social situation means that actors are engaging in some form of activities. As later chapters will show, only actors from the same grade would be actively "involved" in activities with each other: chatting or sharing snacks.

[32] In all three clubs, students did not have their lunch with their instrumental/vocal sections. Instead, members of the same grade always gathered together and had their lunch as a group, in a space that was designated to them. Refer to chapter six.

[33] The ways in which space in different places was used also revealed behavioural patterns in the institutional order of hierarchy. Refer to chapter six.

also presented. I have also introduced the specific clubs and their organisations so that readers will, by now, be familiar with the contexts to which I refer in the following chapters. Indeed, if there is so much *jouge kankei* and socialisation going on in such club contexts, and if club members have little prior knowledge about it, how, then, do they make sense of this new social order through words and deeds? This is the focus of chapter three.

3 Ideologies, power, text, and discourse: *Bukatsudou* as sites of learning and socialisation in language and discourse

Beginning with this chapter, and through to chapter six, I present various types of data gathered during my ethnographic fieldwork and empirical analyses of the discursive constitution of *jouge kankei* in secondary school clubs. In this chapter, I will first show that, upon entering junior high school, students in Japan experience immediate socialisation into the roles and expectations of *jouge kankei* through club activities. Since *jouge kankei* rarely manifests itself in a similar institutional manner on such a collective scale in primary schools, my informants revealed that the experience of learning the conventions and constraints at the outset was like a cultural shock. I present the initial socialisation process by explaining the respective rituals and interactions. Secondly, I introduce some fundamental textual building blocks of the *jouge kankei* social order, and how actors and these macro-level Discourses (see chapter one for the operationalisation of Discourse/discourse) come into play to co-construct a hierarchical order into which new members are to be socialised. This socialisation, as I will then show, is achieved in and through micro-level discourses as special discursive practices are presented and taught right from the commencement of a junior high school student's club stint. This is further complemented by aspects of the surrounding environment that new members are urged to observe: roles and functions falling into an age-based hierarchy. From this chapter onwards, I show "how club activities in high schools and universities prepare students to become competent workers (*shakaijin*)" (Cook 2008: 323).[34] Indeed, the findings demonstrate that new club members are taught from the beginning that what they would learn in clubs would correspond to basic social manners in Japanese society. While new junior members make an effort to learn these hitherto unfamiliar practices in and through discourse, senior club members who are about to graduate are well aware of the usefulness of their club experiences based on such a socialisation.

---

[34] Identified as one of the major lacunae in Japanese language socialisation research, and which extant scholarship has yet to fill.

3.1 First socially meaningful experience of *jouge kankei*

Vignette 3.1: Debriefing session in Tokyo Daiichi Orchestra
After the hustle and bustle of admission procedures and the entrance ceremony in April, the junior high first graders in Tokyo Daiichi finally began to settle down in their new environment for a new chapter in life. Having toured the different club activities on offer during the last week of April, these new first graders made their choice and started attending club activities after school. The choir attracted 65 new members, largely due to its reputation, the orchestra had 19 "applicants" and all were "accepted".[35] Today, the 19 new junior first graders of the orchestra formally joined the practice session for the first time, albeit briefly. They were, however, urged by the teacher to join in the *kaeri no kai*[36] with their junior second and third grade seniors.

The junior high orchestra members concluded their practice by 17:15 (it is the school's policy that junior high students leave the school by 17:30 on weekdays), in order to have enough time to clean up the entrance area of the multipurpose music room and keep their instruments properly so that the debriefing session could be held there. Once they were done, they collected their bags and other personal belongings and gathered punctually outside the music room. Earlier, the junior first graders were briefly told by the teacher where to stand, but when it came to actually lining up for the meeting, they were clueless and started lining up in a single file right in front of the music room. Because there were 19 of them in a single file, the people towards the end of the line were standing too far to be seen from the music room entrance. Some junior third graders took the initiative to tell the new members where to line up (for instance, not to form a line at any place they deemed convenient, but to do so in front of the junior second graders), how to stand (that is, in two single files so as to stay close enough to be seen and also to be able to listen to the announcements, and they should stand at attention, with full and proper attire). Some senior second graders also made gestures to the new

---

35 Auditions were held in both the choir and the orchestra, but not for the purpose of admission. Both clubs conducted auditions to sort new members into different sections (for the choir) or instruments (for the orchestra). In the boys' orchestra, everyone who wished to join was admitted and no audition was held.
36 These are briefing sessions conducted at the end of a day's practice/gathering in all clubs. As is evident from the vignette, procedures are highly ritualised and I have not observed any deviations. For a detailed description of such rituals and how they relate to the construction of *jouge kankei* in social interactions, refer to the sub-section 3.2.1. A special feature of such briefings in Tokyo Daiichi's Orchestra is that there are two sessions of briefings per day because they separate the junior high from the senior high students during briefings (junior high members usually go home about 30 minutes earlier than senior high members).

members as to where they should put their bags (each person puts her bags and belongings right in front of her, the bags should also form a single line). The scene became chaotic for a while, as the 19 new members attempted to get themselves and their belongings in place at the same time.

Once the teacher came back from the staffroom, the newly appointed junior high president, Ishida[37] (J3), announced the beginning of the meeting by saying "*kaeri no kai wa hajimarimasu, yoroshiku onegaishimasu*"[38] (we shall now start the briefing session, let's work together and do a good job) and bowed towards the group, the group then returned the gesture, bowed back, and acknowledged in unison with "*yoroshiku onegaishimasu*" (let's work together and do a good job). At this juncture, the junior first graders realised that they were the only ones not doing it and started looking at each other, wondering if they should respond as well. The teacher intervened and reminded everyone that the new members had just joined the orchestra and they were gathering here for the first time and that the existing members should set a good example. Upon hearing this, the second and third graders responded loudly and in unison "*hai*" (yes), and some new members looked at each other in awe. The teacher then urged the first graders to remember their seniors' names and pointed at the president and officially introduced her as the junior high president "Ishida-*senpai*". At this juncture, Ishida turned to her friends behind her and flushed a little, but quickly resumed her duties by asking if anyone had announcements to make, by saying "*renrakusurukoto wa arimasuka*" (are there announcements). Nobody had anything to announce and so Ishida concluded the session with "*kaeri no kai wa owarimasu, otsukaresamadeshita*" (we shall now end the briefing session, I appreciate your hard work), and then bowed to the group again. The second and third year members bowed and said the same. This time round, some of the new first grade members followed suit, as it began to look increasingly awkward to be the only ones not doing the same actions. A handful of the new comers even started to say "*otsukaresamadeshita*" (I appreciate your hard work) to the second and third year seniors around them, albeit softly.[39]

The vignette above depicts the scenes of a debriefing session. Although they are known in a variety of terms in different clubs, such as *kaeri no kai* (meeting before going home) or *hanseikai* (meeting for reflection), the frequency of such

---

[37] All names are pseudonyms.
[38] Such ritualised and fixed discursive utterances are untranslatable into English, because the concepts and meanings they express are context-dependent in Japanese communication. Most of them either do not make sense or are absent in English language communication contexts. My rough translations in parentheses should only serve as a guide to make sense of what is going on.
[39] Observation in Tokyo Daiichi Orchestra on 10.05.2016.

meetings and their nature are largely identical across schools and clubs. This particular session as shown in section 3.1 illustrates the first debriefing session in which new members in the academic year 2016 took part. It is clearly manifested that, prior to this stage of their life, new members who just entered junior high school and joined a club had been exposed neither to the specific rituals nor to the daily routines of organisational life based on *jouge kankei* in groups. Everything from bodily postures, the use of space, and most importantly, oral expressions, had to be learned and a socialisation process was needed, and was indeed underway. Coming from the language socialisation research paradigm informed by social constructionism, my point of departure is not to consider *jouge kankei* as something that is innate to the Japanese personality. Rather, I ask where and how does it take shape in group dynamics and how do individuals learn to function in it. Evidently, the vignette above shows that primary school graduates have little clue as to the behavioural norms of being implicated in *jouge kankei*, and that the first social training is under way during their very first *bukatsudou* session in junior high school. The norms and expectations of this new life in club *jouge kankei* were so new and unfamiliar that students who had gone through the entirety of their pre-junior high schooling in Japan had little clue about such practices:

> I think it took me around four months to get used to the basic manners in the orchestra. But I don't think that was because of the fact that I was a returnee and had no prior experience in schooling in Japan. As far as I could see back then, we all [the other new members who joined the orchestra with the interviewee] were in a kind of cultural shock. Everyone, including my peers who were schooled entirely in Japan before, had to adapt and we were equally lost. In the beginning, we tried to help each other, like, we checked each other's emails and text messages to make sure that they were written properly before sending them to our seniors. We also helped each other while learning how to behave in debriefing sessions since such practices were new to us. Most of the time parents helped too, at least in my case, like, I asked them what would be the right ways to talk and behave in different situations in which seniors were present. And then of course there was this typical thing of observing the seniors next to you and see how they did it.[40]

The senior second grade clarinettist from Tokyo Daiichi Orchestra, who spent her entire kindergarten and primary school years in the United States of America, revealed that upon joining the orchestra in junior high first grade, everyone was as lost as she was. From her cohort's experience, and from the experience of the new junior club members as shown in vignette 3.1, it is also evident that the socialisation process takes time. This is because various social facts of hierarchy (who is a *senpai* and *kouhai* and what that implies) have to be manifested in the social life of new club members first, presented to them as objectivised facts, and then slowly

---

40 Senior second grade clarinettist in Tokyo Daiichi Orchestra, interview: 14.02.2016.

internalised by them in the process. In the following sections of this chapter, I show how rituals act as the first instance to establish a sense of hierarchy among new club members vis-à-vis their seniors, and how texts (often of unknown origins) serve as building blocks of the *jouge kankei* social order by providing a source of objectivised social facts. A look at such texts, together with the ways in which they are interpreted by both teachers/seniors and juniors themselves offer a first clue as regards the internalisation of such facts in the socialisation process. I argue, by way of illustration, that the social environment of school club settings is conducive to new members' socialisation process in and through language and discursive means. Not only do they observe the "proper" behaviour of their immediate seniors and hence acquire a sense of their obligations as juniors, but more importantly, it is possible for seniors to correct, and even reprimand what they deem as "improper" or "inadequate" behaviour on the part of juniors.

3.2 How are actors socialised into *jouge kankei*?

3.2.1 New members' first encounter with hierarchical orders: Interactions and rituals in clubs

The vignette 3.1 in the previous section depicts the common ritual of a debriefing session conducted at the end of a day's club activities. While existing research on junior and senior high school students in Japan have also mentioned the presence of rituals,[41] they have not put such ritualised practices into the research perspective of *jouge kankei* and language socialisation. In this sub-section, I demonstrate by way of example using the vignette in section 3.1, the ritual of debriefing sessions in clubs and how this represents a milestone experience in the process of new members' discursive socialisation into *jouge kankei*.

As the scene in section 3.1 depicted, the entire debriefing session is highly ritualised and discursive, and consists of the following components:
– Preparation: cleaning up the debriefing area.
– Congregation: gathering together on time and lining up neatly according to grades.
– Commencement: the junior high president (refer to organisational structures of the Tokyo Daiichi Orchestra in chapter two) officially announces

---

[41] See for example Hebert (2012) for a description of the rituals of a combined rehearsal in a middle school orchestra.

the beginning of the debriefing with a standard expression[42] and an accompanying bodily movement.
- Acknowledgement by club members: club members respond in unison to the president's announcement with a standard expression and an accompanying bodily movement.
- Lecturing and/or announcement-making: teachers in charge, or at times senior high club members will use this time to urge members to reflect upon their performance and attitude of the day, remind them of upcoming challenges (concerts, competitions, among others), and make any administrative announcements (regarding the submission of attendance sheets, the distribution of musical scores, urging members not to return home too late, and so on).
- Acknowledgement by club members: club members respond in unison to their teachers/seniors with "*hai*" whenever they sense a need to do so or when hearing an explicit request from teachers/seniors.
- Last call for announcements: the president asks, with a standard expression, if there are still announcements to be made.
- Conclusion: the president officially concludes the debriefing session with a standard expression, accompanied with a corresponding bodily movement.
- Acknowledgement by club members: club members respond in unison to the president's concluding remarks with a standard expression and an accompanying bodily movement.

Rituals have long been regarded by sociologists as paramount to group living and social order (Collins 2005; Durkheim 1912/1995). Collins (2005) posited that, rituals, or the patterned sequences of behaviour, bring together the following elements: bodily co-presence, barrier to outsiders, mutual focus of attention, and shared emotional mood (Allan 2006: 101; Collins 2005). The higher the extent to which these elements are achieved, the higher the effects of rituals, amongst which are group solidarity and group symbols (Allan 2006: 101).

We see from vignette 3.1 that the bodily co-presence during debriefing sessions is not only desired, but also required. When the 19 new junior first graders stand in a single file that extended far beyond the sight of senior students and the teachers, they are made to form two shorter lines in front of the music room. There are practical reasons for being physically close: this facilitates the supervision and correction

---

[42] Such standard formulaic expressions are used by every cohort of new seniors to the same extent and in the same manner. This shows that it is not up to personality or individuality and they form parts of the discursive practices (with accompanying para-linguistic bodily movements) that constitute hierarchy (refer to chapter six for more on extra-linguistic features).

of junior members' ways of standing and how they arrange their belongings and makes sure that new members do not remain out of sight throughout the debriefing session. As the ritual continues, a high degree of focus and attention is demanded throughout, on the part of both the person conducting the session (president) and the audience, because instances of "turn-taking" at the beginning, during, and at the end of the debriefing require that specific expressions and bodily movements be made on the part of both parties. In such on-going exchanges of announcements and acknowledgements between the president/teachers in charge/senior high members and the general audience, we notice that the junior new members are lost, as evidenced by their mutual blank stares while the other junior second and third graders perform the acknowledgements. This is expected behaviour because it is only their first experience of a debriefing session at the end of their very first day in the orchestra, and also because such rituals are absent from primary school clubs. During the announcements, the teacher in charge also reminds the more senior members to set good examples since now they are seniors to the new junior first graders. As a reaction to this, the junior second and third graders express their shared emotional mood of being "promoted" to and acknowledged as seniors and hence perform their duty of being good role models with a loud and particularly unified "*hai*" in acknowledgement. Since all members of the junior orchestra are standing relatively close to each other, as the debriefing progresses, we observe that a handful of junior first graders – the "fast learners" – start to imitate their seniors' behaviour and even pick up some of the standard formulaic expressions.

The effects of such rituals are two-fold: (i) they provide an opportunity for new junior first graders to observe and learn, and (ii) they enable senior members to monitor and correct juniors' comportment. Therefore, these rituals are an important first step in the socialisation process of actors into *jouge kankei*. However, observations and supervisions alone are not enough at this stage, if the hierarchical order is to be maintained and reproduced. This is because new club members who are unfamiliar with the social world of *jouge kankei* have to learn to accept the social facts as an objective given, in order for the hierarchical order to survive and be continuously transmitted from one cohort to the next. Each cohort of new club members need to be able to make sense of their social world to the extent that they internalise the institutional mechanisms of *jouge kankei* and are capable of transmitting it to new generations of club members. In the following sections of this chapter, I show the essential building blocks of hierarchy in clubs and how they, taken together, constitute the social institution of *jouge kankei* that regulates comportment and renders actions predictable in the realm of school clubs.

3.2.2 Texts as basis and building blocks of *jouge kankei*: The specific function of guidebooks/rule books and seniors' right to enforce rules

In the previous sub-section, I have shown that the first instances of *jouge kankei* that new members come across at the beginning of their junior high school career occurred in clubs replete with rituals. Such rituals provide the first learning opportunities for junior new members as they realise how different, or deviant, their own behaviours are vis-à-vis those of their seniors, and hence start to learn and imitate the "correct" behaviour through observation. However, rituals alone are not enough to inculcate institutional values in actors while maintaining and reproducing the institutional hierarchy itself. Not only do new members need to observe their surroundings during such rituals, they also need to be taught how to make sense of what they observe. Reflecting upon their own experience back in junior and senior high school clubs, an overwhelming majority of the interviewees in the first phase of my fieldwork referred to specially arranged teaching sessions for junior new members by club seniors, in which appropriate ways of comporting oneself were explicitly taught. This practice was also present in all the three clubs where I conducted my fieldwork. To substantiate the contents of their teachings, the clubs used special texts that served to establish codes and norms in the club *jouge kankei*. In this sub-section, I present some of the contents of these texts and examine their socialising functions and contexts in which they are used. Such documents have hitherto received little attention in the scholarship on Japanese schools, youth, and socialisation.

Many school clubs in Japan have some sort of established codes of conduct and general club rules in printed form.[43] In all three clubs where I conducted my ethnographic fieldwork, they came in the form of compiled booklets, distributed to every new member at the beginning of the school year. There is, however, no standard appearance, length, or naming, and hence this kind of document could be known simply as a guidebook (*shiori*) in one club, club rules (*busoku*) in another, or even etiquette guide (*reigi gaido*) in yet another club. What they have in common is that they serve to introduce the club, club life and above all, the club rules to new members.

When asked about the origins of such texts (for instance, when did the texts come into existence and who wrote them in the beginning) in the respective clubs, most students I spoke to during the fieldwork said that they were not sure.

---

[43] Similar to the many "how-to" books one would find in major bookstores which provide guidance to new company recruits on proper business etiquette.

What they knew, or at least what they had been told, was that such texts were passed down from generation to generation within their club, at times with some minor amendments by the senior cohort,[44] but the core always remained. The following two quotes from members of the Tokyo Daiichi Choir exemplify the ways in which such texts are held in high regard by club members:

> The foundation of this [the book of club rules] was made by successive generations of seniors, and slight changes have been added to it.[45]

> Such history [of etiquettes and rules as exemplified in rule books] has been present in the choir since the old days, and the seniors have taught us from the year we entered the club.[46]

Terms such as "successive generations of seniors" (*rekidai no senpaigata*), "foundation" (*moto*), "such history" (*sono youna rekishi*), and "since the old days" (*mukashi kara*), as employed by the choir members, underscore the rationale of the ways in which texts with unknown origins could serve as meta narrative or Discourse, thereby legitimising particular social and institutional configurations in groups and organisations (Meyer and Rowan 2006). In addition, and more importantly, they offer a concrete first step in the empirical analysis of how such texts are brought into existence and transmitted. In the case of club activities in Japanese schools, institutional configurations of hierarchy are brought into existence and transmitted via texts consisting of "man-made rules and procedures [serving as] basic building blocks of institutions" (Meyer and Rowan 2006: 6). I will now present some of the "man-made rules and procedures" outlined in the texts.

Materials gathered from my fieldwork sites suggest that much of the contents of such rule books could be divided into several broad categories. The two most important categories that feature prominently in all cases are *greetings* (*aisatsu*) and *proper language use* (*kotobazukai*).[47] Of the club documents I studied, greetings are justified as one of the most important elements because "interpersonal relations (*ningen kankei*) in the club begin with the performance of the basic manners of greetings", and that "the most basic (*kihon*) thing to do in club activities is to be able to perform greetings well" (quotes from Tokyo Daiichi Girls' Orchestra's guide book, all translations are mine). Greetings are

---

44 Refers to the oldest grade of student members who are present and running the club.
45 Acting president (H2) of Tokyo Daiichi Choir.
46 Two junior first graders (J1 in the year 2015–2016) of Tokyo Daiichi Choir.
47 This is by no means peculiar to the clubs I studied. Previous studies on school clubs, notable those by Cave (2004) and Hebert (2012) mentioned the need to greet seniors as part of the basic manners that juniors at the lower end of the hierarchy should do. A large-scale national survey on honorifics in Japanese schools also revealed that students take great care of their expressions towards their seniors in club activities (NINJAL 2002) (see chapter two).

so highly regarded that some guidebooks even encourage students to "aim to be the best in performing greetings in Japan" (as taught by the acting president of Tokyo Daiichi Girls' Choir).[48]

If this is of utmost importance, what, then, are students expected to do in terms of greetings, and who performs and receives greetings? The following are some extracts from the rule books from my fieldwork sites (refer to appendix 2 for detailed translations of two guide books):

- To produce good music and performance, manners are of utmost importance. One must be clearly aware of the interpersonal relations. The initiation of interpersonal relations begins with manners, the first step of which is greetings (*aisatsu*). If you greet and reply (*henji*) in a clear and cheerful (*akarui*) way, just like when you perform music in a clear way, you will be able to express yourself better and get your message across to your interlocutors. As a musician and as a person, try to reflect on your normal behaviour and put more importance on manners:
- Am I capable of greeting teachers and seniors clearly?
- Are my greetings becoming hollow, without emotions?
- Other than seniors and teachers of my club, am I capable of greeting others such as visitors?
- Am I capable of replying?
- When you meet teachers, members of the administration, security guards, visitors, and seniors (*senpai*) in school, greet them with "*ohayougozaimasu*" (good morning) or "*konnichiwa*" (good day). When you are leaving, use "*sayounara*" (goodbye).
- Seniors should also greet juniors cheerfully (*akaruku*).
- Do not greet for the sake of greeting (*katachi dake*), do it with feelings. Besides your seniors and club teachers, greet also other teachers and visitors.
- Be sure to greet seniors, alumni, instructors, and club teachers with "*chiwa*" (a short and crisp version of *konnichiwa*).

The extracts cited above show that proper greetings are expected from juniors at all times. This means that, whenever a younger student comes across someone older, the younger one is expected to perform the greetings in adequate ways. Although it is stated in all texts that students should also greet teachers and other adults (without being prompted), the students I observed did not always follow

---

[48] The fact that clubs place such a heavy emphasis on their members' performing proper greetings is yet another illustration of the educational nature of extra-curricular clubs in Japanese schools. In this instance, clubs start to train their members for the adult corporate world where proper greeting behaviour is generally considered very important.

this rule. Most of the time, students greeted visitors and school leaders, but when it came to their own school teachers, it was quite often the case that teachers[49] were those who took the initiative to greet students, and only then would students return the greeting. Hence, although it is stated in most guide books that teachers should also be greeted, this particular rule has not been followed strictly and there is no enforcement, unlike in the case of failing to greet senior club students, as I show later in this volume. It may seem strange that students would be more careful and show more respect to their seniors than to their teachers, but on closer inspection, the reasons become clear.[50] Most teachers I talked to revealed that they have never reprimanded students in their clubs for not taking the initiative to greet teachers, because they felt that the students were already under pressure with regard to respecting their seniors.

Indeed, as I have observed throughout my fieldwork, senior club members are far stricter about their juniors' adherence to the rules. It is customary in many school clubs that seniors enforce rules and at times even punish juniors for not observing proper rules. This is made possible due to club teachers' minimal participation in running daily routines and managing the clubs, meaning that they do not occupy an institutionalised role in the *jouge kankei* order in club activities (refer to chapter two). A junior first grader in Tokyo Daiichi Orchestra once told me that even though she tried her best to observe the rules and greet her seniors, one of them was so unsatisfied with the junior's soft voice that she wrote frequent messages to her demanding that she improve her greetings by using louder voice. In the same club, a group of junior third graders shared with me their unpleasant experience of being forced to sit on their heels (*seiza*) outside their music room in winter, while listening to a group of senior first graders lecture them about proper greetings for more than half an hour. Throughout my fieldwork, it was rare to see seniors taking the initiative to greet juniors.

It can thus be seen that the bulk of the contents of guidebooks deal with juniors' expected behaviour regarding greetings, and the issue is duly taken up by senior students as they enforce such rules. It is also noteworthy to point out that such rules are not constrained by time and space, that is, even when seniors graduate, they expect juniors to continue the politeness, and juniors should be polite and follow the rules of proper behaviour not only during club activities, but also whenever they come across seniors in and out of school. Existing research has already established that the performance of greetings is

---

49 Teachers here refer to school teachers who are in charge of clubs, not external instructors hired by schools to advise clubs.
50 Students often feel more pressure to abide by the rules governing their behaviour towards seniors than towards teachers. See NINJAL (2002).

heavily emphasised and promoted within diverse social arenas in the Japanese adult (corporate) society (McVeigh 2002). The afore-mentioned data from the club guidebooks show that secondary school clubs prepare their members for the adult society not just by teaching *aisatsu*, but more importantly, by emphasising the rationale behind proper greetings.

A second category of rules regulating oral expressions (*kotobazukai*) also features prominently in guide books[51]:
- You must absolutely use honorific language to seniors, alumni, external instructors, and school teachers.
- Be careful about your language when you write to seniors.
- Be sure to use "*sumimasen*" (excuse me) when you apologise, do not use "*gomennasai*".[52]
- When walking past seniors, alumni, external instructors, and teachers in charge, give a slight bow and say "*shitsureishimasu*" (excuse me).
- Be sure to respond (*henjisuru*) to your seniors politely when they talk to you
- When seniors, alumni, external instructors or teachers in charge come to conduct a practice session, be sure to button your shirt and coat all the way, and say "*renshuuonegaishimasu*" (we would like to start the practice). At the end of the session, say "*renshuuarigatougozaimashita*" (thank you for the practice).
- If you were absent for or left the practice early, be sure to report it during your next practice. When your name is called during attendance taking, answer with "*hai*", get up from the chair, stand straight, and put your hands behind your back, and say "*kinou wa . . . no tame kurabukenseki/chikokushimashita. Doumo sumimasendeshita*" (Because of . . . (reason), I was absent/left early yesterday. Please excuse me).
- When you refer to yourself, use the first-person pronoun of "*watakushi*[53]". [Note: In the guidebook, the character 私 was first written, then a pronunciation guide on top of the character showed that instead of pronouncing the usual "*watashi*", it should be read "watakushi"] [Tokyo Daini Boys' Orchestra's rule]

---

51 Concrete and elaborated examples with recordings of students' actual behaviour will be discussed in later chapters.
52 In many Japanese clubs, a common and explicit rule is to prohibit the use of "*gomennasai*" when juniors want to excuse themselves for some wrongdoings, because this term is considered *tameguchi* (only to be used with friends). "*Sumimasen*" is the preferred, and at times required term, to be used to seniors instead. This point is brought up by both interviewees in my pilot study as well as fieldwork informants.
53 Current research has established that, in corporate and business settings, the first-person pronoun of "*watakushi*" is more desirable than "*watashi*" (Dunn 2011). This represents a clear instance of secondary school clubs moulding members into competent actors in the adult society.

As the opening vignette in section 3.1 illustrates, new students had no prior experience and hence no understanding of rules and routines as well as what was expected of them. During their first day of club activities, none of the new members had an idea of how to respond to the different social situations around them and what to say or do. Yet, most people who have lived through the experience of club activities in Japanese schools, regardless of the nature of activity and type of school, have recalled that norms and conventions on proper language use (*kotobazukai* and *aisatsu*) were the quintessence of hierarchy. As this current sub-section shows, the norms and conventions are clearly spelt out in guide books. Serving as an important learning tool, the section on *kotobazukai* teaches new members a calibrated way of speech: saying what is appropriate in the relevant contexts and to the right people. For instance, the ways in which a junior member should report her/his previous day's absence to seniors, and how to excuse oneself when walking past seniors, all of which would be new to junior high first graders' hitherto social experience. The guide books also made it clear that these rules apply to both spoken and written communication with seniors. On the one hand, this facilitates the socialisation of new members into *jouge kankei* by introducing them to a type of specific discourse. On the other hand, such guidelines also provide newcomers a first instance of making sense of the various social situations in club activities.

In addition, such texts, which are held in high regard and whose legitimacy is not questioned despite having an unknown origin (nobody, not even the most senior students or teachers, know the exact origin), provide the basis for the next essential step in the socialisation process aimed at bringing members of clubs into the hierarchical structure. This is because guidance sessions (which consist of chunks of spoken discourses/lectures by authoritative figures) at the beginning of new members' club life facilitate the bringing to life of such texts and help inculcate corresponding beliefs and value systems in new members that will follow them throughout and beyond their stint in the club. The following section analyses the ways in which such texts are used in clubs: how such texts are interpreted for junior new members by senior authorities in the clubs, the emerging discourse as a consequence, and the ways in which the institutional order of hierarchy is brought to the fore by narrators. My analysis also shows that a specific discourse type peculiar to the institution of *jouge kankei*, again hitherto unfamiliar to new junior first graders, is being presented to these new participants as the "correct" and "legitimate" behaviour. Furthermore, the ways in which they are expected to make full sense of this new institutional order regulating their social world will also be presented.

3.2.3 Macro Discourses as new ways of thinking about the social world: Guidance sessions, meetings, and the "*senpai* know best" approach to create a "common-sense" knowledge

In this section, I offer a glimpse of how cognitive schemata regarding interpersonal relations in the *jouge kankei* hierarchy are constructed based on texts, and the ways in which they help new members to make sense of their social world in club activities by shaping their understanding of the social environment and providing scripts for their actions.

Despite the claim that they are of unknown origin, club rules and procedures (either written or passed down orally) are, in fact, deliberately created human artefacts. I argue that they serve as a fundamental instrument to establish *jouge kankei* as a social institution. In this sense, *jouge kankei* is not seen as an objective structure existing independently of human action:

> Institutions gain an independent existence "out there" by being socially constructed "in here" – that is, in the minds of individual actors who have a stake in them. Before institutions can gain authority as objective social structures they must be endowed with meaning by cognitive acts of individuals. New institutionalists locate the origin of institutions in taken-for-granted classifications, scripts, and schemata that humans use to make sense of a disorderly world. (Meyer and Rowan 2006: 6)

Indeed, the institution of hierarchy needs to be in the minds of individuals first, before such institutional orders could guide individual comportment. In secondary school clubs, the highest ranked *senpai* cohort serves as the main agent of socialisation and enforcement, and is occasionally helped by visiting alumni and teachers in charge, especially at the beginning. Seniors socially and discursively construct the hierarchy in the minds of new members, at the beginning of each school year, so that new juniors could make sense of the "disorderly" and unfamiliar social world as quickly as possible, and be on track to becoming socially competent actors by following the rules set out in guide books.

The social construction first takes place in guidance sessions[54] (*busoku setsumei* or *reigi shidou*). I observed the guidance session of the Tokyo Daiichi Orchestra in early May 2016, right after the Golden Week.[55] The club teacher,

---
54 Such sessions represent the significant first step, but social construction continues in the new members' subsequent daily experiences too, and often lasts for up to a year or more for junior high school students. See later chapters.
55 The other two clubs held it at a later date when I already left the fieldwork site in summer 2016, so my observations here pertain specifically to Tokyo Daiichi Girls' Orchestra. However, follow-up correspondence with informants show that such guidance sessions took largely similar shape and nature. In fact, in the Tokyo Daini Boys' Orchestra, some seniors already started

Shimura, convened the session,[56] which lasted for one hour and 10 minutes with all 19 new members from the junior first grade present (this was held on the same day as these new members started their practice, that is, before the debriefing depicted in vignette 3.1). At the beginning of the session, each new member was given two sets of documents: (i) 12 pages of club rules and regulations (*suisougakubu no shiori: busoku to kokoroe*), and (ii) 31 pages of performance manual (*ensou no tebiki: yoriyoi ensou no tame ni*). The first document received the most attention during the guidance session as Shimura spent more than 50 minutes explaining the rules and regulations and how junior members should behave accordingly. The second document contained much more technical material regarding the reading of musical notes, postures, musical terms in Italian, and some basic exercises. Since the session was supposed to guide members and help them to understand club rules, the second document did not feature prominently and hence will not be discussed here.[57]

As stated earlier, good manners, as expressed through language in the form of specific greetings and ways of responding to seniors formed the cornerstone of rules and routines as outlined in texts. Referring to this as "social manners" (*shakaiteki na maana*), Shimura requested that the students turn to the section on greetings, be prepared to take notes, and started going into the details of the expected behaviour:

Extract 1 of guidance session

This part of the guidebook, the section on good manners, is clearly written, right? Alright, so, as a human being, because we are in a *bukatsudou*, we have to learn some *basic social manners*. In a club, everything starts with manners. Talking about that, what is important is, after all, etiquette. Yes, so, for example, greetings, answering back when someone talks to you, etc, this kind of things, everyone should be able to do it all the time, during and outside of club activities. Yes, so regarding this, what I want to say is that, let's do our best to have good manners. It is very simple, well, for example, when you see your

---

to guide and correct new members' "improper" behaviour on an individual basis before the guidance sessions took place. As for Tokyo Daiichi Girls' Choir, the acting president affirmed that her cohort of seniors taught new members the appropriate expressions in an explicit and detailed manner.

56 Members of Tokyo Daiichi Orchestra revealed that in the previous year it was the senior second year student leaders who convened and conducted the guidance session. It appears that there exist no rules as to who should conduct such sessions, and senior students and teachers in charge alternate. This should not be confused with the daily enforcement of the rules, which are carried out by senior students without teachers' involvement.

57 This very fact also reveals the existential nature of clubs: first and foremost, to socialise new junior members into the club hierarchy, with the aim of empowering them with various social and cultural capitals to be better equipped for later stages of life.

seniors, greet them with "*konnichiwa*", it is just like that, greet them properly. Then, what I would also like you to do, is to respond, if you get the point from your seniors, please respond. Well, it is still the very beginning of your club life so I have no other choice but to use examples that you have yet to experience. For instance, during rehearsals involving the full orchestra, when the (student) conductor gives instructions such as "for this part please play it this way, instrument x", if this is directed to you, the conductor will not know if you understand the instructions or not, so if you do, I want you to respond with "*hai*". That is right, I want you to reply with "*hai*" in a proper way and volume so that your addressee can hear you. Regarding that, I really want you to do it to your best effort. If you do not understand what your senior said, you should tell them by saying "*sumimasen, wakarimasen, mou ikkai ii desu ka*" (excuse me, I do not understand, could you repeat it once more). But again, if you do understand what is being said to you, you must respond to your seniors. This is what I would really like you to do (emphasis added).

The opening vignette at the beginning of section 3.1 demonstrates that new members had started to follow the rules, after having "rightly" interpreted the ways of thinking and orientation guide (that is, Discourse, see chapter one) as discussed above. A critical discourse analytic approach would further reveal the ways in which the interpretation process on the part of new members entering clubs at the beginning of each school year is cognitively played out. The central idea is that interpreters of a text need to find a fit between a given text, or Discourse, and the world – their experiences and assumptions (more on assumptions and ideologies in chapter five) (Fairclough 1989). Using this approach, we could revisit the guidance sessions conducted by Shimura and examine how actors come to interpret Discourses presented to them.

The first important message contained in the Discourse by Shimura is that seniority-based status differences have consequences. That is, they now bring a series of rights and obligations to people implicated in *jouge kankei*. When the text interpreters (that is, new members) draw on their previous experience in primary schools, they would quickly realise that the nature of *senpai-kouhai* relationship that now exists between them and their seniors is something new. This is because, contrary to their prior experience, such relationships now entail obligations on the part of juniors. For instance, it is clearly implied that juniors have the responsibility to initiate greetings whenever they see their seniors ('*when you see your seniors, greet them with "konnichiwa"*') and make acknowledgements when seniors talk to them ('*if you do understand what is being said to you, you must respond to your seniors*'), failure of which would incur sanctions/punishments (see later chapters). This corroborates findings of existing scholarship on language socialisation of primary school pupils in Japan on the importance of being an attentive listener and the ability to provide prompt replies when talked to (Cook 1999, see chapter one). However, contrary to those in primary school classroom settings, interactions in the context of secondary school *bukatsudou* entail power and hierarchical inter-personal dynamics, as new and younger students are explicitly taught to perform such duties to their seniors. Therefore, these verbal expressions of social etiquette facilitate the socialisation of new members into the institutional order of hierarchy in club activities. Moreover, the guidance session instils common sense to accompany the promulgation of rules to guide new members' actions: whenever you come across someone older than you, you are expected to follow the rules, acknowledge the superior status of your seniors, and show them your respect via discursive means.[58]

Another message in the first extract by Shimura is that the new club life is simple to adjust to, and represents the fundamentals of the new members' social encounters henceforth. Based on their experience in primary schools, the new members would have realised that what they have been asked to do consists of something new ('*yet to experience*'), and that, as juniors, they are not knowledgeable about the club mechanisms and need to learn from their seniors (see analysis on extract 2 below). Furthermore, they are taught right from the beginning that everyone is expected to master the standard etiquette because it is very simple and forms the basic foundation for all interactions.

To the interpreters (junior new members), such a Discourse as represented by extract 1 is able to *fit* into the world because in the interpretation process they mobilise their prior experience of dealing with people as juniors and seniors, and then recognise what is required of them.

In an attempt to help the 19 new members better apprehend such a novel way of thinking about the social world, truly understand what was expected of them, and be successfully socialised as quickly as possible, Shimura then offered them the following advice (emphases added):

Extract 2 of guidance session

With regard to how you could do all these, well, in particular, I want you to look at how your seniors from the junior high section (junior second and third graders) do things. They are the seniors who are the closest to you, so look at the kind of things that they do. For example, preparing the music room before and after each practice by arranging the chairs and cleaning up. This also applies to the classrooms we used, be sure to take care of them. From preparations to cleaning up, these are all part and parcel of club activities, and they are all very important, more so than playing music. Like greetings and manners, you should also observe how your junior high seniors perform tasks like preparations and cleaning up, then, you will slowly get used to it and be able to imitate your seniors. I also think that it would be good if you could take the initiative and offer your seniors a helping hand by asking "*nani ka yaru koto ga arimasuka*" (is there anything I could do).

---

[58] This is a quintessence of *jouge kankei* socialisation in secondary school club contexts, and this knowledge accompanies individuals into adulthood.

In this particular guidance session, the message of the importance of proper behaviour for all those involved in the hierarchical relations was not only brought to life from the Discourse, but also communicated to new members (see some of their reactions in vignette 3.1). Juniors should, and as exemplified by the observation of their first attendance in the debriefing session (section 3.1), did start to make an effort to look at and imitate their seniors. It is noteworthy that new members were exhorted not just to observe and imitate the behaviour of any senior, but specifically those of junior high second or third grade, or, in the words of some students in Tokyo Daiichi, immediate seniors (*ikko ue no senpai*) just one or two years older. The rationale is that, while these people serve as seniors to the new members, they are still "young" enough to be juniors to those in the senior high section and hence they too need to observe the guidelines in the rule books assiduously. By telling the new members to observe and learn from these seniors[59] ('*I want you to look at how your seniors from the junior high section do things*'; '*imitate your seniors*'), Shimura also portrayed an internal division of labour (*yakuwari*) along a seniority-based hierarchical order: the most junior grade should observe, imitate, and take the initiative, junior second and third graders need to set good examples for their juniors by showing them how to be good juniors, and senior high students can account for their own actions (discursive and bodily behaviours) and have the right to correct juniors' mistakes. This complements the general tone in the written texts and puts each person in a specific place in the higher-lower relationship. It also helps to reinforce the interpretation of the previous text by emphasising that the junior new members are about to experience something new, but the rules could be mastered because they are simple, and in fact they must be mastered because they are the basics of club activities, '*more so than playing music*'. The new members would, after having listened to the guidance session and digested the written texts,[60] realise that their *senpai* know best in whatever that is going on in clubs and slowly start to watch and learn.[61]

---

[59] On separate occasions, Shimura and club leaders also told these seniors to reflect on what would make them good role models.
[60] Students of all grades and in all three clubs revealed to me that nobody has ever read everything that was handed to them. However, all paid special attention to essential parts of the documents highlighting how they should behave towards seniors and read those parts repeatedly.
[61] This process is further testimony of the important socialising function that secondary school clubs play in Japanese society. Refer to chapter one.

3.2.4 Observing the environment: Who does what?

In the previous sub-section, the Tokyo Daiichi Orchestra's main teacher in charge, Shimura, portrayed a general division of labour in which the senior high school members supervise, those in the middle of the hierarchical order (mostly junior second and third graders) set good examples and perform their duties, while the most junior members watch and learn. It is in this context that Shimura urged the junior new members to observe their seniors and follow suit. In this sub-section, I illustrate some of the specific tasks that new members should observe and learn from their seniors through both ritualised activities and daily routines in clubs. At the end, I show the perspective of senior club members (those who have been successfully socialised into *jouge kankei*), justifying these learning processes as being beneficial in preparing them well for the adult corporate world in Japan.

As manifested in Shimura's speech, the age-based seniority system is central in the assignment of different statuses and functions in clubs, from leadership and/or administrative positions to the duty of running errands and even doing "dirty jobs". Insofar as junior new members are concerned, they ought to learn from their seniors in the ways of arranging chairs before and after practice sessions, as well as the proper ways of cleaning up (*souji*), such as sweeping the floor and emptying rubbish bins. Furthermore, neither this division of labour nor the learning process of junior new members is peculiar to Tokyo Daiichi Girls' Orchestra.

The following vignette depicts what I observed regarding the junior members in Tokyo Daiichi's choir during one of their practice sessions in vocal sections on a Saturday afternoon in November 2015:

Vignette 3.2: "Porters" in Tokyo Daiichi Girls' Choir
An hour into the sectional practice, I decided to focus on a group of junior first year mezzo singers because one of their repeated actions caught my attention. At around 14:00, a group of junior second year members left the music room. As they were leaving, another junior second year singer from the alto section, who was standing right next to the door, held the door for them. Out of a sudden, a junior first year member from the mezzo group, who was standing at least five meters away, literally ran towards the door, bowed to her junior second year senpai, and took over the job to hold the door. I decided to fix my attention to this person, or rather this group of junior first graders, and I counted five

times in the next 35 minutes (from 14:00 to 14:35) where one of the junior first year members rushed to hold the main door or the door to the storeroom whenever people senior to them entered or left.[62]

In the "porters" activity mentioned above, the group of junior first graders were already in the second semester of their junior high school and club career as this particular session was observed in November. Hence, this provided a good opportunity to observe how actors comport themselves in ways that conform to designated duties in the club's institutional hierarchical order six months after the socialisation process began.

In yet another example from the students' daily routines, this time recorded at the Tokyo Daini Boys' Orchestra, junior first and second year members were seen setting up the music room for a combined rehearsal session. Each member, or groups of two to three students, had a specific task to perform, be it arranging chairs or setting up music stands or preparing the right set of scores. A particularly menial job was that a junior French horn player (it was his turn) went around the music room collecting used pieces of "saliva cloths" and replacing them with new ones.[63] While junior club members were busily carrying out their duties, members from the senior high section were nowhere to be seen in the music room (since seniors only come for practice and not for preparations before or after). Just as what seniors and teachers would expect, these good examples would be carried out in the presence of new junior members, in the hope that the latter would quickly imitate and learn from these examples.

In fact, in most cases, the immediate effect of the text and the interpretations by new members can already be seen at a relatively early stage of their club career, for instance, a week into their club life. The more significant manifestation, however, is that such interpretations transform into common-sense beliefs over time. They are not only internalised as members get socialised further into the *jouge kankei* social order, but also reproduced.

Though they might come in different forms and be conducted by different people, these kinds of explicit instructions on what junior new members should do and say, as well as who should they observe, are also reported by interviewees hailing from diverse types of schools and regions across Japan during my initial fieldwork phase. Hence, they are not club- or school-dependent and do not pertain only to the three clubs I worked with. For instance, one of the interviewees revealed that, upon joining the soft tennis club in her junior high school in

---

[62] Observed in Tokyo Daiichi Choir on 21.11.2015.
[63] Brass instruments work when players blow warm air into them. Due to condensation, saliva will form within the instruments and it needs to be emptied from time to time. Hence, a cloth on the floor is needed, onto which saliva is emptied.

Kyoto, she was told in the teaching session that when juniors apologise to seniors, they should use the more formal form of *"sumimasen"* instead of *"gomennasai"*, and were encouraged to listen to and imitate how the junior second year members greeted and talked to the seniors.

Lastly, as regards this series of learning procedures, most junior new members might not understand the rationale behind them at first. They may be following orders, but they might not have seen the connection between these rules and behavioural norms and "basic social manners". However, senior club members who have arrived at the apex of *jouge kankei* are all aware of the rationale for such practices, as one of them in Tokyo Daiichi Orchestra succinctly answered my question on the usefulness of club experiences for their life in the future:

> Well first and foremost it's the manners part, that's going to help me, because in a Japanese company we're going to have the same situation, right? And people who are in clubs, we deal with all these already, and also a lot of other problems, right? So, like, in the future if we face the same issues I think I can overcome them because I've been through many hardships here [in Tokyo Daiichi Orchestra]. And, since I've continued with this club for six years, that gives me self-confidence too. And I've acquired a new hobby maybe.[64] (H2 clarinettist)

The fact that this senior club member attributed the usefulness of her club experience to her increased behavioural competency and self-confidence in the adult society affirms the roles secondary school clubs should fulfil. Indeed, extra-curricular clubs provide *various forms of cultural capital*, such as cultivated manners and calibrated speech, which are linked to the ability to recognise hierarchical interpersonal relations (Miwa 2000). These are valuable because companies explicitly ask about school club experiences during the job-hunting process in the adult corporate world (Van Ommen 2015). In addition, the presence of such an awareness also testifies to the club leadership's successful transmission of common-sense knowledge about the world of *jouge kankei* to new generations of club members. Even though this learning process can be tough at times, club members accept the series of challenges (including the performance of "dirty jobs", see above) because they will slowly come to the realisation that this experience will turn them into more competent actors in the adult society.

---

64 Senior second grade clarinettist in Tokyo Daiichi Orchestra, interview: 14.02.2016.

3.2.5 Efforts, mistakes, reprimands, corrections

The previous section dealt with the ways in which texts serve as the basis of the institutional order of *jouge kankei*, how "incipient knowledge and legitimisation" (Berger and Luckmann 1966: 111–112) of such hierarchical orders are instilled in new members from the outset, and how these have been reproduced and reinforced in the broader social environment of school clubs. In other words, it showed that "processes whereby some people govern or discipline others are frequently closely connected to procedures of identity-constitution and knowledge-production" (Deacon 2002: 89). In the case of club *jouge kankei*, the identities constituted for new juniors are that of socially incompetent young members who should be submissive and willing to learn from their seniors. These juniors should also possess the knowledge of what is expected of them in different club contexts and occasions. In addition, I also presented the wide array of things junior new members ought to observe and learn from their immediate seniors in a variety of club contexts.

Since this represents their very first socially meaningful encounter with hierarchy outside the family,[65] as mentioned in chapter two and in section 3.1 in this present chapter, it is natural that the junior first graders' (and also junior second graders') socialisation process is also a learning process. This involves not being able to memorise the rules all at once, making mistakes along the way, and being reminded or reprimanded by seniors. Junior first and second year members whom I talked to in all the three clubs estimated an average adjustment time of several months, before they could master the basic manners (see following chapters for other detailed examples).

The vignette at the beginning of section 3.1 shows the start of junior new members' learning and socialisation process. This is but one example, because, as mentioned, similar phenomena can generally be observed across the board. For instance, during Tokyo Daini Boys' Orchestra's debriefing, several new members did not know the right sitting posture that were expected of them when seniors lectured, and did not know that they were expected to respond when seniors talked to them. As a reminder, a senior second year student walked across the room and whispered the rules into their ears[66] (refer to chapter six). In all three clubs that I observed, most junior first year members (and

---

[65] For those who come from families with more than one child, they have certainly experienced some sort of unequal relationships between them and their elder or younger siblings. However, the very nature of the hierarchical order within the family and in social organisations such as in club activities is different, as this volume shows.
[66] Observation in Tokyo Daini Boys' Orchestra on 15.04.2016.

some junior second graders) made mistakes along the way. In most cases, seniors did make special efforts to teach juniors in an explicit way, and repeatedly, if necessary. When I interviewed the new cohort of senior second year club leaders in Tokyo Daiichi Girls' Orchestra a week after the new junior first graders joined the orchestra, they revealed:

> **ZW:** I thought what the junior first graders were doing last week, and also yesterday, was interesting. Because whenever you talked to them, for example, when everyone of them gathered in front of you and you told them what time to gather this coming Saturday, there was no response from them at all. Also, greetings were absent. I mean, I understand, as they had a different experience in primary school clubs. When do you think the new members would start to pick things up?
>
> **New senior 1:** When everyone participates in practice sessions, and when junior second and third graders perform greetings and respond to seniors, the new members would think like "so this is what we should do".
>
> **ZW:** So by looking at others?
>
> **New senior 1:** Looking at others, and be mindful that they have to do things like responding to us. And of course, there might be instances when seniors like us tell them things like "be sure to greet and respond to seniors".
>
> **ZW:** Might be?
>
> **New seniors 1, 2, 3, 4:** We will tell them, will certainly tell.
>
> **New senior 2:** We have to.
>
> **ZW:** When you were in junior first grade, did senior club members back then tell you things like that?
>
> **New seniors 1, 2, 3,** 4: Yes, so we also tell our juniors.[67]

In such an age-based seniority system in which everyone has her place, and after being taught in theory (guidance sessions), it is generally expected that the new members should be able to observe role models (their junior second and third year seniors) in practice and also do it themselves. If need be, senior high students act as supervisors to remind and correct them. These new senior second year club leaders from Tokyo Daiichi Orchestra revealed that when they were in their junior first year, they equally felt that those types of etiquette and rules on manners were strange, and only started to pick them up by observing their immediate seniors. Acknowledging this, the group of senior second year students I interviewed also affirmed that they would definitely remind the new members of rules and etiquette in an explicit manner. As this cycle repeats itself, senior members might also, if

---

67 Interview: 20.05.2016.

they deem it necessary, reprimand juniors for their "wrong-doings". Such reprimands could come collectively or individually, and again, is not a phenomenon confined to the clubs I observed.

For instance, Suzuki, a senior third year student at Tokyo Daiichi Orchestra, spent her three junior high school years in Tokyo Daiichi's volleyball club. She reflected on her experience there as one that was full of severe reprimands from entire cohorts of senior club members for new members' tardiness in greeting, helping, and responding to seniors at the early stages, and the fact that seniors repeatedly scolded them for not taking the initiative and observing the stipulated rules from the second month onwards. In Tokyo Daiichi's choir, the acting president revealed that club leaders from her cohort once summoned the entire junior second grade members after practice in November 2015. The reason for this was that the seniors thought that the latter group had not been good role models as immediate seniors to junior first graders because they under-performed their duties in keeping the music room clean and lacked enthusiasm in greeting seniors and affection in coaching junior new members.[68] Such reprimanding could also take place on an individual level. Mai, a junior first year tenor saxophone player in Tokyo Daiichi's orchestra revealed in multiple conversations in January 2016 that she repeatedly received text messages and emails from one of her senior tenor saxophone players in the past several months. This was because, according to the senior's messages, Mai did not perform adequate greetings (in terms of level of politeness and the voice volume) whenever she came across this particular senior. Although rare, such episodes of individual reprimanding do occur, and they show just how far seniors could go, due to enculturated common-sense knowledge of the social world in club *jouge kankei* and seniors' roles in socialising juniors, as well as the extent to which juniors must endure.

Previous qualitative studies on extra-curricular clubs in Japanese schools corroborate this finding by attesting to the strict rules and routines in sports clubs (Blackwood 2016; Cave 2004). The data in this chapter further shows that the basic nature of *jouge kankei* is omnipresent in school club settings, regardless of the type of activity concerned. It is also not surprising that senior students devote much time and energy to correct their juniors' mistakes, since it is apparent that seniors know best what to do and how to behave, hence the entitlement to reprimand. This last point is explored more in-depth in chapter five,

---

[68] I had expressed interest in observing this particular meeting, but my request was denied by one of the teachers in charge, who told me that she did not wish to show the actual intense atmosphere to non-club members. This in itself suggested the nature of the meeting being a severe reprimand rather than merely a normal teaching and briefing session.

when I address the issue on the maintenance of conventions, and the underlying ideologies and power relations.

In this sub-section, I have shown the ways in which generations of new club members go through the cycle from being inexperienced in the institutional order of hierarchy to a transitional phase where they acquire and internalise the common sense of who is who in the club, something which is repeatedly and explicitly highlighted by various Discourses. After being accustomed to the "fact" that there is a common-sense assumption which treats authority and hierarchy as natural (Fairclough 1989: 2), juniors and seniors maintain and reproduce the cycle, as well as reinforce the institution of *jouge kankei* through discursive means (greetings and *kotobazukai*) in daily life and especially when they become seniors. This includes ensuring juniors use proper language and expressions, as well as reprimanding them for repeated "wrong-doings". As Fairclough (1989) concludes, the social world (in this case of interpersonal relations in clubs and beyond) is "textualised" (in the form of spoken Discourse in this case), interpreted, and reproduced in a particular way (Fairclough 1989: 85).

3.3 Seniors' influence on the degree of manifestation of *jougei kankei* in a club and impact on juniors

Thus far in this chapter, I have shown how some texts and Discourses act as the basic building blocks of institutional *jouge kankei* in junior and senior high school clubs. I analysed the ways in which they are interpreted for and taught to new incoming junior members at the beginning of the school year, as well as illustrated the socialisation process aimed at bringing junior new members into the hierarchical order. As I presented, such texts (spoken or written), on which instructions were based, have a comprehensive coverage in terms of regulating diverse aspects of behaviour. In addition, in all cases, it has been claimed that these texts have unknown origins and are modified by the incoming senior club leadership to a certain degree every year. This leads us to examine, in this section, if, and to what extent, senior club leaders could have an influence on such important texts and the production of macro-level Discourses, and by extension, on hierarchy in school clubs.

Throughout my fieldwork, I heard and observed several occasions on which club members claimed that there had been changes as regards strictness (*kibishisa*) of regulations and seniors' rule enforcement. Such instances were always in conjunction with a new cohort of seniors assuming leadership and power. From what I encountered, such changes could be classified into two types. Firstly, it was possible for a new cohort of senior club members to relax, or even abolish, certain unpopular practices that had been established by previous leaders. For instance, one initial study interviewee told me that while she was a junior in her school's orchestra, seniors summoned them for daily lunchtime practices and as a consequence, she and her peers often had little, if any, time to consume their *bento* lunches (refusing to join such practice sessions was not an option). Although practicing during lunchtime was prohibited by the school, none of them spoke up out of fear of being reprimanded or ostracised by seniors in the club. Once this interviewee's cohort arrived at the most senior grade in the orchestra, she and her peers abolished this lunchtime practice at once. A similar experience was made during one of my participant observation sessions at the Tokyo Daiichi Girls' choir. Towards the end of one of their practice sessions on a Saturday evening in November 2015, I approached the acting president as she packed up her bag. When asked if she and other choir members did not feel the need for more regular and longer breaks than what they had (two breaks of 30 seconds each and one longer break of two minutes during the three-hour practice that day), she revealed that, before her cohort took over the club, it was clearly stated in her club's rule book that breaks were limited to one one-minute break for every afternoon practice session of three hours. Therefore, her cohort had already relaxed the rules to a significant extent.

The second type of change that a new senior club leadership could bring about relates more closely to *senpai-kouhai* relations, as the following focus group interview extract with Tokyo Daiichi Girls' orchestra's new senior second grade members revealed:

> **ZW:** Well, so now everyone [of you] has become the most senior in the club, is there anything in this club that you want to change?
>
> **New senior 1:** Well, how can you put it? I guess you can say we don't want to overly restrict our juniors, maybe you can also say we don't want to hurt them, I mean, we don't want to give orders to them like "go do this" or "you have to do that or else". You can say it's more freedom. We just want juniors to be free to speak up and we want to hear their opinions.
>
> **ZW:** I see. What about the others here? What do you think?
>
> **New senior 2:** Juniors shouldn't come to practice thinking that it's a dreadful thing to do. I think everyone likes to play music, that's why they're here. We as seniors should respect this and think about how to help juniors to keep them motivated.
>
> **ZW:** Right. No doubt it's good that seniors think like this. Do you have any concrete ideas on how to achieve this?
>
> **New senior 1:** I think clear channels of communication and consultation are the keys. From our perspective, we should not only communicate with teachers, but also with our juniors, we should make them know that they can rely on us and we all strive together to

make things work. We want a relationship with juniors in which it's easy for them to express their opinions, I think that begins with ambiance (*funiki*), we don't want a strict ambiance. Juniors should feel that they could approach us and talk to us if they're having trouble.

ZW: I understand. How would you create such an ambiance?

New senior 1: Within each instrumental section, there could be more conversations between seniors and juniors, we could do it on a daily basis, like, consultation with juniors.[69]

From the above, it was evident that the new club seniors of Tokyo Daiichi Girls' Orchestra wanted a less strict atmosphere inasmuch as relations between seniors and juniors were concerned. Concretely, the new seniors hoped for more meaningful exchanges of opinion and communication with their juniors as compared to when they themselves were juniors. However, the extent to which there would be such meaningful change in the *senpai-kouhai* relations remains questionable. This is because, in the newest version of Tokyo Daiichi Girls' Orchestra's guidebook that was prepared by these same new seniors and that had just been distributed to new junior members, there was (as had always been) a clear emphasis on appropriate oral expressions and the use of honorifics when juniors spoke to seniors (refer to sub-section 3.2.2). However, as I pointed out earlier, most junior high school students do not receive proper training in honorifics until the second half of junior second grade. This places, on the one hand, restrictions on juniors if they should feel the need to communicate with their seniors. On the other hand, it also gives seniors the role of "teachers": in teaching proper language use to juniors, and in the process, reinforcing the very *jouge kankei* through discursive means (refer to later chapters for cases and examples).

Therefore, it transpires that senior club members do have an influence on a club's hierarchical order.[70] However, their influence is limited in extent, as it mainly pertains to the degree of manifestation of *jouge kankei* in certain aspects of club life, while the basic nature of the discursive constitution of *jouge kankei* in clubs remains largely intact. Furthermore, this nature of *jouge kankei* is manifested both in macro-level Discourses (narratives on and ways of thinking about hierarchy) and in micro-level discourses (forms of talk). The rest of this book will illustrate the workings of the nature of *jouge kankei*.

---

69 Interview: 20.05.2016.
70 A consequence of this is that, since everyone will have her/his turn to be a senior due to automatic "promotion" as one gets older, everyone will have a say in at least some aspects of running the club. Hence, this adds an **egalitarian element to the hierarchy** and makes *jouge kankei* peculiar. Refer to chapter seven.

3.4 Summary of chapter: The textual constitution of *jouge kankei* and socialisation process

As much research on various aspects of Japanese society has shown, *jouge kankei*, as a core social institution, is pervasive in Japanese society (Bestor 1989; Nakane 1970; also refer to chapter one). As regards the stage of life at which individuals acquire knowledge of *jouge kankei*, most recent qualitative social research attribute the formation of actors' cognition of institutional hierarchy from junior high school onwards (Cave 2004; Hebert 2012; LeTendre 2000). While acknowledging the omnipresence and importance of such higher-lower relationships, few, however, have explored the formation of *jouge kankei*, much less *how* such seniority-based interpersonal relations take shape through discursive strategies in social interactions.

In this chapter, I have followed up on an important point revealed by interviewees from the early stage of my study: that school clubs generally place great importance on teaching every cohort of new members on appropriate behaviours. I have shown that such explicit teaching is achieved by means of guidance sessions held at the beginning of each new academic year, conducted by senior authorities in clubs. An important teaching aid are texts outlining detailed rules and regulations as regards proper social comportment (both linguistic and bodily) in accordance to one's status in clubs. Such texts, whose origins remain largely unknown to new members, are held in high regard and passed down to each incoming batch of members, while their contents are interpreted by teachers and/or senior students. In this process, new members are urged to observe and learn, and pay attention to who and what to observe in a variety of social situations and ritualised practices. Lastly, this chapter demonstrated occasions in which juniors made mistakes, and seniors' readiness to reprimand repeated "wrong-doers", evidencing their will and determination to make rules explicit to juniors.

Hence, what I have documented in this chapter concerns the *beginning* of an individual's socialisation process into *jouge kankei* in and through discursive means in Japan. From the next chapter onwards, I show various *processes* of socialisation with more micro-level discursive practices that constitute *jouge kankei* in a concrete manner with snapshots of daily interactions.

4 Address terms, honorific word choices, and the construction of hierarchy

In the previous chapter, I presented macro-level "Discourses" in the form of texts and lectures by club teachers in charge and seniors. I showed how these paved the way to socialise new club members, by and through language, into "new domains of knowledge and cultural practices" (Bayley and Schecter 2003: 2) – namely the interpersonal relations centred around the age-based hierarchical system in the social world of *bukatsudou*. In this chapter, I demonstrate how specific norms and conventions on language use on the micro discursive level are manifested in interactions and how these do their part in constituting *jouge kankei*. To do so, I present and analyse the empirical data of address terms. I will first provide a concise theoretical introduction on the topic at hand from a general perspective (that is, not specifically related to the workings of the Japanese language), followed by a review of important literature and in particular, the ways in which existing empirical research examine address terms in the social contexts of schools. I then narrow down the analytical perspective, and discuss the ways in which these could be applied to the contexts of Japanese secondary schools. This will be followed by the presentation and analysis of data gathered on-site. The goal of this chapter is to demonstrate the social significance of address terms as a micro-level discursive practice and strategy in the enactment of hierarchical interpersonal relations in secondary school clubs.

4.1 Terms of address (ToA): Cognition, legitimisation, and knowledge

As regards the discursive constitution of hierarchy, the type of empirical data I present in this chapter is address terms. The study of address terms is not a novel endeavour in the human and social sciences. Anthropology has a long and distinguished tradition of having kinship terms as an object of investigation.[71] In sociolinguistics and the sociology of language, such terms were first investigated for Western European languages, and these insights have been fruitfully transferred, with adaptations, to non-Western languages, including Japanese.

---

[71] This field of inquiry is sometimes established in the branch of "linguistic anthropology". For a sample selection of seminal works, refer to Geertz (1973) and Agha (2007).

One of the basic concepts of ToA is the notion of address itself. This should be understood as a speaker's linguistic reference to his or her collocutor(s), serving as means to initiate contact (Braun 1988: 7). In most existing studies, ToA include *pronouns*: lexical items that can substitute for a noun or a noun phrase, and pronouns can be personal (including first person self-referent pronouns), possessive, demonstrative; and *nouns*: substantives and adjectives designating collocutors or referring to them in some ways. This is a diverse group and consists of kinship terms, professional titles, occupational terms, and endearment terms (Braun 1988; Mühlhäusler and Harré 1990; Liebscher and Dailey-O'Cain 2013). Since ToA are words or phrases used for addressing and referring to the collocutor, they incorporate a strong element of deixis, which highlights the process "by which reference is made to spatial, temporal, social or personal aspects of a situation" (Mühlhäusler and Harré 1990: 9). What is relevant is above all *social deixis*, which is understood as "those aspects of language structure that are anchored to the social identities of participants (including bystanders) in the speech event, or to relations between them, or to relations between them and other referents" (Levinson 1979: 206). Put into the practice of everyday interactional situations, the act of addressing someone can thus be seen as a deictic act. Examples of deictic acts in a Western language include a waiter's addressing a customer with the formal, singular, second-person pronoun *vous* in a Parisian restaurant and the French Socialist Party's members' mutual addressing with the informal, singular, second-person pronoun *tu* (proximity of social relationships). In a Japanese context, a junior member of the orchestra addressing a senior member using the senior's name and the suffix *-senpai* while getting addressed by this same senior with simply the name is an example of a deictic act showing the distance in their social relationship according to their relative standing in the *jouge kankei* hierarchical order.

The existence of a wide range of ToA as well as their varied usage imply that, more than being just linguistic tools, ToA are also resources in social interactions to convey positions, relationships, and categories in a variety of contexts (Liebscher and Dailey-O'Cain 2013). In other words, address terms construct and reinforce social relationships among interlocutors (Leech 1999).

It is important to bear in mind that such ToA usages constitute speakers' "choices", at least to some extent and for some speakers, as I will show in this chapter. The "choice" of specific ToA or vocabulary and the non-use of others highlight the need to examine the interlocutors' "shared assumptions about what is appropriate behaviour in the situation at hand, based on their knowledge about the world, their partly shared histories and cultural experiences" (Clyne et al. 2009: 25).

4.1.1 Analysing ToA: Theoretical frameworks and previous studies

To date, research in a variety of disciplines such as psychology, psycholinguistics, sociology and sociolinguistics have all contributed to studies of ToA. In existing literature on Western languages, an important focus has been on the examination of second-person pronouns. Early and influential works are Brown and Gilman's (1960) study on pronouns, and Ervin-Tripp et al.'s (1973) attempt to reconstruct rules of address. Insofar as second-person pronouns are concerned, Brown and Gilman (1960) suggest that there exists a T/V differentiation in Western European languages, and that this distinction first appeared in Latin antiquity usage of both *tu* and *vos* in the singular as an address term, while a set of norms crystallised regarding the informal/formal distinction of *tu/vos* in the various Western European languages from the twelfth to the fourteenth centuries (Brown and Gilman 1960: 188). The authors point out that such a differentiation in second-person address terms implied a connection between social structure, group ideology and address terms of ToA in general and pronouns in particular (Brown and Gilman 1960: 252). Regarded by some as "forefathers" in the domain of ToA research (Braun 1988: 17), their seminal work in 1960 on *The Pronouns of Power and Solidarity* highlight the "power semantic" of ToA at work in Western European languages. They argue that, if we understand power of one person over another in the degree that the more powerful person is able to control the behaviour of the other, then power is asymmetric, since both cannot have power in the same area of behaviour. In this case "the superior says T and receives V" (Brown and Gilman 1960: 255). This asymmetry would disappear in social interactions between equals, in which case choice depends mostly on the social status – upper level people mutually exchange V and lower class people T (Brown and Gilman 1960). In contrast to the "power semantic", there is also a "solidarity semantic", which is symmetrical. What determines the extent of similarities between any two collocutors and the ensuing decision to employ mutual T (instead of V) would, according to their study, be "political membership, family, religion, profession, sex, and birthplace" (Brown and Gilman 1960: 258). In other words, group membership that offers a particular sense of common identity and belonging is key to solidarity.[72] In terms of contemporary relevance when their research was conducted, they revealed interesting tendencies and changes. In particular, their brief claim (unfortunately without detailed follow-up study) that "once solidarity has been established as the single dimension distinguishing T from V the province of T proceeds to expand . . . In general, the mutual T is advancing among

---

[72] My findings show that, in the case of Japanese school clubs, solidarity as expressed through ToA is often based on membership in age groups. See analyses that follow.

... members of the same political group." (Brown and Gilman 1960: 261–262). Such a concept of reciprocity might have been a common assumption at the time Brown and Gilman conducted their study, and has left its mark in later studies by other researchers.

Prominent sociologists and sociolinguists who have written on the subject also show us the social salience of ToA and how closely it is related to interpersonal relations. For instance, Bourdieu and Thompson (1991) affirm that the varied use of the two forms of second person pronouns in French – *vous* and *tu* – occurs depending on the social relations between the speakers. Such relationships are defined by variables such as age, social status, and the level of intimacy of their interaction. This manifests clearly the relationship between linguistic forms (different ToA) and social relations, that is, they are interdependent and mutually constitute one another. Mühlhäusler and Harré (1990) point out similar traits in Japanese, as they observe that "characteristic features of the Japanese social system are very fully represented in the grammar of Japanese forms of address. Almost every social distinction possible between speakers [. . .] is overtly expressed in language choice. [. . .] A Japanese must learn the local hierarchies of respect and condescension and where he or she belongs within them"[73] (Mühlhäusler and Harré 1990: 133).

In sum, most literature on ToA adopt one of the two major analytical models in understanding the mechanisms of ToA usage. The first model is a system-based approach with opposing ends. For example, Bayer (1979) proposes that there exist two systems of ToA in German: one with *du* (T) and *Sie* (V) usage to distinguish between intimacy/informality and hierarchy/formality, and one in which *du* and *Sie* do not necessarily reflect an intimate relationship, but rather group belonging and solidarity. The second model is a context-based approach with varying social contexts. For instance, again as regards the German language, Clyne et al (2009) suggest the existence of three interactional contexts of (i) a stable *du* context for family and close friends, (ii) a stable *Sie* for formal interactions with strangers above a certain age, and (iii) a fuzzy context in which *du* and *Sie* usage is to be negotiated (Clyne et al. 2009: 79; Liebscher and Dailey-O'Cain 2013: 136–137). The primary (though not the sole) basis of negotiating the *du/Sie* usage is not age or status, but rather "sameness", understood as "a common ground and a sense of common identity" (Clyne et al. 2009: 79), not unlike Brown and Gilman's (1960) concept of the solidary and mutual use of T. In all the above-mentioned studies on pronouns as ToA in Western European languages thus far, it has been established

---

73 This book shows precisely how they learn such "local hierarchies" and (are expected to) apply what they have learned in interactions during club activities from junior high school onwards.

that the usage of various T/V pronouns necessarily requires a speaker to refer to an interlocutor and to define social relationships simultaneously (Liebscher and Dailey-O'Cain 2013: 135), hence highlighting the constitutive nature of ToA in interpersonal relations. In this light, ToA in interactions do not only communicate information about the interlocutors, but also establish rapport between the very interlocutors implicated in the interactions.

Since ToA are markers of social relationships and their usage is governed by power and/or solidarity (Brown and Gilman 1960: 254), a closer look at "who is calling whom how" in specific organisational setups under particular circumstances will shed light on how speakers seek to create, represent, perpetuate, and even challenge interpersonal relations and social facts.

A recent work by Clyne et al (2009), in the form of an edited volume, represents one of the most comprehensive analyses to date, in which address terms and their expression of social relationships and distances are examined in a wide variety of institutional contexts across four languages: English, French, German, and Swedish. With the aim of examining the social significance of address practices and how they work in different domains and index to different identities and facts, Clyne et al (2009) select four institutional contexts: the family, workplace, university, and school. Out of these, the authors claim that the family and the school contexts are those with "well-established address practices not requiring choices" (Clyne et al. 2009: 125). By way of example, Clyne et al (2009) demonstrate that, speakers employ either mutual T or non-reciprocal T-V in the family: the former practice being used by immediate family members to mark inclusivity, whereas the latter being used largely among extended family members, and at times even with parents of one's partner (in the case of French). Such established practices in the institutional context of family correspond to the expression of respect and formality, rather than unequal relations with power semantic at play between interlocutors. As regards schools, Clyne et al (2009) record similar behavioural trends in French and German, and the address practices in both languages appear highly predictable according to established conventions. For instance, an overwhelming majority of students (more than 90 percent) address teachers in V, while teachers address younger students (younger than 12 or 14 years old) in T and older students in V (Clyne et al. 2009). The authors also observe that the solidarity among teachers as belonging to the same group of people practicing the same profession leads them to use T with each other, with V only reserved in most cases for members of the administration and the senior management in the school. Hence, ToA in schools can highlight either unequal relations, formality, or solidarity.

Major psychologists and social scientists whose works I have surveyed above point out the deictic nature of ToA in social interactions. I claim that this also implies that ToA are indexical to social institutions, therefore by using ToA we reinforce specific institutional setups, as Leech (1999), Searle (2010), and Clyne et al (2009) have demonstrated. However, whenever conventional studies on ToA and language use have a focus on school contexts, the emphasis has almost exclusively been on interactions and corresponding relations between students and teachers, or between teachers and their superiors. Therefore, there is a lack of focus on social organisational structures that bind students of different grades into groups and processes in which students themselves take on different statuses. To a certain degree, this research gap in Western literature is understandable, for, unlike secondary students in Japan, students in Europe and North America do not generally experience the same level of organisational and institutional life in secondary school extra-curricular clubs (refer to chapter two). This warrants attention when we transpose theories and methodologies originated in Western literature to Japanese contexts. In addition, whether or not the above-mentioned existing studies and their contributions could be readily applied to the analysis of the discursive constitution of *jouge kankei* in secondary school clubs in particular, remains to be explored. The next sub-section bridges the gap by examining what has been done on Japanese ToA, hierarchical relations and ways in which to go about analysing potential data in the context of student-to-student interactions in extra-curricular club settings in Japanese secondary schools.

4.1.2 ToA in Japanese contexts

The previous sub-section surveyed a highly developed literature on the use of pronouns as ToA in Western European languages and how such usage constitutes interpersonal relations of power, solidarity, and intimacy. Although in Japanese there is an abundance of pronouns with nuanced indexicalities, it is also a language in which one tends to avoid second-person pronouns as ToA (Enyo 2015). Instead, a variety of suffixes attached to names are used to index roles and interpersonal relations (Enyo 2015; Martin 1964; Morita 2003; Niyekawa 1991). Such terms, made up of names plus suffixation, serve as the most common address and referent terms in daily lives (Morita 2003).

In this sub-section, I aim to pin-point important works that address the issues of ToA in Japanese from a perspective of the linguistic construction of hierarchical interpersonal relations and/or asymmetric power balances between speakers, viz. works that are pertinent to the topic of this book, as well as their achievements and shortcomings. Traditionally, such studies have focussed on the important aspects of showing politeness, formality, and deference in the utilisation of ToA

4.1 Terms of address (ToA): Cognition, legitimisation, and knowledge — 91

(Enyo 2015). As regards the social significance of ToA in Japanese society and how they could have been compared to Western usage, Nakane (1970) expressly points out that:

> This categorization [of splitting the world into three categories consisting of seniors, juniors, and people of the same rank] is demonstrated in the three methods of addressing a second or third person; for example, Mr Tanaka may be addressed as Tanaka-*san*, Tanaka-*kun*, or Tanaka (i.e. without suffix). *San* is used for *sempai* [senior], *kun* for *kohai* [junior], and the name without suffix is reserved for *doryo*[74] [people of the same rank]. The last form is comparable with the English usage of addressing by the Christian name. But the use of this form is carefully restricted to those who are very close to oneself. Even among *doryo*, *san* is used towards those with whom one is not sufficiently familiar, while *kun* is used between those closer than those addressed by *san*, former class-mates, for example. A relationship which permits of address by surname only is of a specifically familiar nature, not unlike the French usage of *tu*. Therefore, a man may also address very intimate *kohai* in this way, but these *kohai* will use the *san* form of address to him . . . It is important to note that this usage of terms of address, once determined by relationships in the earlier stages of a man's life or career, remains unchanged for the rest of his life.
> (Nakane 1970: 26–27)

The passage above illustrates that the social world of interpersonal relations in Japan is as socially as it is linguistically divided. Usage of the suffix -*san* to address seniors and those with whom one is not sufficiently familiar creates deference and distance between interlocutors; while employing the suffix -*kun* to juniors or those with whom one is on more familiar terms, as well as surname only address, constructs intimacy (though non-reciprocal for juniors). The study by Nakane (1970) also affirms that the discursive practices of employing different ToA are constitutive of the very social relations between speakers, since ToA usage remains as enduring as the nature of the relationship itself.

While no research has refuted the constitutive nature of ToA in the hierarchical social world in Japan, later works attest to different usages and conclusions. One such example is noted in Niyekawa (1991), in which the author observes that first name plus the suffix -*san* is the most commonly used ToA among students of equal statuses, while seniors are addressed by title only. A common characteristic of early research on ToA is a tendency to assume that particular ToA have fixed and pre-determined meanings and are hence only suitable to be used by certain profiles of speakers to address certain others. Recent research, both on Japanese and on Western European languages and societies, tend to reject this notion and

---

[74] Nakane (1970) highlighted at this point that the different address terms discussed here pertained only to men, as women did not apply such fine-grained differentiations in general social life. Data in this volume suggest that this is not the case, insofar as secondary school club contexts in contemporary Japan are concerned.

examine variations and negotiations in meaning and usage of ToA under diverse circumstances. Enyo's (2013; 2015) works on the ways in which ToA are used and how they construct *senpai-kouhai* relationships in a university movie club represents an important and relevant recent study. Firstly, in her research, Enyo (2013) found that honorific titles, such as *senpai*, were never used by participants. Instead, when juniors addressed seniors, either surname plus the suffix *-san* or first name plus the suffix *-san* was used. Secondly, the ToA of first name plus *-san* or *-chan* were used by seniors to juniors, the latter being more intimate. She also observed that the surname or first name only ToA was almost always used by seniors to juniors and was never reciprocated, just like the usage of the suffix *-chan* (Enyo 2013: 99). What sets Enyo's study apart from the afore-mentioned earlier works is that Enyo also took into account the distinction between on- and off-stage talk and corresponding ToA usage by same pairs of speakers. For instance, a senior club member used the suffix *-san* when addressing a junior member during an official meeting (on-stage official talk and personae), but later reversed to addressing this same junior with the suffix *-chan* to construct the *senpai-kouhai* relationship between them (Enyo 2013: 100). This work demonstrates that, in addition to ToA per se, it is the ways in which speakers employ them in a variety of situations and frames that determine their functions; in this case the construction of hierarchy in off-stage talk and the fore-grounding of a formal and official identity in on-stage talk.

In extant literature, insofar as the discursive construction of hierarchy is concerned, Enyo's (2013) study is the most similar in nature to my research. There are, however, crucial differences.[75] One of them is that, being university students and alumni, the speakers in Enyo's study are all seasoned users of various aspects of the Japanese language compared to speakers in my study. As mentioned earlier in this volume, the ability to employ discursive strategies also means the ability to recognise hierarchy (Miwa 2000). In addition, there exist other reasons to call some of the conclusions of Enyo's research into question. For instance, we know that speakers do not possess the same extent of knowledge in social rules governing ToA usage, and this is in addition to the fact that the very repertoire of ToA might vary from speaker to speaker (Braun 1988). Indeed, as I have shown in the previous chapter, the very existence of the socialisation and learning process at

---

75 Other significant differences not mentioned in this chapter include my incorporation of a more encompassing "discursive" approach (language plus complementary extra-linguistic meaning-making signs and symbols) to the constitution of hierarchy vis-à-vis Enyo's approach, which is limited only to the linguistic features of ToA and *desu/masu* forms. In addition, such hierarchical social life in clubs occupy a much more central role in students' lives in secondary schools as compared to in universities. Refer to chapter two.

the beginning of a student's club stint exemplifies the effort to standardise the unequal knowledge, and in many instances, to fill the "knowledge gap" with regard to social rules governing ToA usage. The ways in which a junior high school club member acquires and masters ToA usage (as well as other discursive practices) at the same time as she/he gets involved into the *jouge kankei* of her/his club has so far not been studied. In the next section, I present my data and show the different dynamics of ToA constitution of hierarchy among speakers who are much younger than in Enyo's (2013) study, and for whom the socialisation process into *jouge kankei* is at its very beginning.

4.2 ToA in Japanese secondary school clubs

In this section, I illustrate the ways in which ToA are used by secondary school club members in Japan as part of the micro-level discursive practice to construct hierarchy. Data for this chapter were collected in two ways: (i) self-reported use of ToA in secondary school clubs, and (ii) everyday ToA usage. The first way entails data obtained through interviews with high school graduates and university students in the initial phase of my fieldwork and secondary school students during the main ethnographic fieldwork phase. The second way entails data observed and heard in the three student clubs throughout my participant observation sessions. Self-reported language use has been a major part of data collection in empirical surveys in Japan, the most notable of which are the NINJAL (2002) survey on honorifics in Japanese schools and the Agency for Cultural Affairs' annual honorifics attitude survey. Surveys or studies that rely solely on reported language use have manifested weaknesses in their explanatory power. This is because, in interviews, people often think through carefully before they respond, whereas in actual linguistic and social interactions, most speakers hardly go through the same process of reflection before uttering an address term. However, despite the afore-mentioned insufficiency, I maintain that self-reported language use data as obtained from interviews do serve important purposes. This is because speakers' own comments on language use, in this case ToA use, not only provide a good basis to understand language and society, but also enhance linguists' claim to objective analysis by underscoring communities' (speakers') beliefs about language use (Niedzielski and Preston 2003). In order to ensure that multiple perspectives and comprehensive viewpoints are taken into account, reliance on self-reported language use as the main data source should always be qualified, and if possible, accompanied by supplementary verification methods like participant observation. This is where my extended on-site presence in the student clubs prove useful.

In what follows, I first present a general overview of what secondary school graduates recalled as their ToA use in their secondary school days, followed by my observation of ToA use of current junior and senior high students in the three secondary school clubs. Then, I explain the different scenarios in the institutional order of *jouge kankei* and the ways in which one goes about employing an appropriate address term. These parts will be exemplified by interview data.

The Table 4.1 below presents information gathered through interviews with high school graduates and university students, where I asked interviewees to recall their experience in their respective secondary school club activities and asked questions focussing on the micro-level discourse of ToA practice:

Table 4.1: High school graduates and university students on ToA usage in their secondary school club activities. LN denotes last name/surname, FN denotes first name.

Juniors to seniors	Seniors to juniors	Between equals	Remarks
LN + *senpai*;	LN + *san*;	LN only;	No rules for seniors to juniors and between equals;
LN + *san*;	FN + *san/chan*;	FN only;	1 person reported gender difference in her club: seniors called female juniors FN + *san* and male juniors LN + *san*
FN + *senpai*;	Nicknames	Nicknames	
Senpai			

Since most of these interviews were conducted right before I ventured into the fieldwork sites of secondary school clubs, the data gathered served to provide some background information as to what to expect. Furthermore, I noted that, although there was a 15-year gap between the data collection period for the NINJAL (2002) survey (late 1980s) and the period when my interviewees attended junior and senior high school (mid to late 2000s), results in both cases as regards ToA use corroborated each other.[76] This consistency in ToA norms and conventions of usage provided useful clues as to the enduring nature of hierarchy which I could look for in my fieldwork sites.

Observations from the three student clubs during my fieldwork further illustrated the persistent social order of *jouge kankei* and its discursive constitution. Regarding ToA usage in the three clubs in Tokyo Daiichi and Tokyo Daini, the following practices as shown in Table 4.2 have been observed:

---

[76] The NINJAL (2002) survey showed an overwhelming majority of respondents in Tokyo, Osaka, and Yamagata using the suffix *senpai* as part of the ToA to their seniors in clubs. Refer to chapter two for more details.

Table 4.2: Summary of ToA usage observed in the three clubs. Data obtained from November 2015 to May 2016.

Club	Juniors to seniors	Seniors to juniors	Between equals	Remarks
Tokyo Daiichi Orchestra	FN + *senpai*	FN only/FN + *chan*	No rules, LN only/ nicknames* common	*Omae*+ commonly used between equals among seniors
Tokyo Daiichi Choir	LN + *senpai*	LN only/LN + *chan*	No rules, LN only/ nicknames common	
Tokyo Daini Orchestra	LN + *san*	LN only	No rules, LN common	Teacher calls everyone *omae*, except the student conductor (Last name)

*Nicknames included abbreviated surnames. +*Omae* is a second-person pronoun that has traditionally been considered informal, coarse, and masculine (SturtzSreetharan 2009).

With data presented, the rest of this chapter will consist of detailed analysis of particular ToA usage and choice, and more importantly, the social context in which particular ToA are practiced. The central question guiding the analysis is, who is using which ToA to whom, when and why?

4.2.1 Seniors to juniors

From the tables above, we can see that a relatively wide range of possible ToA exist for seniors addressing juniors. These can be classified into the following:
- First name (FN)
- Last name (LN)
- Nickname (including abbreviated first name or last name)
- First name + *chan*
- Last name + *chan*
- Last name + *san*

From the above, we notice that in groups with female students, the suffix -*chan* was overwhelmingly used by seniors to address juniors. This observation corroborates with existing research that affirmed -*chan* as an endearing version of -*san* and that it is more often used to refer to females (Martin 1964). Its frequent usage to refer or address children in the family (Niyekawa 1991) also extends in this context to a form of ToA for seniors addressing juniors. Contrary to Enyo's (2013) observation that -*chan* was never attached to the last name in the university movie club, my data show that, in the context of junior and senior high school clubs, the form of last name + *chan* was not only a possible option, but also the normal ToA employed by seniors in Tokyo Daiichi Girls' Choir to address their juniors. As for male juniors, either last name alone or last name + *san* was observed.

In addition, both interview and fieldwork observation data in the three secondary school clubs revealed that the above ToA were not reciprocated by juniors. Furthermore, since there are no conventions as to how a senior should address a junior, seniors were free to use their creativity as well, and at times did come up with nicknames for their juniors.

4.2.2 Juniors to seniors

When it comes to ToA for juniors to address seniors, we could see that, in all instances, the role of seniors must be acknowledged by juniors in one way or another. Possible ToA for juniors to address seniors are:
– First name + *senpai*
– Last name + *senpai*
– Last name + *san*
– (*Senpai*[77])
– Titles: e.g. *buchou* (president)

The acknowledgement of a club member's seniority is expressed through the above ToA, as seniors must be addressed at least with the suffix -*senpai* or -*san* following last names or first names. Generally speaking, the observable trend is that there is much less variation in the ToA for juniors to address seniors than for seniors to address juniors. This is consonant with the nature of the *jouge*

---

[77] According to some interviewees (graduates) who were in smaller clubs, the term *senpai* was reported to be used as a stand-alone ToA for juniors addressing seniors. However, my observations revealed that this practice would, in reality, be impractical in larger clubs. If there are several seniors present, a particular junior would be forced to include the last name/first name in the ToA. Hence, I do not consider *senpai* as an altogether different ToA classification, but rather a contextualisation to the situation of whether or not there are more than one senior present.

kankei in requiring juniors to show respect and deference, as well as the discursive constitution of such hierarchical interpersonal relations.

Contrasting the data in this sub-section to those in the earlier sub-section (4.2.1.) on senior-to-junior ToA, it is apt to apply Brown and Gilman's (1960) non-reciprocal "power semantic", which, in this case, is based on age cohort. The character of the non-reciprocal power semantic between a senior and junior implicated in a secondary school club activity is manifested in the senior's relative freedom to use intimate terms or create nicknames for juniors, while on the other hand the junior is expected to utilise one of the few accepted ToA towards the senior.

I observed that juniors were expected to address seniors in such ways whenever they came across their seniors. In other words, this social relationship extends beyond the confines of club activities. The extent to which this is etched into the cognition of juniors is so large that when juniors walk past their seniors in school or in the neighbourhood, they are expected to address seniors as such. This behaviour echoes Nakane's (1970) claim that once such a relationship based on seniority is established, it persists over time and space. Such rules concerning proper (discursive) behaviour among club members are strictly enforced in and out of the club. One of the teachers in charge of the Tokyo Daiichi Choir explained the need for the strict observance of rules:

> Our club gets into the national finals every year and we aim to be Japan's top school choir. Without strict rules [pertaining to how juniors behave, including how they address seniors] it would not be possible to achieve this. We want to maintain order at all times, and instil a constant sense of urgency [that something decisive, such as an important competition, is coming up] and discipline in our members.[78]

The teacher in charge of Tokyo Daiichi Choir justified her club's strict behavioural rules based on their collective ambitions to reach the national finals every year, hence the need to have a disciplined and orderly group to maximise training efficiency. Though this applied to the choir, it did not mean that clubs with a "lower" level of ambition were different in *nature* as regards hierarchical interpersonal relations and corresponding discursive practices. When I asked a member of the clarinet section in Tokyo Daiichi Orchestra about club rules regarding ToA and whether or not the orchestra was one of the top-performing clubs supposedly with the strictest rules, she revealed:

> I thought our club is rather average in terms of performance and nobody really expects much from us in terms of results. I also think that rules for juniors to follow in our

---

[78] Interview conducted on 18.11.2015.

98 — 4 Address terms, honorific word choices, and the construction of hierarchy

orchestra are not among the strictest. They just need to ensure that they address us with first name + *senpai*, talk to us properly, and always greet us with appropriate expressions [according to the time of the day] whenever they see us in or outside of school/club.[79]

In effect, though this book shows that some clubs do have more regulations than others, the underlying principle and nature of *jouge kankei* remain largely consistent across different types of clubs. This is manifested by the largely consistent practice of ToA usage from juniors to seniors. The constant and pervasive nature of this institutional hierarchy and its discursive constitution (ToA in this case) are also exemplified by juniors' practice of using (and being expected to use) the appropriate terms when mentioning or referring to seniors, even when the latter are not physically present, as the following scene illustrates:

Vignette 4.1: Addressing and referring to an alumnus in Tokyo Daini Boys'Orchestra
The clarinet section today had their practice session supervised by an OB ("old boy", which means alumnus). When he arrived, I was already in the room with the clarinettists. As we had not met before, he first thought that I was an even older alumnus he had not personally known, hence he started to bow and greet me. His actions stirred laughter from the rest of the current club members, because they, as juniors, had not seen this particular alumnus behaving in such a humble and respectful manner. I cleared the matter by briefly introducing myself to him, and he went on to conduct the session (during which time there were little oral communication, let alone opportunities to observe ToA usage). When the practice came to an end, the clarinettists packed up their instruments and (junior members) quickly proceeded to clean the classroom. At this juncture, I saw that the senior clarinettists were walking back towards the music room. I followed and walked up to the two senior second year students, Daimaru and Mitsuhashi, who were also the president and vice president of the club respectively. I asked them about the alumnus present during the practice, such as his age and the frequency with which he came back to visit his juniors. Mitsuhashi became excited and started talking about how good relations were between alumni like him and the rest of the current students in the clarinet section. His voice became particularly loud when he started talking about the *yakiniku*[80] outing with this alumnus last week. He mentioned how the junior first and second graders had been asking the section's senior members to bring them out to a restaurant for a round of *yakiniku*,

---

79 Interview conducted on 20.11.2015.
80 Grilled meat typically enjoyed in groups in special restaurants equipped with table grills.

but that most active members from the senior high section hesitated, until this particular alumnus who is already in university came back to visit. He not only agreed to organise, but also paid most of the bill for this event. While explaining, Mitsuhashi used "*ano hito*" (that person) to refer to the alumnus. Daimaru intervened immediately and warned that the alumnus might be walking several meters behind us and he might hear us. Mitsuhashi suddenly realised what he has gotten into and the potential "danger" of using such disrespectful language when talking about seniors. He instantly stopped talking, covered his mouth, turned his head around to make sure that we were far enough from the alumnus, and then resumed by saying "Oh yes, we are very close to Tanaka-san (the alumnus) and so he is still treating us like his juniors and taking care of the entire section."[81]

The above scenario demonstrated that, what was expected of juniors was that they be polite to their seniors and show reverence even when the seniors were not present. Not only were juniors required to refer to seniors with the appropriate ToA, but also to use honorific language as much as possible when talking *about* seniors. This instance demonstrates the persistent nature of *jouge kankei* between a senior and a junior once such a relationship is established in the secondary school club setting, as well as the discursive construction of it. On the "role of the vocabulary" (in this case ToA), Searle (2010) affirms:

> One sees the role of the vocabulary in the activities of revolutionary and reformist movements. They try to get hold of the vocabulary in order to alter the system of status functions. The feminists were right to see that the vocabulary of "lady" and "gentleman" involves a deontology that they wanted to reject. Again, the Communists in Russia wanted people to address each other as "comrade" as a way of creating new status functions and destroying old ones. The continued use of vocabulary maintains and reinforces the existing status functions. (Searle 2010: 104)

As Searle (2010) argues, ToA are used to create and maintain basic social facts, that is to say, specific social relationships, within the respective organisational settings, in this case the established *jouge kankei* between a senior and a junior. The more a specific set of vocabulary is used, the stronger the relevant statuses in the institution become. Therefore, the hierarchical organisational structure of club activities, in which seniority-based functions (such as president and section leader), as well as roles and statuses (such as *senpai* and *kouhai*) are observed (refer to chapter two), is concomitantly constituted and sustained by the micro-level discursive system of ToA between seniors and juniors.

Moreover, as "appropriate" ToA are taught to new juniors, a process of legitimation (of *jouge kankei*) is underway. In the process of transmitting the

---

[81] Observation and conversation in Tokyo Daini's orchestra on 20.01.2016.

institutional order to a new generation of actors, a series of explanations and justifications occur and these further consolidate the institutional structure in question (Berger and Luckmann 1966). Legitimation here refers to the act of explaining and inserting normative elements into the social order, as well as providing individuals with relevant knowledge about the very order (Berger and Luckmann 1966). The ToA practices contribute to this by emphasising to an individual that she/he is a part of the *jouge kankei* system. The normative elements, such as what is allowed and what is prohibited, would then become clear once new members have read and digested the guidelines stated in their clubs' rule books. In this light, the discursive practice of ToA is an important part of "incipient legitimation":

> Incipient legitimation is present as soon as a system of linguistic objectifications of human experience is transmitted. For example, the transmission of a kinship vocabulary *ipso facto* legitimates the kinship structure. The fundamental legitimating 'explanations' are, so to speak, built into the vocabulary. Thus a child learns that another child *is* a 'cousin', a piece of information that immediately and inherently legitimates the conduct with regard to 'cousins' that is learned along with the designation.
>
> (Berger and Luckmann 1966: 112)

What Berger and Luckmann stipulate here applies to the roles and status functions of *senpai* and *kouhai* in the hierarchical order of school clubs as well, as I show in this book. As a micro-level discursive practice, the ToA usage brings *jouge kankei* into being by instilling incipient knowledge to ToA users and reinforcing status functions through its range of designated vocabulary.

4.2.3 Between equals

According to my observations, there are no rules governing ToA use between equals and ToA choice here is most prone to negotiation based on a variety of factors and contexts. Since it concerns a flat hierarchy among people from the same grade, the suffixes -*senpai* and -*san* were not observed throughout my fieldwork. The commonly used ToA between equals were:
– Last name
– Last name + *chan*
– Nickname
– Nickname + *chan*
– Second-person pronoun *omae*

Between equals in Tokyo Daini Boys' Orchestra, last name alone was the norm, while in Tokyo Daiichi Girls' Choir, a mixture of last name and last name +

chan was most commonly heard. In Tokyo Daiichi Orchestra, last name, nickname, and the second-person pronoun *omae* were overwhelmingly used.

4.3 Similarities and differences of ToA use in secondary school clubs: At the intersection of social roles and gender

In the previous sub-sections, I presented the ToA usage and data collected from my fieldwork. In this section, I point out and analyse some of the similarities and differences in ToA usage across groups. To do so, I refer back to the central guiding question of "who is using which ToA to whom and why".

The first major similarity across clubs was that, when addressing and referring to seniors, juniors were to always show respect and acknowledge the seniors' higher status by using appropriate ToA. This was evident in the fact that last name, nickname, or first name only ToA for juniors to address seniors were not accepted in any of the clubs. A junior was to always use one of the polite suffixes and/or a title, and the available range of ToA was limited. Such respectful ToA vocabulary served to maintain and reinforce specific status functions in institutional contexts (Searle 2010), in this case the *senpai*'s seniority vis-à-vis juniors once this relationship was established.

Secondly, as regards the ways in which seniors addressed or referred to juniors, there existed no rules to regulate such ToA and as a consequence, a much wider range of address terms was available. The same also applied to those of equal ranks.

The differences in ToA practice across clubs are equally worthy of examination. In particular, my three fieldwork sites in two single-sex junior and senior high schools allowed for the observation of gender differences in the discursive practice of ToA use.[82] A notable phenomenon was the existence and utilisation of far more varieties in ToA by club members in both Tokyo Daiichi Girls' Orchestra and Choir, as compared to seniors in Tokyo Daini Boys' Orchestra. This practice was especially so for seniors addressing juniors and between equals. For instance, seniors in the boys' orchestra at Tokyo Daini always addressed their juniors with last name only, while last name or first name was used among people from the same grade. Suffixation, such as the use of *-kun*, as well as abbreviations of names or the

---

[82] This does not, however, cover gender differences (if any) within the same group, due to the single-sex nature of my fieldwork sites. I discuss the benefits, limits, as well as future research potentials as a result of my research site selection in chapters two and seven.

invention of nicknames, and the use of pronouns like *omae* were rarely, if ever, used in club activity settings. As the various sub-sections in 4.2 have shown, this stands in stark contrast to the discursive practices of ToA usage in the two girls' groups in Tokyo Daiichi, where last names, first names, nicknames plus suffixes, and *omae* (only between equals) were common practices.

While the social world of students in Japanese secondary school clubs is divided into the three broad categories of seniors, juniors, and people of equal rank, the usage of ToA, in particular the difference across gender, contradicts to what Nakane (1970) claims about ToA differences between men and women; that "the differentiations here discussed apply only to men: women do not use such elaborate address terms in general social life" (Nakane 1970: 27). My empirical findings show the contrary and highlight the need to recognise that higher-lower relationships exist and are institutionalised in male as well as in female groups by way of various discursive practices. If there are any differences, survey results by NINJAL (2002) and my findings illustrate that girls tend to be more conscious of their social behaviour of speaking to seniors and varieties in the two female clubs are more elaborate than in the male orchestra in general. To be sure, exceptions have been observed: in the clarinet section of Tokyo Daini Boys' Orchestra, seniors occasionally referred to juniors with "last name + *chan*". Although uncommon, this reminds us that insofar as gender is taken into account, intra-group variations do exist and we should avoid making clear-cut divisions across gender lines alone in an outright manner.

4.3.1 Different in manifestation, similar in nature

Insofar as the discursive construction of hierarchy is concerned, it is important to note that, while differences in ToA exist, this is more a question of the degree of manifestation of *jouge kankei*, rather than the very nature of it in different clubs. For even in clubs where seniors explicitly told juniors that they favoured a "flat hierarchy", certain baseline protocol was still in place, without which the social world of *jouge kankei* in *bukatsudou* would be inconceivable. This point is put forward succinctly by an interviewee (a university student as she recalled her secondary school club experience), when I asked her about her thoughts on hierarchy in her broadcasting club (in which she served as president in her secondary school days):

ZW: When you were the *buchou* (president), did people show respect to you?
Interviewee: Yes.

ZW: How did they call you? For example, if a junior member wanted to talk to you?

Interviewee: Just "*senpai*".

ZW: They didn't have to say "*buchou*"?

Interviewee: Sometimes, like, junior first graders did call me "*buchou*", because I didn't know them very well. As for the others, well, we did have grades, but we were sort of very friendly to each other, so we only had "*senpai*".

ZW: Just "*senpai*". And how did you call them?

Interviewee: Just family name + *san*. That is also a traditional thing I guess.
[. . .]
Interviewee: In the *housoubu* (broadcasting club), in the year when I became the president, it was very ridiculous. Seven new students came in, which was like the same as the total number of members then, like, there were seven or eight students in the other grades. They were so many, and we had to do things strict. I mean, because there were so many people.

ZW: So at that point in time, what happened? Like, did you introduce anything new? Or?

Interviewee: Not really, but we started doing things more, automatically [systematically], like, teaching them rules. Because in the other years there were like one or two or three new students coming, so we sort of took turns in teaching, and like each *senpai* would take care of one *kouhai*. But because there were so many new students, we could not do that in the last year, we had to gather all the new students and teach at once. That sort of changed the atmosphere very much, that never happened before.

ZW: So it became more formal?

Interviewee: Yes, I didn't really like that, because it was a very friendly club until then. It was still friendly enough, but not like before.

ZW: I see. How did it change in terms of daily life? Except the fact that there were so many juniors, did they act really respectfully, or?

Interviewee: No, not really, because I didn't like that.

ZW: Did you actually say that to the juniors? Was it part of the teaching?

Interviewee: Yes, it was. And I don't like this kind of strict things, so don't, they don't have to be super respectful or polite to me, I thought.

ZW: You actually said that to them?

Interviewee: Yes, I mean it depends on the person. But I personally didn't like it, so I said like, you don't have to be super polite, but, like, fairly polite is fine.

ZW: So I'm interested in your understanding of "fairly polite". What does it mean to you? What is acceptable as "fairly polite" behaviour on the part of juniors?

Interviewee: Well, for example, calling me "*naninani-senpai*" (literally, "so-and-so"+*senpai*), and the other seniors too, calling them "*senpai*", and using some sort of *keigo*, if you see what I mean . . . I wanted, like, the smallest [flattest] hierarchy possible, but I didn't want none.

> **ZW:** Right, so, to you, what is acceptable as "fairly polite" behaviour would be to acknowledge the seniority of you and your cohort by referring to you as *senpai*, and use some form of *keigo*. Can you give me some examples?
>
> **Interviewee:** Like, in addition to addressing seniors properly, juniors should not talk to us in *tameguchi* (refers to the way in which two equals talk), not like friends. But other than that, just saying "*desu/masu*", that was enough.[83]

This particular interviewee took great pride in the fact that her broadcasting club in secondary school had a very unique atmosphere where people across different grades were on friendly terms with each other. She also mentioned that, because of her personality, she explicitly told junior members in her club not to be "super polite" to her and the other seniors, as what would normally be expected, because all she wanted was just a fair amount of politeness and respect. This should be, according to her, manifested first and foremost in ToA from juniors to seniors, such as attaching the suffix *senpai* to seniors' names. In this regard, this club with a friendly atmosphere was no different from other clubs. The main difference was that the interviewee accepted the simple use of sentence-final "*desu/masu*" form (as opposed to the plain form) from juniors to seniors, and juniors were not required to perform other conversational routines set out in some rule books (refer to chapter three) or more "advanced" forms of honorifics (refer to chapter five). However, the difference in the degree of formality between this interviewee's club and most other clubs does not call into question the existence of the very nature of the institutional arrangements of higher-lower relationships, for there was a clearly defined baseline: special vocabularies such as various stipulated ToA practices were used to acknowledge certain statuses in the club. Furthermore, the friendly atmosphere did not mean that seniors and juniors in this club could behave like friends, that is to say, to address or talk to each other in a way that friends or people from the same grade would do. The enduring asymmetric discursive practice of ToA from juniors to seniors ultimately kept this institutional setup intact.

4.4 When deviant cases occur: The impossibility of ToA transition in school clubs

Existing studies on address terms have often posited that, when two speakers start off with V as the default address term, a "transition" might be possible after a certain point in time, that is, this same pair of speakers would switch to a

---

[83] Interview conducted on 27.10.2015.

mutual T. In-group membership and sentiments, such as solidarity, age, pursuing common hobbies/activities, political alignment and the like, are decisive factors that enable the transition from V to T between speakers (Brown and Gilman 1960; Clyne et al. 2009). This is also attributed to the fact that, during the process in which two speakers transform from strangers to those with important common grounds/group membership, the social distance created by the V address term diminishes (Cylne et al. 2009). Such transitions could happen in an "official" manner, in which explicit and fixed expressions are used to signal this transition,[84] or it could happen in a more "natural" way without a formally marked moment of transition (Clyne et al. 2009).

From the data presented in this chapter thus far, we can see some basic mechanisms of ToA in various club contexts in secondary schools in Japan. The greatest difference as compared to existing studies on ToA examining the possibility of a transition in ToA use is that *secondary school club contexts have much more rigid codes of conduct* that do not leave the possibility of a ToA transition between speakers open for negotiation. For instance, although slight variations in ToA practice exist in different clubs and schools across Japan, the baseline principle reigns in all groups: juniors are expected to address seniors in a way that shows reverence. Juniors are expected to uphold this code of conduct to all seniors at all times. To be sure, such regulatory conventions and behavioural norms are learned by individuals during the socialisation processes in junior high school clubs. More intimate ToA expressing a high degree of familiarity and solidarity between two people of different age status certainly exist and pre-date the socialisation into institutional hierarchy in clubs. During my fieldwork, I observed that this was especially the case for childhood friends who, upon entering the same junior high school and the same club, became implicated in the system of *jouge kankei* by virtue of their age difference. The pertinent issue then becomes, how do individuals comport themselves when prior practices confront and conflict with norms in *jouge kankei*? Do they attempt a "transition", and if so, would they be successful?

It transpires that, on occasions where deviance occurs, it is hardly tolerated, as one other interviewee (in her third year of university at the time of interview) recounted to me her experience in her junior high school basketball club:

---

[84] For instance, the phrases such as *Wir könnten uns ja duzen* (we could say *du* to each other, couldn't we?) or *Sollen wir uns duzen?* (Should we use *du*?) in German, as well as *on peut se tutoyer* (we can say *tu* to each other) or *on se tutoie?* (shall we say *tu* to each other?) in French are still commonly used to initiate the transition from from V to T (Clyne et al. 2009).

> **ZW:** In your case, when you were in junior and senior high school, could you address your seniors in casual terms?
>
> **Interviewee:** No, in the basketball club, no. Because, actually, when I was in junior second year, there were people from the first year who came and joined the club, and I knew one of the new members really well. We basically lived in the same neighbourhood, grew up together, and were best friends in primary school. So naturally I urged her to join my basketball club once she entered the same junior high school one year after me. After she joined the club all the new members, herself included, were taught proper manners. Like how to talk to seniors. But, since we were really close I just let her address and talk to me in casual ways, just like before, like, just nicknames and no *-san* or *-senpai* attached to my surname. Afterwards, seniors from the third grade heard it and they reprimanded me for this and told me that I shouldn't do that.
>
> **ZW:** Oh really? What did they say?
>
> **Interviewee:** Yes. Well, the seniors said that even if I made this exception to just one particular junior, it would break the club atmosphere (*funiki*), so I shouldn't let juniors talk to us seniors in improper ways.[85]

In the extract above, this particular interviewee was apparently severely reproached by her seniors and she left the basketball club at the end of her junior high years (she was in a school with a six-year programme). After the interview, she confided that it was hard for her to accept that she had done something "wrong", because she had been very close to the new junior and they had been childhood friends who grew up together in the same neighbourhood and attended the same primary school. However, despite the fact that it felt weird for the interviewee when her childhood-friend-turned-junior addressed her with "surname + *san/senpai*", they had to act in accordance with club rules. Indeed, such rules were so important in her club that when new students joined the club each spring, the top theme during the welcome information sessions for new members was the importance of addressing seniors properly. Heavy sanctions were in place to deal with deviant cases. What was more instructive was that even when deviant behaviours were initiated by seniors and aimed only at particular juniors based on their private friendship, as what this interviewee did, sanctions were nonetheless applied collectively by other seniors in an attempt to correct the "wrong" behaviour and to maintain the appropriate *jouge kankei* social orders in the club.

In fact, exceptions like this, as based on individuals' private relationships, have not been tolerated elsewhere either. The degree to which ToA usage has been enforced in various school clubs has occasionally been so strict that it has even created "troubles" among siblings. On a separate occasion, in one of the focus

---

85 Interview conducted on 29.10.2015.

group discussions I conducted at the Tokyo Daiichi Orchestra in Spring 2016, a senior first grade flautist revealed that she had originally wanted to join Tokyo Daiichi's badminton club, as everyone in her family was an active player. After several trial sessions,[86] however, she had to give up the dream of playing badminton in her secondary school years. The main concern, as she mentioned, was that her elder sister was already in the same school's badminton club, hence if she were to join the badminton club, it would mean that her elder sister would become her *senpai* in the club. For her, the consequence of addressing her own sister with "last name + *senpai*", as well as the obligatory observance of rules and codes of conduct when interacting with club seniors (her sister included), were prospects that deeply annoyed her (*iyada*). This case, together with the aforementioned situation where the interviewee recounting her experience in the basketball club, further testifies the *institutional and impersonal nature of jouge kankei*: constitutive rules (such as ToA practices) are not to be violated, and routines render the behaviour of individuals who are implicated in *jouge kankei predictable*, hence stabilising the very institutional setup of the social facts of who is *senpai* and who is *kouhai*.

As regards micro-level discursive practices, the data presented in this chapter reveal that, ToA practices among actors in secondary school clubs in Japan defy the conclusions of most existing empirical studies on address terms and social relations. In the social organisation of school clubs in Japan, the hierarchical system of *jouge kankei* takes *precedence* over group solidarity, common interests, the closeness of age, and even kinship, all of which would, according to existing literature on Western languages and society, promote a transition between two interlocutors from V to (mutual) T at some point in time (refer to sub-section 4.1.1). In Japanese school club contexts, however, ToA practices are much less negotiable: a *kouhai* has to stick to prescribed ways of behaviour towards her/his *senpai* (and the latter must respect it, as various data in this chapter revealed), regardless of common club membership, how much common interest they share, and the nature of their prior relationship. This comparatively rigid discursive practice of ToA usage in school clubs corresponds to what has been claimed about the rigidity and endurance of *jouge kankei* in Japanese society in general: once a person recognises another as a *senpai*, this relationship continues (Nakane 1970).

---

86 In many junior high schools, new junior first graders are typically given two to three weeks' time to freely explore the range of extra-curricular club activities on offer. During this time, they could choose and attend trial sessions in as many clubs as they wish, before they finally make their choice (in writing) to join a certain club. Once this is done, however, members are generally expected to stay in the same club until graduation. Refer to chapter two.

4.5 Summary of chapter: ToA maintain, strengthen, and legitimise hierarchy

In this chapter, I have discussed the ways in which asymmetric power relations and hierarchy are constituted through ToA use by speakers occupying different social positions. I examined a prior study, Enyo (2013), which shares a similar theoretical vantage point with my research and is conducted in an extra-curricular club setting as well, albeit in a different stage of life: university. My findings revealed that ToA practices are far from similar between university club members and secondary school club members, even though a similar fabric of social world comprising *senpai*, *kouhai*, and those of equal rank exists. From the data obtained through various phases of my fieldwork sites, we clearly observe that titles (*senpai*, *buchou*) are much more commonly used by juniors to seniors in secondary school settings as compared to a university setting. Furthermore, there is little, if any, difference between ToA in on-stage and off-stage talk in secondary school club contexts: a pair of senior and junior club members always used the same ToA irrespective of social contexts. A full inquiry into the reasons for such differences between secondary school and university club members would be beyond the scope of this book. However, if ToA are part of the micro-level discursive strategies to constitute *jouge kankei*, it could be inferred that such institutional hierarchy resembles to a greater extent a "total institutional" nature in secondary school clubs as compared to in university clubs, since the range of social conventions in secondary school clubs (such as a person's status) exerts far more overwhelming constraints on an individual's interactional/discursive choice of ToA. Indeed, such conventions are so comprehensively enforced that *even siblings are affected*, if they are in the same club. As I mentioned in chapter two, one of the unique features of secondary school clubs is that this is the milieu where individuals in their crucial adolescent years come into contact with *jouge kankei* (hierarchy outside the family) on a large, collective scale, and learn the discursive practices that constitute it. In the process of learning how to use appropriate ToA in their social life of club activities, secondary school students in Japan also acquire "shared assumptions and cultural experiences" (Clyne et al. 2009: 25) of the right way to do and say things in clubs. To fully understand club members' knowledge of the world of seniors, juniors and people of equal ranks, as well as to grasp the dynamics of the discursive construction of hierarchy, our analysis also needs to include the very ideologies behind such language use and social behaviour, of which ToA are a part. In the next chapter, I extend the analysis to what I term the language-ideology-power nexus, in order to understand the "common-sense knowledge" instilled in club members when they are taught the club rules and appropriate behaviour. Such proper behaviour extends to a full range of micro-level linguistic discursive practices such as honorific word choices and different forms of talk. By examining them, I shed light on the ways in which they further support and strengthen *jouge kankei*. Extra-linguistic discursive practices, such as corresponding bodily movements and the use of signs, symbols, and objects, as well as the ways in which they complement linguistic discursive practices in constituting hierarchy, will be analysed in chapter six.

5 The linguistic constitution of *jouge kankei*: Ideology in micro-level discourse and epistemic orders

In chapter four, I discussed and showed how ToA index statuses and how ToA practices contribute to the co-construction of higher-lower relationships in secondary school clubs in Japan. This is, however, just one part of the whole set of micro-level discourses that together constitute the hierarchical order in daily interactional routines. In the present chapter, I show other aspects of micro-level language use and expected (linguistic) behaviours that also constitute such relationships. Prior to the discussion of empirical data, it would be instructive to address some theoretical concerns, which would also facilitate a better appreciation of the data that follow. We have witnessed in the two previous chapters that, upon joining an extracurricular club, new junior high first grade members adapt and conform to established conventions and norms in their discursive practices. How, then, do such norms/conventions and actual discursive practices relate to each other? Before I examine the bulk of micro-level discourses (in the form of naturally-occurring conversations) in this chapter, I first introduce a framework that links social structure (the hierarchical order of *jouge kankei*) to forms of micro-level discourse. In my analysis, I shall refer to this as the "*language-ideology-power nexus*" at work in discursive practices and in the constitution of social relations. Against this backdrop, this chapter proceeds as follows. I start by surveying some general notions of ideology and power (notably in and behind discourse), in order to lay the foundation on which to examine the ways in which ideology and power connect to language and how this nexus is manifested through discursive practices. In particular, I will illustrate that power here does not only limit itself to the "power semantic" of non-reciprocal formal and informal ToA usage between a junior and a senior, but also in the introduction and maintenance of an entire "discourse type" that is deemed acceptable and appropriate in *jouge kankei*. The constituent parts of such a discourse type, apart from appropriate ToA already presented in the previous chapter, are different aspects of honorific language, which are the foci of this chapter. I then present a concise overview of politeness theories, how honorifics have been brought together with certain notions of politeness, and why this could be problematic in analysing contextual data. Following the theoretical discussion on the language-ideology-power nexus as well as politeness and honorifics, I present data pertaining to two aspects of honorific language: (i) exalting words, and (ii) plain and *desu/masu* forms of talk. I then utilise discourse analysis to illustrate how the language-ideology-power nexus functions in the discursive practice of employing honorifics in linking conventions and norms to actual interactional behaviour, thereby bringing about and strengthening the social structure of *jouge kankei* and the institutionalised roles in it.

5.1 Ideology and language

What are ideologies and how are they manifested in society? One influential strand of scholarship originates from Karl Mannheim's (1991) work on ideology and utopia. As opposed to understandings of ideology from the Marxist tradition (refer to arguments further down the section) with emphasis on *the* dominant ideology, Mannheim stipulates that, in advanced societies, it is possible to have, and indeed there have been, different and competing ideological systems of thought (Ackroyd 2002; Mannheim 1991). In order that it be sustained, transmitted, or imposed by one group on another, an ideology has to correspond, at least partially, to what exists in society, and act as a framework which individuals rely on to orientate their actions and make sense of the social world. The survival of the ideology is dependent on people's not being conscious of its operations in their systems of thought, because once they do, the immediate reaction would be to "escape" from it (Ackroyd 2002). In other words, ideologies are often transmitted and acquired as part of legitimised common-sense knowledge about the world which people inhabit. Ideologies have the function of maintaining social order, for as long as they persist, they contribute to the stabilisation of social orders around particular sets of institutions and organisational principles (Ackroyd 2002). Looking at this, and in connection to what I have shown thus far, we can see that there is a certain type of ideology at work behind the discursive behaviours of secondary school club members. For instance, a certain ideology functioned when we witnessed the strict social orders brought about by the specific rules of address terms in the clubs, as well as the rationale given by teachers to substantiate such behavioural conventions (refer to the choir teacher's quote in chapter four). Seen in this light, ideologies can be considered sets of beliefs that affect our *Weltanschauung*, helping us make "common senses" of the social and political worlds which we inhabit (Freeden 2003: 2).

According to scholars of ideology, the making of such common sense in the form of a "complex of ideas" about the social world and the appropriate ways to comport in it, are instilled in the minds of individuals through both political and social semiotic processes (Blommaert 1999: 31). This highlights the place of language in the transmission of ideology. However, language does not only serve as a communication tool in the transmission of common-sense knowledge that is ideology. On a more significant level, language is also constitutive of the very social facts of which the common-sense knowledge seeks to make sense. The Marxist literature on ideology attests to the important function of language and power with regard to ideology:

> They [Marx and Engels] associated ideology and class, asserting that the ideas of the ruling class were the ruling ideas. Ideological illusions were an instrument in the hands of the rulers, through the state, and were employed to exercise control and domination; indeed, *to* "manufacture history" according to their interests. Moreover, the filtering of interests through a container – ideology – permitted them, and ideology itself, to be represented as if they were truth-claims that possessed universal, rational validity. That representation assisted the wielders of ideology in forging the myth of a unified political community, through illusory laws, cultural direction, and "verbal masquerading" – that is, *the power over language*. (Freeden 2003: 6, emphases added)

One may or may not fully agree with the scholarship from this tradition,[87] but what Marx and Engels posit is more than worth considering as it offers a useful vantage point from which to approach data analysis and social theorising in this book.[88] As we have already witnessed in chapters three and four, senior club members and teachers in charge have an interest in running the club and maintaining a peaceful social order where statuses and roles would be duly recognised, and this is facilitated with the aid of the codes of conduct (*shiori*) (which are themselves constituted by language in the form of texts), whose unknown, but presumably dated origins are portrayed as "history" to each new cohort. Their contents are not (supposed to be) questioned by the new members and they confer upon seniors the right to see to it that rules are followed and conventions upheld. For juniors, not following the properly set out conventions of *aisatsu*, for instance, would be considered as lacking common sense and failing to comport in a normal, acceptable way.

---

[87] The Marxist tradition and main proponents of critical discourse analysis (CDA) tend to view ideology in a negative light. While parts of my work borrow their insight on ideology, I do not view it with negative connotations insofar as this present research is concerned. I consider it from a more neutral perspective, as will be discussed in section 5.2.

[88] A significant potential in social theorising lies in what I call the "varieties of hierarchy": for instance, the meanings and manifestations of the "ruling class", (re)production of power, unique features of *jouge kankei* hierarchy, and so on. More on future research orientations in this direction is presented in the final chapter.

5.1.1 Forming the language-ideology-power nexus in discourse: Power, power semantic, power in and behind discourse

In the beginning of this chapter, I mentioned that a new framework of language-ideology-power nexus would be useful in the analysis of the discursive constitution of hierarchy. In section 5.1, we have seen the form of existence of ideology (as knowledge and ideas about the world), its functions (to guide actions and stabilise social orders), as well as its relations to language (language not just transmits ideology, but also makes up the very social facts of which ideology helps individuals make sense). In this sub-section, I introduce the notion of power and connect it to language and ideology to form a cohesive analytical framework. In the process, I survey and adapt existing relevant social research on power, as well as the discourse analytic approach to language, ideology, and power. My aim in this sub-section is to show how this new framework could be usefully applied to the analysis of micro-level discourses (various aspects of honorifics in interactions) in the constitution of *jouge kankei*.

My discussion here on power will touch on relevant literature to show how theories and concepts of power developed in a variety of disciplinary perspectives have been transplanted to the study on language, discourse, and society. That discussions and theorising of power (and hierarchy in organisations) have a rich and varied tradition across diverse fields of inquiry (notably in management and organisation studies as well as in psychology) is not surprising. This is because, power is often considered as one of the bases of society (Roberts 2003), representing a "basic force in social relationships" (Keltner, Gruenfeld and Anderson 2003: 265; Magee and Galinsky 2008), and an "inescapable feature of human social life and structure" (Turner 2005: 1). With regard to what could help us in our understanding of the discursive constitution of *jouge kankei* (and the workings of the language-ideology-power nexus in this framework), I limit my discussions to power in interpersonal relationships. In this light, the following theorists and concepts are worth mentioning.

In his discussion on the meaning of having power over other people or in social institutions, Searle (2010) remarked:

> [T]he core notion of power concerning the power of some people over others. . .is that it involves the ability of an agent of power to get subjects to do what the agent wants them to do whether the subjects want to do so or not. (Searle 2010: 146–147)

In this succinct discussion, Searle (2010) summarises the meaning and manifestation of power as the ability to influence others' behaviour and desire. But how does the agent get the subjects to do something? Several strands of thought and dimensions of power have been developed on the basis of this question. One such relevant idea is what Lukes (2004) labels as the latent dimension of power. According to this perspective, an agent of power gets subjects of power to do what the agent wants them to do by making them perceive only certain interests/ actions (which serve the interests of the agent) as available courses of action. Lukes (2004) terms this the *latent* dimension of power, because it is difficult for people who are influenced by this latent dimension of power (that is, subjects of power) to discover or identify its existence. Based on the same basic principle of power as discussed above, and focussing on the nature of power that emerges from interpersonal relationships, Turner (2005) proposes a framework through which to examine the nature of power through people, highlighting the fact that the use of force does not necessarily have to be present, as Figure 5.1 illustrates:

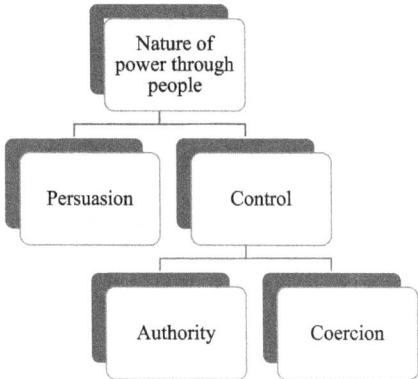

Figure 5.1: Framework to understand the nature of power through people. Adapted from Turner (2005: 7).

Under this framework, the ability to affect people by getting them to perform at one's will can be divided into persuasion and control. Persuasion refers to the "capacity to persuade people that some decision, judgement, action is correct, right, valid" (Turner 2005: 7). On the other hand, control refers to the "capacity to get people to do what one wants when they are not persuaded of or are uninterested in the validity in the desired act" (Turner 2005: 7). The capacity to control can be further sub-divided into authority and coercion, whereby authority refers to wielding the right to control by defining in-group norms and codes of conduct, and coercion refers to the exercise of control against the will of others (Turner 2005: 7). In the context of this book, such a framework is more empirically applicable and it facilitates the connection of our discussions on the nature and concept of power to the topic at hand: the workings of the language-ideology-power nexus in the discursive constitution of hierarchy.

For instance, in chapter four, I presented and examined the ways in which people use the "power over language" to forge a unified and tightly knit social structure with harmonious status orders, as well as to legitimise the social order of *jouge kankei* in the process of transmitting it to new generations of individuals in secondary school student clubs. The case in point was the "power semantic" of the ToA vocabulary (Brown and Gilman 1960), manifested by the non-reciprocal ToA usage between a senior and a junior in secondary school clubs in Japan, a usage that simultaneously indexes the interlocutors' relative social statuses and their interpersonal relationships. For the most part, this is achieved through a combination of persuasion and control (authority): teachers and seniors employ meta narratives during guidance sessions (Discourse, see chapter three) to "persuade" each cohort of new junior members that certain discursive practices of addressing seniors (discourse) are the correct ways. At the same time, they also exercise their power through authority; defining the very discursive norms in the first place. Furthermore, my data have shown who has the right and power to uphold established discursive conventions (coercion): older seniors could reproach younger seniors with respect to the latter's "improper" behaviour with new junior members, hence control as exercised through authority and coercion. Such capacities to influence others and the power relations between agents and subjects of power need to be sustained, and this brings us closer to the language-ideology-power nexus, because discourse scholars have posited that ideological assumptions, taken as common-sense knowledge, is what sustains the power relations among human agents (Fairclough 1989).

Discourse scholars, especially those using the critical discourse analysis (CDA) approach, often approach the decoding of texts and language structures by putting particular emphases on "common-sense assumptions which are implicit in the conventions according to which people interact linguistically, and of which people are generally not consciously aware" (Fairclough 1989: 2). In elaborating the relationship between language (discourse), ideology, and power, Fairclough (1989) posits that "conventions routinely drawn upon in discourse embody ideological assumptions which come to be taken as mere 'common sense', and which contribute to sustaining existing power relations"[89] (Fairclough 1989: 77).

---

[89] Refer to chapter three to see an illustration of how the macro-level Discourse in club guidance sessions for new members impart ideological assumptions to new junior members and how they are expected to take these as common-sense knowledge to navigate themselves through the club hierarchical order (their social world).

In keeping with these considerations, I introduce the "power" element in the equation and complete the analytical framework of language-ideology-power nexus. To achieve this, I examine the relevant common-sense assumptions underlying the conventions of discourse and language use in Japanese school clubs. Such an analysis can show that ideologically charged discourses (where the ideology is almost always hidden) could be power-laden in two ways:
- Power *in* discourse: powerful participants control and constrain the less powerful participants' contribution in terms of contents, relations, and subjects (Fairclough 1989: 46–47)
- Power *behind* discourse: a particular discourse type (with its properties) is "imposed" on all those who are implicated in a social institution concerned. In addition, power holders in the institutional setup or organisation retain the right to uphold the conventions (Fairclough 1989: 61)

This is where ideology and power meet language and the language-ideology-power nexus takes shape, for discursive approaches contribute to the analysis of ideologies and power in language. In fact, we have already had a first glimpse of the power behind discourse at work in chapter three, where properties of one discourse type, together with its ideological common-sense assumptions, were taught to new members. The data presented in chapter four and those to be presented in this chapter deal primarily with the actual manifestations of power in and behind discourse in club members' behaviour and interactions in daily club life. In this chapter in particular, I extend the analysis to two linguistic aspects (within Japanese honorifics) in the discursive constitution of *jouge kankei*: exalting words and plain/"polite" forms of talk. In my analysis, I show how these discursive practices are backed by ideologies ("common-sense knowledge") and the power relations that come with them, as well as the various capacities exercised by holders of power (club seniors) to subjects of power (juniors) in social interactions, hence the existence of a language-ideology-power nexus in the discursive constitution of *jouge kankei*.

5.2 Politeness, honorifics, and ideology: Theories and conceptual links

One type of data gathered for this study was recordings of conversations among club members during their normal practice sessions. In the participants' interactions among themselves, a variety of linguistically indexed hierarchical relationships became apparent. To identify and analyse them, I clarify concepts of politeness, honorifics, the (misrepresented) link between them, and connections to ideology and power. In this vein, the data pertaining to politeness in this chapter represent a case in point in linguistic and social interactions that work in accordance with common-sense assumptions. Such assumptions consider the hierarchy of roles and statuses, and the accompanying authority or duties (in the institution of *jouge kankei*), as legitimate and the "normal" order of things (Fairclough 1989: 2) in the social world of school clubs. They also show the ways in which contents and interpersonal relations (and multiple identities) are constrained.

Contrary to conventional CDA approaches, I avoid making normative implications and judgement on ideologies behind language. In the light of what has been said about the pervasive nature of ideologies (and also power) in language and discourse, I seek to adopt as normatively disinterested a point of view as possible. In this light, the common-sense assumptions constituting ideologies are but bases of social representations shared by members of a particular group, guiding them in making sense of their social and political worlds (Van Dijk 1998: 8; Harris 1970; Woolard 1992). For the purpose of operationalisation and data analysis in this chapter, one can adopt a loose working definition of "politeness". For example, politeness as "routines and strategies which are used to enhance cooperative interaction" (Kienpointer 1999: 2) by "establishing and/or maintaining in a state of equilibrium the personal relationships between the individuals of a social group . . . during the ongoing process of interaction" (Watts 2005: 50). Hence, it can be said that politeness is intricately linked to ideology and power, because it is the underlying common-sense assumptions that inform and shape strategies of interaction in specific contexts (such as, but not limited to, senior-junior interactions), so that interactional orders conform to conventions,[90] and with this, the establishment and/or the maintenance of social relationships of power. Indeed, it is even suggested that not only do politeness formulae stabilise and regulate hierarchical structures, but speakers also use them to express submission, hence reflecting power differentials in social relationships (Held 1999).

As regards approaching politeness in empirical social research, Holtgraves (2001) suggested three different views on politeness:

i. Social normative: to be polite means to behave according to a specific set of rules deemed appropriate to the particular context at hand.
ii. Pragmatic: Politeness is an element constituting pragmatic competence – speakers' ability to use language effectively in a given context.

---

90 Throughout my fieldwork, there were instances when social actors did not interact in a way that conformed to established conventions. Hence, deviations could and in fact did occur. But such "impolite behaviour and utterance", as they are often considered, attest precisely to a certain assumption of how social interactions under a particular circumstance ought to be carried out, therefore an underlying ideology at work.

iii. Face management: "face" is an important underlying principle governing polite behaviour in interactions (see discussion below).

Insofar as the study on language and society in Japan is concerned, there has been an established, though increasingly controversial tradition in the literature to link politeness to honorifics. In Japanese, honorifics can be broadly understood as morphemes that are "affixed to verbs, nouns, adjectives and adverbs. The most extensive markings are found on verbs, which are divided into two categories: the referent honorifics (respect and humble forms) and the addressee honorific *masu* form" (Cook 2011: 3656). The Table 5.1 below illustrates a general classification of honorifics in Japanese, which also corresponds to the various types of honorifics used by club members in my data:

Table 5.1: General classification of Japanese honorifics. Adapted from Cook 2011 and Hudson 2011.

Honorifics		Structure	Examples
Referent honorifics	Respect/exalting form (*sonkeigo*)	*o*-VERB *ni naru*/ Verb-*(r)areru*;	*o-yomi ni naru* (to read)
		Suppletive form	*ossharu* (to say)
	Humble form (*kenjougo*)	*o*-VERB *suru/itasu*	*o-machi suru/itasu* (to wait)
		Suppletive form	*moushi ageru* (to say)
Addressee honorifics	"Polite" form (*teineigo*)	NOUN/ADJECTIVE-*desu*	*gakki desu* (musical instrument)
		VERB-*masu*	*tabemasu* (to eat)

As Table 5.1 above shows, referent honorifics in Japanese could be further subdivided into respect form and humble form. Usage of the former implies the speaker's deference to the addressees and their group by elevating their position (hence also known as exalting forms). Usage of the latter, humble form, on the other hand, shows deference by lowering the speaker's own actions (Cook 2011). In addressee honorifics, it has been analysed that the *desu/masu* endings following nouns, adjectives, and verbs are employed to show politeness to the addressees (Comrie 1976; Martin 1964), and the name of this addressee honorifics in Japanese, *teineigo*, has been correspondingly translated as "polite" form. However, it would be too sweeping to assume the natural equation of addressee honorifics to politeness. A survey on the three broad theoretical standpoints on Japanese honorifics and how it relates (or not) to politeness reveals that recent literature has become increasingly sceptical of this assumed link.

An early theoretical perspective based on politeness research stipulates that honorifics are part of negative politeness strategies, that is, part of the "face management" view of politeness as mentioned above. This is based on Brown and Levinson's (1987) politeness theory that regards politeness as "an outcome of mitigation of a face-threatening act (FTA)" (Cook 2011: 3657). Centred on the concept of "face", Brown and Levinson (1987) posit that face as one's public self-image is common to every member of a given society, and a politeness strategy is used when a speaker decides to commit an act which would cause the hearer (or the speaker) to lose face (Brown and Levinson 1987: 59–60). The concept of face is further classified into two categories: (i) positive face which is "the positive consistent self-image or 'personality' (crucially including the desire that this self-image be appreciated and approved of) claimed by interactants", and (ii) negative face which is "the basic claim to territories, personal preserves, rights to non-destruction – i.e. to freedom of action and freedom from imposition" (Brown and Levinson 1987: 61). Corresponding to positive and negative face, there exist positive and negative politeness strategies: positive politeness strategies are friendly acts that can include noticing the addressee's needs and identifying common grounds, whereas negative politeness strategies represent deferent acts that could include indirect expressions and hedges (Cook 2011). According to this line of thought, the decisive elements to consider, before performing a FTA, would be the social distance and relative power between the interlocutors, as well as the scale of imposition of such an act (Brown and Levinson 1987).

Following this theoretical standpoint, there have been studies that classify Japanese honorifics as negative politeness strategy. For instance, Fukada and Asato (2004) affirmed that the addressee honorific of *masu* form talk was one such instance of performing a face-threatening act. They justified their argument by claiming that, while it was common practice for teachers to use plain forms when talking to their students, they would switch to the addressee honorific *masu* form when they had favours to ask from their students, and such a practice was interpreted as a face-saving act on the part of teachers (Fukada and Asato 2004: 1998). Recent literature has pointed out the problematic nature of this viewpoint. This is because, if the point of departure is the assumption that honorifics equal to politeness strategies, it would then also imply that honorifics are directly connected to social status. However, this perception would not allow researchers to promptly recognise the fluidity of the statuses of the interlocutors and the ways in which they could emerge in interactions (Cook 2011). Furthermore, social meanings of honorifics do not remain fixed in most social contexts (Agha 2007; Cook 2008), hence it would not always be possible to predict if and how a speaker of lower status uses honorifics to an addressee of higher status.

In addition, both notions of face and one's social interaction oriented to them are, according to this theoretical standpoint, universal (Brown and Levinson 1987: 61; Fukada and Asato 2004: 1992). Such a universalistic approach that only considers differences in degree rather than nature has also invited criticism. This is due to the existence of socio-culturally specific ideologies of politeness (and what constitutes "politeness" to begin with) influencing social interactions. With regard to what concerns my research the most, we could also question the extent to which this framework is suitable for Japan. For instance, the use of honorifics (*keigo*) is more about being sensitive to social contexts and acting as a "relation-acknowledging device" to indicate the interlocutors' status differences (Fukada and Asato 2004: 1993; Matsumoto 1988). Therefore, the direct "mapping" of Japanese honorifics to politeness should be questioned, since utilisation of honorifics does not necessarily equate to a solution to a face threatening act. As a matter of fact, face threatening acts do not have to be present for the employment of honorifics in Japanese, for honorifics is about placing emphasis on showing human relationships, and not minimising imposition due to face threatening acts (Matsumoto 1988).

The second theoretical standpoint concerning honorifics and politeness argues that, instead of a politeness strategy as part of face management, honorifics is a manifestation of discernment (Cook 2011). This viewpoint is brought forward in Japanese honorific studies by Sachiko Ide (1982) and her proposal of the "*wakimae*" (roughly translated to discernment) concept. As a culmination of a wave of post-war Japanese honorifics research, Ide (1982) concluded that there were three basic rules that determined honorific usage (which manifests *wakimae*) in Japanese speech: (1) be polite to people of higher social status, (2) be polite to people of power, and (3) be polite to elderly people. However, she also noted that these three rules succumb to the imperative that one should always be polite in formal situations, implying that, for instance, a more powerful and older superior should in effect be polite to his younger inferior at the latter's wedding ceremony. Accordingly, honorifics are seen as "linguistic forms to index the speaker's acknowledgment of this sense of place toward the addressee/referent" (Ide and Yoshida 1999: 448). This linkage of honorifics to discernment partly originates from the assumption that honorifics directly index politeness, which is in turn fixated to the social statuses of the interlocutors (Cook 2011). In this sense, this second viewpoint also presupposes given social rules and a rather static hearer-speaker relationship, as well as the absence of agency on the part of the interlocutors. Furthermore, this perspective cannot account for deviations from prescribed, normative usage of honorifics in actual interactions, hence providing limited explanatory capability as regards honorifics in Japanese (Cook 2011).

The third major theoretical perspective that has been emerging in recent literature is one that espouses an element of social constructionism: that honorifics are linguistic tools for the construction of social facts. This is in line with linguistic anthropological perspectives as put forward by Duranti (1992):

> If we conceive of words not only as labels for already existing reality but also as *ideologically loaded tools* for defining the situations in which speakers qua social actors co-construct their context, we can better appreciate the social (hence pragmatic) function of linguistic subsystems such as the Samoan RW's [Respect Words]
> (Duranti 1992: 89, emphasis added)

According to this perspective, individual speakers are active agents who choose to use (or not to use) honorifics to achieve their interactional goals. In other words, honorifics go beyond politeness or discernment, because they not only reflect existing social facts, but also create them. In addition, such a social constructionist take on honorifics also allows for the analysis of ideological elements in and behind honorifics. Because honorifics like exalting and humbling forms construct hierarchical lines of authority (McVeigh 2002), student club members do not only learn to use honorifics and recognise various social statuses and ranks in clubs, but are also primed to be ideologically receptive to such social facts in the socialisation process. This is furthermore in line with findings of recent studies that, for instance, the addressee honorific of *masu* form of talk has multiple functions and serves as a linguistic resource for the construction of interlocutors' identities, on-stage personae, and so on (Cook 1996; 1998; Enyo 2013; Geyer 2008). I adopt, in principle, this third theoretical viewpoint in analysing my data. Evidently, this relates to what I hypothesised in chapter one about the discursive constitution of *jouge kankei*, as well as the ideology and power asymmetries at play in determining discursive choices on the part of speakers. In the following sections, I present and analyse two aspects of Japanese honorifics observed and gathered under circumstances of actual interactions in the three student clubs in Tokyo: referent honorifics (in the form of respect/exalting words) and addressee honorifics (in the *masu* form of talk). I show the contexts and ways in which they are used, as well as the interlocutors involved. My goal is to show the ways in which the language-ideology-power nexus works in the form of honorifics, and how this in turn contributes to the construction of hierarchy in secondary school clubs. At the very end of my analysis, I reveal the peculiarities of junior and senior high school club activities as regards the discursive constitution of *jouge kankei*: how they defy current scholarship and how we might go about explaining and understanding them.

5.3 Ideology and honorifics: The cases of exalting words and "polite" forms of talk

This section marks the beginning of my data presentation and analysis. I focus my attention on the following two groups of honorifics: (i) exalting words, and (ii) "polite" *masu* forms, known as *teineigo* in Japanese (literally means polite, courteous, respectful language).

5.3.1 Exalting words

Throughout anthropological studies (which includes linguistic anthropology), it is well-established that vocabulary choices other than pronouns and simple ToA titles indicate social statuses in an elaborate manner (Duranti 1992; Geertz 1973). As the data in this volume thus far have shown, the Japanese language is no exception. Such discursive strategies of constructing identities and relationships in Japanese include the use of referent honorifics, in particular, the respect form, in order to exalt and elevate the actions of addressees and referents. In the context of *jouge kankei* in secondary school *bukatsudou*, such forms are used by juniors to seniors. As I observed during my fieldwork, the usage of respect forms was present in club members' daily discursive practices and it included commonplace verbs of action and motion, the two most commonly used of which are listed below:
- The motion verb "to come":
  - "Normal" form: *kuru*
  - Respect form: *irassharu*
- The action verb "to say":
  - "Normal" form: *iu*
  - Respect form: *ossharu*

Though expressing the same motion or action, the different forms in each category carry different social meanings as they index the respective statuses between interlocutors or between speakers and referents. Therefore, the respect forms of *irassharu* or *ossharu*, when used, express the acts of coming or saying for a higher status person (vis-à-vis the speaker) and simultaneously construct the asymmetrical relationship between interlocutors or speakers and referents.

The fact that this discursive practice belongs to part of the expected code of conduct from juniors to seniors is manifested in the club rule books' specifying the obligatory use of honorifics (to which respect forms belong) to those of higher status (refer to chapter four). On this topic, the acting president of the Tokyo Daiichi Choir further revealed:

> **ZW**: So I see that you have strict rules regarding the way of speaking [*kotobazukai*] in the choir?
>
> **Choir president**: That's right, and this is clearly stated in our rule book.
>
> **ZW**: Would you share with me what is stated in there with regard to language use?
>
> **Choir president**: Sure. So it specifies when, where, and how juniors must greet seniors, what kind of language they should use when they talk and write to us, how they should respond to us when addressed.
>
> **ZW**: Alright, that's a lot. Can you give me some examples?
>
> **Choir president**: They basically must use honorifics [*keigo*] whenever they talk to us or about us.
>
> **ZW**: Do juniors, especially new members, know *keigo*?
>
> **Choir president**: Not really, so we teach them. For example, it is stated that they must use *desu/masu*, they must not use *gomennasai* when they excuse themselves, and what we call *sonkeigo* (respect form).
>
> **ZW**: It seems a lot for them to learn.
>
> **Choir president**: True, but we all did it. And I try to show them by example. For instance, when I brief the entire choir everyday before and after practice, and when I talk about our instructor or OGs ["old girls", meaning alumni], like, when I tell them that some *senpai* OGs will come tomorrow, I don't use "*kuru*", but "*irassharu*", or if I ask the choir if they remember what our seniors said to us during practice, I don't use "*iu*", but "*ossharu*". They will get used to it.[91]

As the interview extract above once again affirms, new club members in junior high school first come into contact with extra-curricular club life with the discursive practices of honorific usage, before properly learning honorifics in classrooms. Club seniors are conscious of this, but the constitutive nature of such language use in the club *jouge kankei* implies that clubs in junior high schools assume the primary responsibility of teaching students *kotobazukai* during their formative years. Contrary to classroom teaching, club members directly sense the need and the ways in which to apply these *keigo* learned: that is, to anyone who is more senior, regardless of context and location (in or out of school). As we have seen, such respect forms of referent honorifics form but a part of the "appropriate" behaviour, because they are most often used in

---

91 Interview conducted on 25.11.2015.

conjunction with the addressee honorifics of the *masu*, or "polite" form of talk (Cook 2011). This will be explained and examined in the following sub-sections.

5.3.2 "Polite" forms of talk

As I have illustrated in Table 5.1 in section 5.2., the second analytical perspective I consider in this empirical chapter is the *teineigo*, manifested in the *desu/masu* forms. The different forms here refer to "morphological markings on nouns, adjectives, and verb stems appearing in the clause-final position" (Geyer 2008: 39). As the Table 5.1 shows, the *masu* form follows verbs and makes the ending longer than would be in the plain form. The *desu* form follows adjectives and nouns. In this work, the *desu/masu* forms are both referred to as "polite" form[92] when I cite informants' explanations, as this was the term that was commonly used by them during my fieldwork. However, when I discuss literature, I adopt, just like in most sociolinguistic literature, the terms of addressee honorifics, i.e., a speech style that carries a different *social* meaning and highlights the speaker's relative status towards and identity vis-à-vis the addressee (who can be of a different social status[93]) (Cook 2011; Enyo 2015; Geyer 2008; Niyekawa 1991).

In order that we make better sense out of the data, consider first the following two simple examples:

1. *Senpai ga honru o fuki masu*
   Senior SBJ French OBJ blow MASU
         horn   FORM
   'The senior plays a French horn.'

2. *Senpai ga honru o fuku*
   Senior SBJ French o blow-PLAIN
         horn
   'The senior plays a French horn.'

---

[92] In most literature, *teineigo* is commonly translated as polite forms of talk. In this book, however, I write it as "polite" form because a straightforward literal translation would be misleading. As data here and my arguments throughout the book will show, such forms of talk are more about formality of context and, in the case of secondary school club activities, the bringing into existence of diverse social identities and statuses.

[93] We should, however, be careful not to link honorifics to relative social status all the time. As my empirical data will show, without sufficient contextual knowledge, we cannot always easily predict the form used based on status alone.

The above examples express the same content, but in (1), the "polite" form ending *masu* is used, whereas in (2) the plain form of the verb is used. Plain and "polite" forms do not alter the referential meaning, but the *social* meaning (Cook 2011). The mechanisms by which this works will be explored in section 5.4.

How do these forms manifest themselves in practice? As I have discussed in section 5.2, using the "polite" form of *desu/masu* does not necessarily imply politeness or face-threatening acts. The ability of a speaker to employ plain forms of talk and addressee honorifics would instead imply her/his having a sound knowledge of social etiquette on the part of the speaker and the ability to recognise social relations and contexts (Ide 1982; Ide and Yoshida 1999; Miwa 2000). In addition, honorifics serve as linguistic resources for the social construction of speaker identities: that speakers are also active agents who, in strategic ways, use honorifics to achieve certain interactional goals (Cook 2011). This point is particularly relevant as it brings us closer to the empirical data below, as well as the broader theoretical framework on the discursive construction of *jouge kankei*. If honorifics are used in a fluid way and their usage depends on interactional goals and contexts, then their usage, and in general, language use, do not simply reflect existing social reality, but also construct it (Duranti 1992). While I embrace this as a point of departure, I also emphasise in my analysis that honorifics, as part of the discursive practices, construct the institutional orders of *jouge kankei*, but at the same time these hierarchical orders also exert influence on the very discursive practices. Consider the following extract of a focus group interview on the topic of polite language use with the same group of new senior members in Tokyo Daiichi Girls' Orchestra at the beginning of the school year of 2016:

> **ZW**: Now I would like to go back to your junior high school days, in particular, your first year. Did you feel that you had to mind your language when you talked to seniors?
>
> **New senior 2**: I thought we had to use honorifics.
>
> **ZW**: But was that part of the rules?
>
> **New senior 3**: It was alright if we did not use perfect honorifics, so long as we tried as much as possible . . .
>
> **New senior 2**: I thought it would be good to add "*desu*" to sentence endings.
>
> **ZW**: Was that your own feeling? Or did someone teach or tell you so?
>
> **New senior 4**: Everyone did it . . .
>
> **New senior 2**: Um, somehow everyone thought like, "should add it [the *desu/masu* ending]".
>
> **New senior 3**: It was the same in every club.

New senior 2: Um, in Japan.

All: That's right, that's Japan.

New senior 2: [There is] this *jouge kankei*.

New senior 3: It's also like this in companies.[94]

From the extract above, we can tell that in Tokyo Daiichi Girls' Orchestra, specific ways of language use (*desu/masu* forms) are seen as *the* common-sense way of communicating with seniors. In other words, the seniority of a senior and the asymmetrical interpersonal relationship go together with the stipulated discursive practice, which is seen as the "normal" practice. Furthermore, what is equally revealing are the interviewees' interpretations for this kind of social behaviour: that it is normal in all clubs and across Japan. They justify the practice by arguing that there exists a similar hierarchy and it is present in the Japanese corporate culture too. From this, we could tease out the ideology at work: generations of club members are inculcated with common-sense beliefs about particular discursive practices (in this case addressee honorifics), and that such practices link to social reality (as regards status and ranks in clubs).

5.4 Plain and *desu/masu* forms of talk and their constitution of *senpai* and *kouhai* identities and interpersonal relations

In the previous three sections, I discussed theoretical concepts as well as operational notions of ideology, power, and discourse (focussing on politeness and honorifics as part of discursive practices). I have also shown the ways in which observed usage of referent honorifics, in the form of exalting words, index social roles. In addition, I illustrated the ideology behind the "polite" form of speech and how members justified their usage of this form. In the following two sub-sections, I present two data sets consisting of recorded conversations among club members in Tokyo Daiichi Girls' Orchestra and Tokyo Daini Boys' Orchestra. This will be followed by a discourse analysis of such interactions. Just like in the process of understanding ToA usage, a central question to bear in mind in my analyses of such micro-level discourse will be: who is using which form to whom, when, how, and why.

---

94 Interview conducted on 20.05.2016.

5.4.1 Active identity construction with the addressee honorific *desu/masu* form

The following excerpts were taken from recordings of practice sessions in Tokyo Daiichi Girls' Orchestra on a Sunday morning in January 2016. I made the recordings with members of the orchestra's saxophone section, one of the larger groups with members from diverse grades and covering different roles in the orchestra. On the day of the recording, six members showed up for practice. These included two senior second year members (Leader and Tenor H2 respectively), a junior third year tenor player (tenor J3), two junior second year members, and one junior first year player (all grades at the time of recording). The participant identifiers were made for easy referencing in the transcript, and they include information about a member's age/grade group and instrument type. For instance, 'H2 AS' represents a member from high school (H) second grade (the number "2") who plays the alto saxophone (AS). For an overview of the participants, see Table 5.2 below:

Table 5.2: Members of Tokyo Daiichi Orchestra's Saxophone Section present on the day of recording.

Grade	Instrument	Other Administrative Roles in Club	Participant Identifier in Transcript
High School 2	Alto Saxophone	Saxophone Leader	H2 AS
High School 2	Tenor Saxophone	Club Vice President	H2 TS
Junior High 3	Tenor Saxophone	NA	J3 TS
Junior High 2	Alto Saxophone	NA	J2 AS 1
Junior High 2	Alto Saxophone	NA	J2 AS 2
Junior High 1	Tenor Saxophone	NA	J1 TS

Their annual concert was about two months away and by the time of the recording they had started to practice only concert pieces. After around 40 minutes of individual warm up exercises, the members started to gather around and prepare for the ensuing group practice. They sat in a circle so that they could see each other. In the centre, there were several tables arranged together so that additional scores and metronomes could be placed. Throughout the entire recording session, the two digital audio recording devices were put on the tables in the centre. The exact seating arrangement, which was typical and did not change throughout my stay with this group at the Tokyo Daiichi Orchestra, is illustrated in Figure 5.2 below:

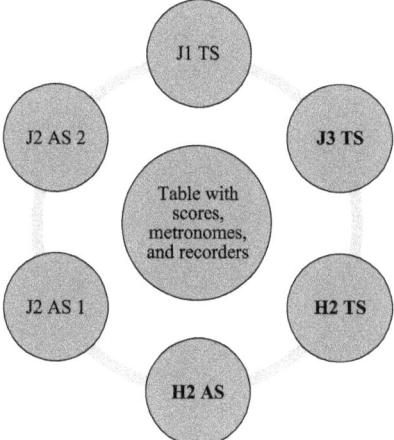

Figure 5.2: Seating arrangement of Tokyo Daiichi Orchestra's saxophone section for part I.

The recording was done in two parts. Part I consists of a full group practice, whereas Part II consists of only junior members' practice led by J3 TS (during this time the two seniors were doing individual practices in the far corner and were thus uninvolved in the junior practice session). The emphasis is on the interactions among H2 AS (who led the session in Part I as group leader), H2 TS (also present in Part I) and J3 TS (whose roles changed after the transition from Part I to Part II), showing how participants could be active agents in creating various identities by employing (or not) the addressee honorific of *desu/masu* form.

Part I (Tenor J3 as junior)

1. H2 AS: *Ja,　　E　no　　nishou-　kara. Sono　mae　　aru?*
   　　　　　　　　　　　　　　setsume
   　　　　Then,　E　POSS　second　from.　That　before　have-
   　　　　　　　　　　　　　　bar　　　　　　　　　　　　　PLAIN?
   'Well, let's start from the second bar in E. Do you have anything before that?'

2. J2 TS: *Nai desu.*
　　　　No　MASU FORM
　　'No.' [falling volume]

3. H2 AS: *C, no,　E no　nishou-　kara yatte kudasai.*
　　　　　　　　　　　　setsume
　　　　　C, POSS E POSS second　from do　please
　　　　　　　　　　　　bar
　　'Please play from second bar in C [error], E.'

4. All: *Hai.*
　　'Yes.'

5. H2 AS: *Iki ma::su. Ichi, ni, san.*
　　　　Go MASU　One, two, three.
　　　　　FORM
　　'Let's play. One, two, three.'

[The section plays, omitted]

6. H2 AS: *Muzu- sou kashi*
　　　　Diffi-　seems
　　　　cult
　　'It seems difficult.'

7. H2 TS: *Muzu- sou kashi*
　　　　Diffi-　seems
　　　　cult
　　'It seems difficult.'

8. H2 TS: *Nan　no　oto　nano?*
　　　　What POSS tune Q-
　　　　　　　　　　　PLAIN
　　'What tune is that?'

9. J3 TS: *Re, re desu*
         Re, re MASU-FORM
    're, it's re.' [falling volume]

10. H2 AS: *De,   Suraa   tsuiteru?   Ah, Tenaa ni tsuiteru?   tsuitenai?*
           And,   slur   attached-   Ah, tenor to attached-   not attached-
                            PLAIN   PLAIN   PLAIN FORM
                            FORM   FORM
    'And is a slur attached? Ah, is a slur attached to the tenor part? No?'

11. J3 TS: *Tsuite   masen*
           Attached   Not-MASE FORM
    'No, not attached'

The above portrays an interaction among three members: H2 AS, H2 TS, and J3 TS, with the exception in line 4 where everyone present uttered in unison as a response to their leader, H2 AS' request. The first observation that could be made is that, whenever there is a question-answer sequence between one of the two senior second graders (H2 AS or H2 TS) and the junior third year tenor player (J3 TS), the two seniors always used the plain form (lines 1, 8, and 10) while the junior always utilised the addressee honorific *desu/masu* form in her response (lines 2, 9, and 11). This corresponds to one of the functions of the *desu/masu* form, that is, the construction of social identities and statuses. In this case, the H2 AS and H2 TS' usage of plain forms indexed their identity as seniors in the club *jouge kankei*, whereas J3 TS' use of the addressee honorifics not only symbolised her recognition of the asymmetrical relationship between her and her seniors, but also her mastery of basic social etiquette and codes of conduct required to be a competent actor along club hierarchical lines.

In addition to the binary opposition of plain and "polite" *desu/masu* forms of talk, there was also a third style "in between". This style was formed by combining the plain form ending of verbs, adjectives, or copulas with the "polite" morpheme of *desu* (*masu* here is not an option). For instance, we could notice that in Line 2, J3 TS answered her senior's question with the utterance of *naidesu*, which is the combination of the plain form *nai* (instead of *arimasen* in the *desu/masu* form) and the morpheme of *desu*. This usage has frequently been termed as a "semi polite form"[95] (Hudson 2008), and scholars have observed the pervasiveness of this usage from as early as the 1990s, especially among young speakers. This form allegedly emerged as a consequence of a long and gradual process of the simplification of honorifics that corresponded to simultaneous social change in the Japanese society since the mid-nineteenth century (Hudson 2008). With the advent of democratic ideas in Japan, the honorific language gradually changed from a "class-based" to a "social-based" language, and with this, an increasing emphasis on addressee honorification and "polite language" (*teineigo*) (Hudson 2008; Inoue 1998), from where this "semi polite form" developed by adding the "polite" *desu* morpheme to plain forms (Hudson 2008). Even though it is not clearly classified in the addressee honorifics category of *keigo*, it is recognised that this form of talk produces "psychological distance" on the part of the speaker, which is understood as "the speaker's assessment that the hearer is not a member of his/her in-group at the time of the utterance and so sounding familiar would be inappropriate. In other words, the major effect of adding *desu* is to avoid being too familiar or rude" (Hudson 2008: 151). Hence, although it is less "sophisticated" or elegant as compared to the addressee honorific *desu/masu* form, its usage by juniors in their interactions with seniors is largely accepted by the latter, since the socially obligatory use of the added *desu* morpheme, as well as seniors' non-reciprocal use of the plain form, constitute discursive practices that bring about and reinforce various unequal statuses and hierarchical relations.

In all instances in the above excerpt, the junior speaker, J3 TS, used either the addressee honorific *desu/masu* form or the "semi polite form" effortlessly, since she has been in the club for about three years and had gotten used to the various forms of talk.[96] This stands in stark contrast to the ways in which new members who just joined the club behaved. Moreover, this instance once again illustrates the crucial role of a secondary school club in Japan: to socialise young adults into the social order of *jouge kankei* in and through language, so that they become competent actors in a variety of social situations both in school clubs and, it is hoped, adult society.

From the above, we notice that the non-reciprocal use of the plain and addressee honorific *desu/masu* styles of speech between the senior second graders

---

95 In this case, it is also important to bear in mind that "politeness" is not necessarily expressed automatically with the use of such "semi polite forms", especially if there is no power asymmetry in interpersonal relations between interlocutors.
96 During a focus group interview conducted by me with her and a group of her friends from the same grade at a later date, she almost exclusively used plain form and informal talk.

and the junior third grader also constructs the hierarchical relationship between them. To be sure, it is *linguistically* possible that the above-mentioned interaction occurred otherwise: that is, everyone used the plain form or everyone used the addressee honorific form, without altering the *referent* meaning of their utterances. The fact that the H2 AS and H2 TS did not employ the *desu/masu* form and the J3 TS' non-use of the plain form reflected their adoption of the respective chosen forms of speech as discursive practices in constituting their interpersonal relations and senior-junior identities in interactions. Hence, in the institutional life of *jouge kankei* in this instance, it is *socially* not possible that the interlocutors spoke otherwise, because doing so would alter the *social* meaning of their utterances, which goes against the nature of their interpersonal relationship.

In addition to using the *desu/masu* form to her seniors, J3 TS also employed some "extra-linguistic" discursive features to mark her relative lower status and power in comparison to H2 AS and H2 TS. For instance, we observe in line 2 that, in conjunction with her use of the "semi polite" form (*naidesu*), she also began with a volume that was softer than usual, and the volume kept decreasing. In line 9, J3 TS' response was almost inaudible. Contrary to one's behaviour while talking to equals (friends or club mates from the same grade), there was no direct eye contact in either instance, in fact, J3 TS was not looking at her seniors while she responded.[97]

Before moving on to analyse the recorded data in part II, one additional, relevant point needs to be discussed. There is an addressee honorific form in line 5 (*ikimasu*). If one were to follow the conventional wisdom that this form necessarily equates to politeness, and that social meanings of utterances are fixed, as are speakers' identities, then it would lead us to assume that this particular utterance from line 5 was from a junior to a senior. However, a look at the transcript reveals that it was indeed one of the two senior second graders (H2 AS) who said this. A suitable point of departure to understand this is to recognise that meanings and functions of such addressee honorific forms are not presupposed. Hence, we should neither detach a text from its context, nor assume that a certain style of speaking or honorific form necessarily comes from a certain type of speaker. This case shows that the leader of the group, H2 AS, used this *desu/masu* form to the entire group. This highlights another function of the addressee honorific form, which is to index social activities (and not social identities pertaining to status and power alone, as what the J3 TS had done) (Cook 2006). In this social activity, whoever addressing the group could

---

[97] I was present throughout the recording session and was sitting at the side of the classroom in order that I could take note of the 'extra-linguistic' features.

use the *desu/masu* form to mark the nature of the utterance and the fact that she/he is speaking from an "official frame", or assuming an official capacity/identity (such as that of a section leader) (Geyer 2008). In instances like this, the utilisation of the *desu/masu* form have little regard as to status and power differentials, and it is not used as a marker of deference either (Geyer 2008). Therefore, not all instances of addressee honorific *desu/masu* form could be categorised as part of the discursive constitution of hierarchical relations. Occurrences like the one in line 5 should not confuse our analysis of the discursive constitution of hierarchy in club activities.

Returning to the recorded data, what happens when one's status changes from that of a junior to that of a senior? The data in part II show parts of the conversation among junior high saxophone members only, as they split with H2 AS and H2 TS to form their own practice group after a 10-minute break. Being the most senior, J3 TS led the session, and their seating arrangement is shown in Figure 5.3.

Part II (the same tenor J3 as senior)

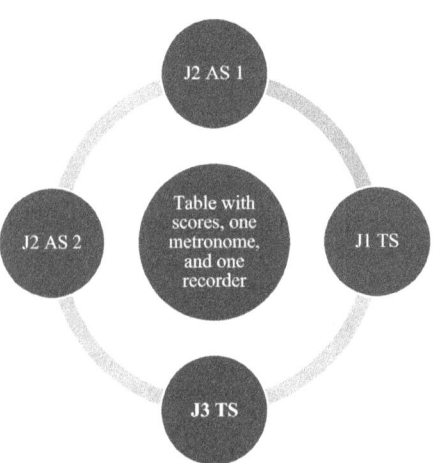

Figure 5.3: Seating arrangement of Tokyo Daiichi Orchestra's saxophone section for part II.

[The section was divided into two: the two senior students went for individual practice, while the tenor J3 led the rest of the junior high students and carried on with group practice]

12. J3 TS: *Eee, mae   saa, doko   made yatta   oboeteru?*
    　　　　Eh,　before　　　where　till　did-PRF　remember-PLAIN FORM
    'Eh, do you remember until where did we play the last time?' [much louder volume and more assertive tone than when she responded as a junior previously]

13. *Doko   yatta   kana?*
    Where　Did-PRF　I wonder
    'I wonder where could it be?'

14. *Hyaku-rokujuu toka yatta   yone?*
    160　　　　　　etc　Did-PRF　Right-Q-PLAIN FORM
    'We did section 160, right?'

15. *Dou   shiyou   kana?*
    What　should do　I wonder
    'I wonder what should we do?'

16. *Dou   shiyou   kana?*
    What　should do-PLAIN FORM　I wonder
    'I wonder what should we do?'

17. *Kojin-ren   shitai?*
    Individual　want do-PLAIN FORM
    practice
    'Do you want to do individual practice?'

18. *Kojin-ren   shitai?   Shitai?*
    Individual　want do-PLAIN FORM　want do-PLAIN FORM
    practice
    'Do you want to do individual practice?'

19. *Dochira   mo   ii   kedo zenzen,   suru?*
    Which-ever　also　fine　but　not at all　do-PRS-PLAIN FORM
    'Whichever is completely fine with me, shall we [do individual practices]?'

20. *Ah, demo kojin-ren   no   jikan aru   noka?*
    Ah, but　Individual　POSS　time　Have-PLAIN　Q
    　　　　 practice
    'Ah, but do we even have time for individual practice?'

21. *Tabun   saisho   kara yaru   jan,   gassou   wa. Ja. . .*
    Maybe beginning from do-PLAIN FORM isn't it combined SBJ So
                                                               practice
    'Maybe we will play from the beginning during the combined practice. So. . .'

22. Juniors: *Hai.*
             Yes

23. J3 TS: *Ikutsu gurai   dake   wakaru?   Hachi-juu kana?*
           How   roughly   know-PLAIN FORM 80   I wonder
    'Do you know the approximate tempo? 80 I guess?'

24. *Ja, nishou-setsume kara juuni mae   made yatte kuda-sai.*
    So, second   from   12   before till   do   please
         bar
    'So, please play from second bar till before section 12.'

25. Juniors: *Hai.*
             Yes

26. J3 TS: *Ichi, ni,   san.*
           One,   two, theee.

The data in part II shows how J3 TS, who only a while ago was still a junior, now led the junior high saxophone members in the practice session as their leader and the most senior member in the group. Following a change in context with new interlocutors and the ensuing emergence of new interpersonal dynamics between J3 TS and the rest of the members present, it is not surprising to note her exclusive use of plain form when asking questions (lines 12, 14, 17, 18, 19, 20, and 23). Other informal styles of speaking, which usually supplement the use of plain form to foreground the identity of a senior, were also extensively employed. These include the informal suffix *sa* (line 12), as well as the informal and truncated *jan* (line 21). The term *jan* here is the truncated form for *janai* (literally "isn't it"), which is considered very colloquial. The complete form is in the *desu/masu* style and as club members have been taught, should be used from juniors to seniors. The fact that J3 TS cut off the *desu/masu* ending and used the truncated colloquial form concomitantly with other plain form usages in her speech reflects the discursive practice to construct a *jouge kankei*

5.4 Plain and *desu/masu* forms of talk — 137

in which she emerges as a senior, in contrast to Part I. Indeed, throughout the entire duration of my fieldwork, the afore-mentioned terms were heard only when a person was talking in plain form, either to people from the same cohort or to juniors. There was little variation across the clubs as regards usage of addressee (and also referent) honorifics and non-reciprocal plain forms insofar as asymmetrical interpersonal relations were concerned.[98] In addition, and accompanying the switch to plain form, we could observe the emergence of a dominant personality in J3 TS, as she not only spoke in a significantly louder volume than before the break, but also hardly gave her addressees any chance to reply to her questions as she continued with her monologue after posing a question: in line 14, she immediately suggested her knowledge to the right answer to her question in line 12 without displaying any interest in knowing what the others had to say; while from lines 17 to 19, J3 TS first asked the same question four times ('do you want to do individual practice?'), before proceeding right away to state her own opinion in lines 20 and 21, soliciting a polite response (*hai*) from the juniors (refer to chapter three for learning process and contents). Such behaviours, which come in accordance with the use of plain style, contribute to the active construction of a *senpai* identity on the part of J3 TS. We could thus conclude that J3 TS made choices that seemed adequate to her in various situations by combining her "linguistic ability" (mastery of the Japanese language) and her common-sense knowledge of social norms and conventions governing proper behaviour towards seniors and juniors.

Thus far, I have shown the ways in which Japanese adolescents acting within the framework of *jouge kankei* utilise honorifics (respect forms/exalting words, plain or *desu/masu* form, plus corresponding extra-linguistic features) in accordance with their relative status in the group and their relationship with the addressee(s). To engage with the data critically, it is imperative to ask *why* do actors do this and *why* does it happen, in addition to how they do it and how it happens. To answer the why question, we return to the language-ideology-power nexus discussed at the beginning of this chapter, and try to make explicit the ideologies and power relations underlying the conventions of the conversations analysed here. In "designing" their conversational turns and how they react to others, participants orientate to both the micro structures of conversation routines and the macro structures of societies and institutions

---

98 In this case, the same discursive rule of who is to use which form of speech to whom reigned in all three clubs, as well as in clubs of those interviewees in my pilot study. Hence, in this regard, there was little, if any, variation across gender (comparing Tokyo Daiichi and Tokyo Daini) and age (in secondary school clubs in my research and in the university club in Enyo 2013).

(in the case of my research, *jouge kankei*) (Fairclough 1989: 12). Social actors' orientation is largely based on common-sense assumptions and knowledge that constitute their ideology and which facilitates their making sense of the world in which they live. As we have seen, upon entering a club, junior members are inculcated with behavioural conventions, values such as respect, discipline and diligence, and sets of norms to help them conform to the new social life as quickly as possible. These are achieved by portraying such ways of comportment as commonsensical, to the extent that they no longer question it and expect their own juniors to follow suit once they become seniors in the future.

Power, in turn, is present in an ideology that looks at the social world through the lens of *jouge kankei*, because status and functional differences are sustained by such an ideology. The critical discourse analysis approach understands power in discourse in terms of "powerful participants [indirectly] controlling and constraining the contributions of non-powerful participants." (Fairclough, 1989: 46). As mentioned in the sub-section 5.1.1, this is manifested in three overlapping aspects: (i) contents – what is said or done; (ii) relations – the social relations people enter into in discourse; and (iii) subject positions – positions people occupy (Fairclough 1989: 46). All these can be observed in parts I and II of the recorded data. As to what pertains to the various exchanges among H2 AS, H2 TS, and J3 TS in part I, we notice that in the process of the practice session, a routine was followed, in which seniors led, and what could be said by whom (seniors free to say things, juniors only able to reply) and how it was said (plain or *desu/masu* forms) were respected. As regards the overlapping social and subject relations, the three members operated in a superior-subordinate relationship in their interactions (social), as well as positions, or identities, of section leader, alto saxophone or tenor saxophone players (subject positions). Linguistically speaking, the exchanges in Part I could have taken place all in the plain form as well, without changing much of the referent meanings of the things said. However, the presence of the language-ideology-power nexus as described above means that such an occurrence would have been socially unacceptable in the context of *jouge kankei*. Therefore, we could observe the non-reciprocal, contrastive use of plain form by the seniors and the addressee honorific *desu/masu* form by the J3 TS in return, and with this, the discursive enactment of the *senpai-kouhai* relationship.

For most of part II, J3 TS performed a quasi-monologue, and her lines of utterances without significant breaks (more than one second) made it difficult for any of the juniors to make meaningful contributions to the conversation content. In addition, in line 21, J3 TS' use of the grammatical form of a negative question (*yaru jan*) in a high pitch and significantly louder volume implies that the juniors had no idea of what would come up during the combined session, they had no time management skills, and that they had wanted to go for individual practice. This facilitates the bringing into being of a "senior knows best" image and a superior status vis-à-vis her addressees in their social relationship.[99] This in turn puts her in an authoritative position to command and her addressees in a subordinate position to comply. The analysis above may lead to the conclusion that more powerful actors in any given situation actively control and constrain the less powerful participants. We should, however, note that such control during social interactions is of an *indirect* nature, because the main constraints derive from the conventions of the particular discourse type being used (in this case the plain and "polite" discourse used in hierarchical relations). Hence, the more powerful actors' active role lies rather in determining a particular discourse type to be used, making it the legitimate one, and making others recognise the need to employ this.[100]

It is equally worthwhile to highlight that scholars from the traditional CDA approach often portray themselves, in analysing diverse features of texts, as those who know best about what is happening by decoding the texts and that they are there to help reveal power structures and ideologies imbued in language so as to ultimately help emancipate the oppressed (Breeze 2011; Fairclough 1989). In this regard, the discourse analytic approach employed in my research departs from CDA in two important ways. Firstly, the aim of my research is to highlight the nature of *jouge kankei* (how does it come into being in secondary school clubs, how is it maintained, etc), and not to facilitate the emancipation of those who are implicated in the hierarchical order. As oppressive as it may ostensibly seem to be, this particular social structure does have certain unique features that can be enabling even to those who are situated at the lower end. This point is taken up again in chapter seven. Secondly, analyses of spoken and written texts throughout my research are backed up by other forms of empirical data such as vignettes from participant observations, interviews, as well as secondary data such as survey results. This ensures a more comprehensive coverage of the diverse contexts, specific reasons for action and norms that altogether enable the discursive practices in constituting *jouge kankei*.

---

99 Research on the establishment of authority and power relations by people assuming different roles through talk and language socialisation has been conducted in English-speaking contexts in the institution of family. Refer to Ochs and Taylor (1995) and Schieffelin (1990).
100 This may sound dictatorial, but it does not reveal the full dynamics of *jouge kankei*. What makes this institutional hierarchy special is that everyone implicated in it has her/his chance of arriving at the top. Refer to chapter seven.

5.5 Language-ideology-power and the epistemic order in discourse

In the previous sub-section, I discussed the ways in which ideology guides actors' interactional behaviours, creates and sustains power relationships in and through talk by examining plain and *desu/masu* forms. In this section, ideology and power at work in language to co-construct social realities and identities is explored from a different angle: that of "epistemic order" in discourse (Heritage 2008: 309; Heritage 2013). According to Heritage (2008), when speakers convey information, they position themselves according to an epistemic order: a matter of expressing what interlocutors know relative to others and what they are entitled to know, as well as what they are entitled to describe or communicate in any given context. Such positioning is done with reference to other "co-interactants in the here and now" (Heritage 2008: 309). Hence, the language-ideology-power nexus comes into play as well, because the data presented here reveal that status differences and power relations among members influence the epistemic ordering in an interaction.

The excerpts in this section were taken from a recording session in the Tokyo Daini Orchestra in November 2015. The recording session was conducted with the orchestra's bass section, consisting of the following five members at the time of the recording, as Table 5.3 documents:

Table 5.3: Members of Tokyo Daini Orchestra's Bass Section present on the day of recording.

Grade	Instrument	Other Roles in Club	Participant Identifier in Transcript
High School 2	Bass Trombone	Bass Group Leader	H2 BT
High School 2	Tuba	NA	H2 TU
High School 1	Euphonium	NA	H1 EU
Junior High 2	Trombone	NA	J2 TB
Junior High 1	Tuba	NA	J1 TU

The recording procedure was the same as in Tokyo Daiichi Orchestra. Just like members of the Tokyo Daiichi Orchestra, this group of boys from Tokyo Daini Orchestra were practicing in an empty classroom. But unlike their peers in Tokyo Daiichi, this bass section adopted a slightly different seating arrangement as shown in Figure 5.4:

5.5 Language-ideology-power and the epistemic order in discourse — 141

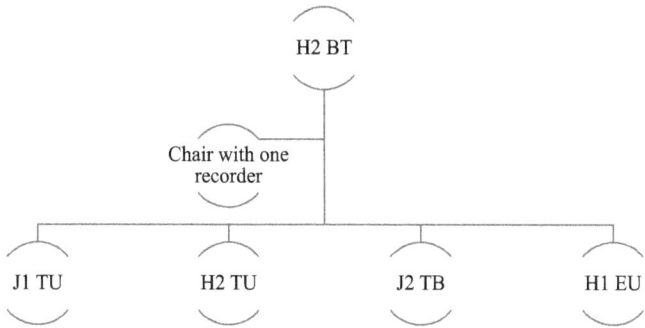

Figure 5.4: Seating arrangement of Tokyo Daini Orchestra's bass section.

The recording was done while they practiced one of their concert pieces, "Songs of Sailor and Sea".

[H2 BT set the metronome to 60s/minute, metronome started to tick, all members had their scores open and instruments in place, H2 BT flipped through the full score, and got ready to give the cue to start]

27. H2 BT: *Etto, dou shiyou?   Juugo-ban kara iki masu.*
    So,   what should do   15th   from go MASU FORM
    'So, what should we do? Let's start from the 15th.'

28. J1 TU: *Hai.*
    Yes

29. J2 TB: *Hai.*
    Yes

30. H1 EU: *Hai.*
    Yes

31. H2 TU: *Ah, dekitara   Juuyon kara*
    Ah, can-COND   14   From
    'Ah, let's start from 14 if possible.' [falling volume]

32. H2 BT: *Juuyon kara*
    14   from
    'From 14.' [flips back a page, looks at section 14 and realises his mistake]

33. *Ja, Juuyon kara iki masu*
    So   14   from go MASU FORM
    'So let's start from 14.'

34. All: *Hai.*
        Yes

In the above excerpt, when H2 BT gave an initial instruction in line 27, he actually overlooked a portion of additional music marked in the tuba section. To start playing from where H2 BT had initially ordered would be highly unnatural for the tuba players. Nonetheless, the first tuba player, J1 TU, who was within two meters from me (hence I could see his score and facial expression) and who responded first, simply said "*hai*" and was preparing to follow the instruction by H2 BT. His facial expressions at the moment clearly indicated the fact that he knew his senior had overlooked the tuba's part. However, he did not raise the concern, and instead, it was only until line 31, the moment when his tuba senior, H2 TU, also realising the mistake by H2 BT, that a request was made, by H2 TU, to H2 BT. The data reveal two important issues as regards epistemic order in discourses involving *jouge kankei* in club contexts. Firstly, the fact that J1 TU knew something, but did not raise the point against his senior, H2 BT, but instead acknowledged the latter's instructions, illustrates that juniors are not expected to express their knowledge to their seniors. Indeed, juniors are taught not only the appropriate ways of responding to their seniors right at the onset of the socialisation process, but also if and when they should speak up. In this case, J1 TU followed the common-sense logic of appropriate behaviour vis-à-vis seniors. Secondly, even when H2 TU, who was the only other senior second grade member in the room, raised the concern, he was careful in his choice of expression, speech volume, and intonation. Instead of using declaratives to assert his utterance and indirectly insisting on the fact that he knew something that the recipient did not know, his choice of a more request-like formulation ("Ah, let's start from fourteen if possible") adjusted the "epistemic gradient" in the interaction, so that the level of assertion and certainty was downgraded (Heritage 2008: 309). In line 31, H2 TU's intervention was indeed a way of saying "you are wrong" to the leader, albeit in a very indirect way. The justification for his action was that he was on an equal status with the leader age wise, hence he was entitled to know something and to express his knowledge to H2 BT.

Having been trained to accept and internalise a particular way of making sense of the social world (*jouge kankei*) around them at the beginning of their club stint, junior members would naturally tend to think that they are not entitled to such communications, even if they happen to know something that their seniors had overlooked. Hence, the excerpt in this section shows a clear general epistemic order in interactions among actors occupying different positions along the institutional hierarchy of *jouge kankei*: seniors have ownership of knowledge and experiences, as well as the right to express them.

On a side note, the above transcription presents a potential pitfall that we need to avoid. If we simply follow the denotational reference of the plain and "polite" forms in texts without additional observations and extra-linguistic, contextual information, we would be led to assume that H2 TU is a senior and occupies a superior role than H2 BT because H2 TU not only interrupted H2 BT, but also that the former used plain form and the latter polite form. However, they were in fact of an equal status, with H2 BT occupying a more important institutional role of the group leader in this context. Therefore, if we consider the interactional reference of the entire context, as opposed to the denotational reference alone (Pizziconi 2011), we notice the similar function of the use of *desu/masu* form by the senior leader H2 BT – to foreground the social identity of a section leader addressing an entire group – as it was used by the two senior saxophone players in Tokyo Daiichi Girls' Orchestra (section 5.4).

5.5.1 When age and length of service do not correspond

In sections 5.4 and 5.5, I demonstrated the ways in which discursive strategies in the form of honorifics construct hierarchy in clubs. The hierarchical relation in the student clubs addressed in this chapter, as it is throughout this volume, pertains to the age-based *jouge kankei*. This *jouge kankei* could be conceived in ideal terms where all parameters coincide and boundaries clearly drawn, in which case every individual in a group would know with ease her/his exact place in the hierarchical order, and correspondingly, the exact behaviour as expected of her/him. In reality, however, it is not always easy to have the ideal situation in which everything could be clear-cut. This applies not only to the adult society, but also to secondary school student clubs. For instance, I was reminded by an interviewee, right from the beginning during my initial study, that it was possible and not uncommon to see the mismatch between an individual's age and the length of membership in a club:

> I wouldn't say that our choir had strict rules compared to most other clubs in my school, or even compared to choirs elsewhere. Among junior high students, once you get to the second grade, you are allowed to take part in discussions with third graders from time to time, and we discuss topics like what to play for our annual concert, whether or not to make club t-shirts for summer, etc. The third graders always had the final say, but at

least second graders could talk. I remember just one incident where someone who joined us in her second year and came straightaway to one of the meetings. The third grade seniors and most of us second graders didn't feel good. Like, we thought she didn't really qualify to be here in the discussion. So we mostly ignored her.

This was indeed not uncommon, and during my main fieldwork phase in the two junior and senior high schools, I realised that, especially in schools that provided a six-year combined junior and senior high education under one roof, such instances were present in almost every other club. In fact, this was the case for H2 TU in Tokyo Daini Boys' Orchestra during my fieldwork.[101] H2 TU was a "transferred" student: he spent the first three years of junior high school in Tokyo Daini's football club, and transferred to the orchestra only in his senior first year. This means that, at the time of my field work and the recording of the practice session in section 5.5, H2 TU's length of membership in the orchestra was only about two years (similar to J2 TB and less than H1 EU), even though he was the most senior member (together with H2 BT) in terms of age. As I have shown at the beginning of this book, the basic principle around which *jouge kankei* in secondary school clubs operates is age. Such a mismatch between biological age and organisational membership renders the business of negotiating relationships delicate, because actors involved are conscious about this mismatch, and it is reflected in discursive practices. From the exchange in section 5.5, we notice that, being a senior member, H2 TU did exercise his right to the expression of a certain knowledge. However, he was also exercising constraint and caution to some extent, as manifested by his falling volume, mild intonation, and his downgrading of the level of assertion, all of which would normally not be present (at least not all at once in an utterance) between two equals in a secondary school club context.

In Tokyo Daiichi Girls' Orchestra, the senior second grade trombone section leader, by the name of Suzuki, was also "only" in her second year in the orchestra, after having spent three junior high years in Tokyo Daiichi's volley ball club:

Our trombone section seniors chose me as the trombone section leader because the only other person who was in the same grade was already going to serve as the new club president. So I have been leading our section since becoming a senior second grade student. But it is also true that the senior high first grader and the junior high third grader have been in the section for four and three years respectively. I am aware that in some ways

---

101 He was not the only "transferred member" I met, all three clubs had such members. This again highlights the importance of conducting my research in schools with six-year programmes as this provides students the possibility to transfer to another club while remaining in the same school.

they are my seniors since they have both been here longer. So I have decided from the beginning [when she became the section leader] that I will not give them orders or harsh criticisms like I would to juniors.[102]

Suzuki revealed that transferred students like her do feel the mismatch and are conscious that in their clubs, there are people who are of the same age, or younger than them, but with more experience. Just like H2 TU in Tokyo Daini Boys' Orchestra, such transferred students do tend to play down their behaviour and make adjustments to their discursive practices. However, a crucial point to note is that, despite such consciousness on the part of these transferred students, basic norms and conventions that are spelt out in clubs continue to play the decisive and regulatory role: in no instance did Suzuki or H2 TU receive "inadequate" or "inappropriate" treatment by those who are in lower grades, be it in terms of using addressee and referent honorifics, greetings, or other etiquettes juniors should display to seniors. This implies that the institutional nature of *jouge kankei* and its discursive constitution in secondary school clubs are determined first and foremost by age cohort. Experience does play a role in injecting intricacies in interpersonal relations and nuances in discursive practices, but when it disagrees with age, age prevails insofar as the discursive construction of hierarchy in secondary school clubs is concerned.

5.6 Deviation from the conventions

What happens when behaviours deviate from established conventions? Just like the incident on ToA mentioned by one of the university interviewees in chapter four, "unusual" behaviour also occurred regarding a disrupted epistemic order during one of my participant observation sessions, in which a junior first grade member "crossed the red line" and interrupted her seniors' conversation to express her knowledge about certain information:

Vignette 5.1: Junior first grader at Tokyo Daiichi Orchestra breaking the epistemic order
The Tokyo Daiichi Girls' Orchestra's trombone section had a full attendance today and I stayed with this section most of the time. Contrary to last week, when I just started my fieldwork here, some students have been getting less shy and taking the initiative to approach me for a chat. Most of the time, the topics of our conversation revolved around techniques of playing the trombone,

---

[102] Interview conducted on 14.02.2016.

since I had told the entire orchestra on my first day here that I used to play the trombone and tuba. For instance, we talked about proper ways of using the slide (the part of a trombone where pushing or pulling it helps produce different notes), breathing techniques, as well as the names of the different parts of a trombone in English and Japanese. This was when I thought I should start to memorise as many members' names as possible, so as to build better rapport. Hence, during one of the breaks today, I started by asking for the names of the two senior high second grade members. As I was sitting quite far from these two senior members, the section leader shouted her name across: Suzuki. I then turned to the other senior member, who also happened to be the orchestra's president. Partly because she was wearing a mask and partly because the trumpets in the far corner in the same room were still practising, I could not get her name. Even though she repeated it several times, increasing her volume each time, I did not catch it. At this juncture, the junior first grade member, a bass trombone player by the name of Edogawa (her name was written on her indoor shoes), who was literally right in front of me, turned to me and said loudly that her senior's name was "Matsushita". A moment of awkward silence ensued as I was jotting down the president's name. Probably sensing something wrong, Edogawa started apologising to Matsushita, uttering profusely: *sumimasen, ichiban chikai node* . . . (I am sorry, I thought I was the nearest to him, so . . .).[103]

From the scene depicted above, we could notice that, as I failed to get the name of one of the senior second grade members, (Matsushita, who was also the club's president) after her repeated attempts which became louder and louder, Edogawa, a junior first grade member who was nearest to me turned over, faced me, and relayed the information to me by saying "Matsushita". This was the moment when she disrupted the epistemic order of who is entitled to have knowledge about something and who has the right to express what she knows in the hierarchical order. Just as how the mechanism works in Tokyo Daini Boys' Orchestra, not only are junior members not expected to know more than, or as much as, their seniors, but more importantly, they are not entitled to express what they know as long as seniors are present and are participating in the same social activity/engaged in the same conversation. Whenever interactions between seniors and juniors take place, seniors control the conversation contents as well as juniors' contribution. Juniors, on the other hand, are taught from the onset that they should not communicate their opinion or what they know if unsolicited (as data in section 5.5 have shown). In the event that seniors conduct a conversation or interact among themselves, such as in this

---

103 Observation in Tokyo Daiichi Orchestra on 20.11.2015.

case (an interaction between Matsushita and me), juniors are simply not expected to contribute in any way unless solicited. Edogawa was therefore obliged to apologise formally and justify her unexpected, deviant behaviour. This once again showed the language-ideology-power nexus at work, as the power to control contents, ways of interacting, and common-sense behaviours are highlighted. Such transgressions also help us to find out and confirm established conventions of language and social behaviour for individuals implicated in the *jouge kankei*.

5.7 Summary of chapter

From the examples mentioned throughout this chapter, we could draw up some preliminary conclusions regarding ideology and power in (honorific) language. Once a particular discourse type (the non-reciprocal use of honorific language between seniors and juniors) is established as the main form of talk (micro-level discourse) in *jouge kankei*, its conventions are expected to be followed. As a consequence, certain types of power relations, such as that between seniors and juniors, as well as a variety of social personae, are brought into being by relevant discursive practices.

Specifically, as regards the dichotomy of plain and "polite" forms, I have illustrated that we could not fully grasp their meanings in interactions if we rely solely on politeness theory. To gain a more complete picture, we also need to take into account the language-ideology-power dynamics in interactions, so as to realise the ways in which such addressee honorific forms are also used by speakers to discursively construct identities (for example, when senior students used the *desu/masu* form to highlight their changing social personae).

At the beginning of this chapter, I surveyed several research traditions adopting various perspectives on honorifics and interpersonal relations. From my introductory chapter and the empirical chapters thus far, it is evident that I adopt the constructionist approach to studying honorifics. However, the data gathered during my fieldwork revealed a peculiarity in secondary school club contexts that is absent in the context of adult society. As previous research mentioned, social meanings of honorific terms are not always fixed and it is not always possible to predict, for instance, a lower status speaker using honorifics to a higher status speaker (Cook 2011). Furthermore, it has been observed that "speakers shift back and forth between the two forms [plain and addressee honorific *masu* form] in most speech situations, if not all. When speakers mix the two forms, in some social contexts the *masu* form indexes the addressee's higher social status, but in others, it indexes instead the speaker's self-presentation display" (Cook,

1998: 87). Such a *leeway for flexibility* in language choice and the agency in speakers' being able to choose the form and style of speech are largely *absent* in the cases I studied. Interviews, observations, as well as my recorded data all show that this room for negotiation and choice of forms of talk do not apply to juniors who are at the lower end of the *jouge kankei* pecking order. In addition, the specific discourse type (of which honorifics are a part) that new junior members learn at the beginning of their club stint does assume *fixed* social meanings across contexts. We can not only predict, but also know that a lower status speaker in a secondary school club *jouge kankei* must follow the specified codes of conduct. Only people of higher status, usually senior high school members, have the "choice" of alternating forms and styles of talk depending on contexts and social activities. Hence, in sections 5.4 and 5.5, my analyses of interactions between juniors and seniors further attest to the fact that, in secondary school clubs, such exchanges both represent the predominant form of social interaction and serve as the main medium of communication to which junior new members are exposed and through which socialisation into *jouge kankei* occurs.[104] At this crucial, initial stage of talking the social structure of *jouge kankei* into being, strict codes and regulations are in place and social meanings in discursive practices are fixed, thereby reducing the extent to which speakers, especially junior club members, could exercise their agency (cf. Cook 2011; Enyo 2013).

Lastly, it is often suggested by scholars that nowadays younger speakers of Japanese are becoming less and less capable of using honorifics, so much so that they tend to avoid using it altogether most of the time[105] (Inoue 1998, Shibamoto-Smith and Cook 2011). In fact, in a recent opinion poll on honorifics conducted by the Agency for Cultural Affairs (2015), an overwhelming majority of 72.8 percent of those surveyed held the opinion that junior and senior high school students around them had corrupted (*midareteiru*) manners of speaking. The aforementioned public and expert opinions notwithstanding, empirical data presented throughout this book in general, and in this present chapter in particular, show the contrary. Through "induction programmes" at the beginning of their club

---

104 This is because, other than such sectional practices as recorded in sections 5.4 and 5.5, there is often little, if any, meaningful exchange and talk between students of different grades (that is, when *jouge kankei* is present). See next chapter.
105 These claims are ubiquitous among Japanese (socio)linguists. During one of my regular research visits to the National Institute for Japanese Language and Linguistics (NINJAL) in Tokyo in December 2015, the director of NINJAL gently warned me, upon hearing my research topic, that I should be careful not to take young speakers' language too seriously, because he doubted that young people nowadays would use honorific language on a daily basis, let alone "correctly".

career (which also coincide with the commencement of their junior high school life), young speakers come into contact with proper manners of speaking (*kotobazukai*) and honorifics, together with their underlying ideology in the discursive practice. They are then socialised into the hierarchical social order in and through talk on a daily basis. Most of them are able to recognise status and power differentials in their clubs after several months, and as such recognition is inextricably linked to the use of honorifics (Miwa 2000), evidence of such parlance is aplenty in an average student's time in junior and senior high school extra-curricular club activity. Since prior research on honorifics among youths in Japan has relied primarily on surveys[106] and has not normally involved researchers spending significant amounts of time doing participant observation with the students while they engage in club activities, it might be that impressions of young speakers using less "polite language" have come from observing and listening to them in public, that is, out of school. The complicating factor is that there exists a segregation according to grades and one would always tend to be with people from the same grade, if interaction with *senpai* (or also *kouhai*) could be avoided. This book affirms that, when people interact with others from the same grade, the established convention guides them to use informal talk and plain forms, and a very colloquial manner. This is because, among people of a same age-grade, no hierarchy of the *jouge kankei* sort is present, hence the difficulty of hearing young speakers using "polite language" if one simply observes a group, say, going home together or hanging out after school. However, why is there a segregation according to grades, and could this have anything to do with the discursive constitution of hierarchy? This will be the main topic of the next chapter.

---

106 NINJAL (2002) did publish a report on honorifics in schools, where the main data source was a series of recordings (in addition to surveys and interviews) of students' conversations in school settings, including in clubs. The results revealed that honorific language was well and alive in schools, but since the recordings of club interactions were done without taking note of the profiles of the participants present as well as interactional contexts, we could unfortunately not conclude much about interactional dynamics from them.

6 Space, signs, symbols, and objects used in conjunction with discourse

In the preceding chapters, I illustrated the ways in which new club members in junior high schools were socialised into the hierarchical order in and through language, as well as the daily discursive and behavioural practices that enacted the interpersonal *jouge kankei* in such settings. In other words, I mainly demonstrated how the actors involved in this hierarchical system "talked the talk". However, making language and discursive choices is not just a matter of being more or less polite or formal; specific ways of using certain forms of talk and styles of language bring into existence social relations among actors – in the case at hand, among seniors and juniors in *bukatsudou*. Hence, to be able to use the different forms and styles would mean that one is competent enough to recognise one's own roles and identities vis-à-vis those of the interlocutors. From my observations, we can conclude that, much to the contrary of existing claims by scholars (Inuoe 1998; Shibamoto-Smith and Cook 2011), Japanese junior and senior high school students who engage in club activities are in fact competent users of diverse styles and forms of talk (that is, the micro-level discourses that constitute *jouge kankei*). However, if they could, they would also try to avoid interacting with people from other grades. This is especially so for juniors, who would either avoid interacting with seniors or accept not enjoying the same rights when using available space while interacting with them. This is notably manifested in a general *spatial segregation* which I observed in all three clubs studied (though to a lesser degree in the boys' orchestra), for instance, before and after practice sessions, during short breaks and lunch time.

Furthermore, it appeared that usage of signs and symbols on school uniforms, as well as certain available objects in clubs, were also designated along the age-status hierarchy. This chapter focuses on this other aspect of the discursive constitution of *jouge kankei* and explores the ways in which the use of space, objects, and signs constitute parts of broader discursive practices in the enactment of hierarchical relations in extra-curricular clubs. At first sight, such everyday routines might not seem to be related to discursive practices. However, a closer analysis of (i) the ways in which the club members made use of space (and objects), and (ii) their rationale for such usage, reveal that macro-level Discourse was at play, albeit in a more indirect way. As a result, this book is the first in existing scholarship that analyses students' use of space, objects (blackboard, bags) and symbols (colour coding on school uniforms) in the construction and maintenance of hierarchy.

https://doi.org/10.1515/9781501514876-006

6.1 An analytical framework for the use of space

In ethnographic and anthropological accounts, "space" is usually regarded as an analytic category in which to examine the production and reproduction of social relations (Keating 2000; Zhang and Spicer 2014). In this regard, there is an emphasis on the social construction of space: in addition to a "physical space" existing out there, there is also a dimension of a socially constructed space in which human beings orientate themselves, decide the ways in which to make use of the physical space, and by extension, draw up social boundaries (Baur et al. 2014). A decisive figure in this strand of scholarship is Lefebvre (1991: 38–39), who argues that space is intricately linked to power relations because:
- Space is first and foremost conceived of and ordered by planners to satisfy specific needs and ways of assigning usage ("representations of space").
- Space is lived in and deciphered by users who seek to appropriate the social space ("representational space").
- Space is practised by both planners and users in their daily routines ("spatial practice").

Since power is understood as the ability to make others do what a power holder wants (where they were not already going to do it on their own, see chapter five), the afore-mentioned three points create power. For instance, the planners/power holders prescribe a specific set of actions to users within the space which they are compelled (by social facts, such as being superiors or subordinates) to comply with. This framework of analysing the social construction and usage of space has been widely applied. For instance, mirroring Lefebvre (1991)'s analytic triad, Dale and Burrell (2008) outline three dimensions to explicate how socio-cultural forces in office buildings produce power relations in organisational lives:
- Organisation members are assigned to different places according to roles, statuses and functions.
- Space has encoded meanings.
- Space prescribes patterns of mobility in the workplace.

Dale and Burrell (2008) therefore provide an applicable framework to examine the ways in which macro socio-cultural forces produce organisational space, and how the latter produces power relations (Zhang and Spicer 2014).

In this chapter, I apply this approach to analyse various club members' use of space. In the process, I put my focus on two analytical perspectives: *territoriality* and *social distance*. Territoriality is considered as an act of laying claim to a territory (Hall 1973), and I show, in sections 6.2 and 6.3, the elaborate ways in which secondary school club members, especially senior members, draw up boundaries to make their exclusive claim to a reserved territory clear to the junior members. In section 6.4, on the other hand, I illustrate that the spatial segregation we observe between juniors and seniors during informal social situations is not simply a matter of physical distance, but a matter of social distance as well. In addition, based on club members' justification of juniors' unwillingness to mix with seniors during such informal situations, I combine the dimensions of discourse and discursive practices that prove decisive in the carving out of social spaces by club members while performing different activities. My observations of the different club members' use of space are also guided by parts of the ethnographic "descriptive question matrix" by Spradley (1980: 82–83). Notably, I follow guiding questions such as "how is space organised by activities?", "how is space used by actors?", and "are there any spatial changes over time".

6.2 The allocation and use of space during lunchtime on Sundays

In order to have a more concrete look at the conceptualisation of space as a materialisation of social (and power) relations in the *bukatsudou* hierarchy, consider the following scenario:

Vignette 6.1: Lunchbreak with senior students at Tokyo Daiichi Orchestra
Today is Sunday, and usually on two Sundays per month the orchestra has full-day practice sessions from 09:00 to 16:00. On such occasions, there is a lunchbreak of one hour, from 12:00 to 13:00. The school does not provide food for clubs, as there is no cafeteria or canteen on campus. And even though there are shops, restaurants, and several convenience stores in the immediate neighbourhood, students are not allowed to patronise shops in their school district, according to school rules. Therefore, all club members bring their own lunch when they come for practice/activities on Sundays, not unlike on any other usual school day. I gathered this information prior to my observation and hence bought my bento (lunch pack) beforehand in one of the convenience stores nearby.

Today's agenda started with morning sectional practices and the sections went to their respective locations after attendance-taking. I stayed with the saxophone and French horn sections, located in the same classroom on the second floor. At 12 o'clock, the saxophone and French horn players cleaned their instruments and left them on the tables/chairs, and started packing their bags for lunch. They then left the room where they had been having their practice, and as I walked out with them, I saw members from other sections doing the same. The club members were in fact moving to their "designated" lunch rooms, which were two designated locations: an empty classroom on one of the higher floors of the school building (5th to 8th storey) for the senior second year members, and the multi-purpose music room for the rest of the orchestra.[107] I followed the senior second year members to a classroom on the 5th floor, since they promptly invited me to join their group.

Out of 15 active senior second grade members, 10 were present today. About half of them brought homemade bento food, while the other half had bought food from convenience stores, like I had. They sat quite close to each other and some even started to share food with others. Once they began eating, the member in charge of the club's annual concert committee took out a piece of paper with a list of possible pieces of music for the concert. She first read out the titles of all these pieces, and then they started discussing which pieces should be chosen for the finalised concert programme. Some of the girls had different opinions and the group decided to vote on their top three most-preferred pieces. This was a genuinely egalitarian voting process, as all voters were from the same grade with virtually no hierarchy observed, and they seemed to have expressed their true personal preferences, with one of the choices receiving only one or two votes. At the end of the vote, I asked if their decision was final, to which the girl behind me explained that it was, because as members of the most senior grade present, they had the right and duty to set most of the agenda for the annual concert.

When this most serious business (lasting about 10 minutes) was done, the group started chatting. Most of the time, topics centred around club-related issues, but occasionally other topics were brought up as well. Five of the members were particularly active and dominated much of the conversation throughout, while others chipped in from time to time. Though prohibited by school rules, they started to use their smartphones to send chat messages to friends and look at images from online fashion magazines. However, they did so in a somewhat discreet manner, for fear that at any time someone might come in and spot their action of using phones in school. Towards the end of the lunch break, they tidied up the classroom and descended to their respective practice locations to join their juniors for the afternoon session.[108]

Based on the above-mentioned practice of assigning space during lunchbreaks in Tokyo Daiichi Orchestra, several observations could be made. Firstly, the

---

107 Though the four remaining grades share the multi-purpose music room, boundaries and the use of available space and objects were clearly demarcated according to seniority. See illustration in later sections in this chapter.
108 Observed in Tokyo Daiichi Orchestra on 21.02.2016.

principle based on which space is allocated changed from one social situation to another. During the formal social situation of sectional practices, available classrooms on any given day were randomly allocated to instrumental sections, largely out of practical concerns[109] rather than seniority of certain members. However, when it was time for the informal social situation of lunchbreaks on Sundays, the four grades of relatively junior club members (from junior first to senior first grades) would "descend" to the music room at the basement level, while the most senior members (senior second graders) would proceed to one of the reserved empty classrooms located on the higher floors. This usually meant that the basement music room would have to be shared by approximately 60 to 70 members, while the upper classroom, normally spacious enough to fit 40 people, was reserved for around 10 to 15 senior second graders.

Secondly, the ways in which actors made use of space and objects revealed hierarchical orders. In the music room, for instance, although the space was shared by members from four grades, designated areas were carved out, with accompanying designations regarding the use of objects and equipment. For example, only senior first graders could sit on chairs during lunchbreak. Junior first graders were not only not allowed chairs (they were only allowed to use, that is, sit on, the floor), but designated the least amount of space (often in a far corner in the music room), despite their numerical superiority. Throughout my fieldwork, this allocation persisted. Furthermore, during my observations of the Sunday lunchbreak scene in the music room, it was easy to notice how members sat neatly in grades and kept a distance from groups of other grades. Also, interactions, mostly whispers, were almost exclusively within each cohort group. Such "eating and whispering" constituted the main activities in the music room during lunchbreaks.

On the other hand, in the empty classroom allocated to senior second grade members, they could freely arrange tables and chairs to their liking. Besides eating, they also conducted business related to their prerogatives as club seniors (such as choosing concert pieces and deciding the repertoire on behalf of the orchestra). They also made use of this special space to break their school's strict rules concerning the use of mobile phones. The seniors did not have a fixed classroom for Sunday lunches, but they would always get such an empty classroom somewhere on the higher floors in their school building. On each Sunday morning, the seniors' allocated lunch space was written on the white board in the music room, as shown in Figure 6.1 below:

---

109 For instance, since the percussion and bass sections have heavy and bulky instruments, they would stay put and practice in the multi-purpose music room, whereas sections whose instruments are small and light, such as flutes and clarinets, will be assigned an empty classroom on one of the higher floors.

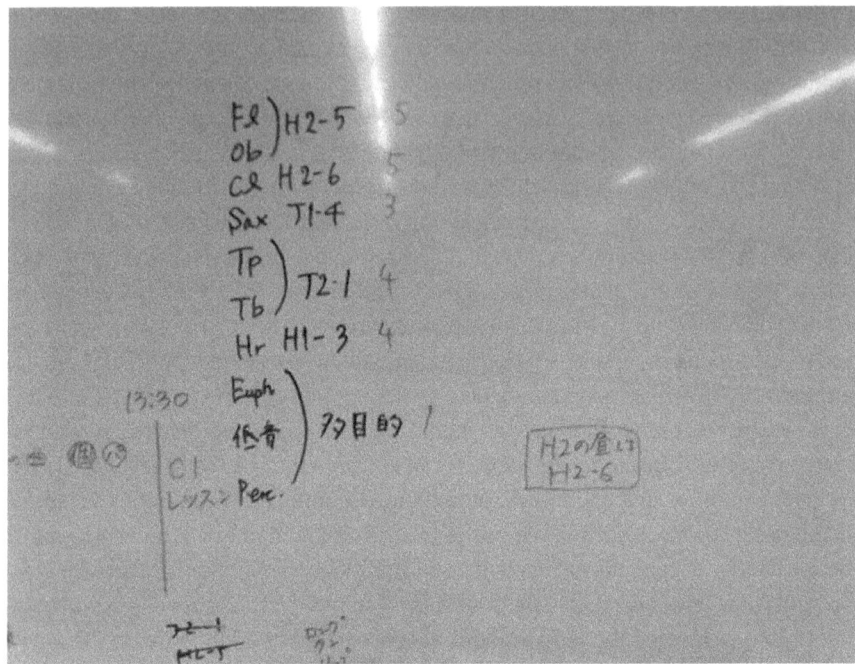

Figure 6.1: The allocation of rooms on a typical Sunday with full-day practice. Texts written in blue denote sections and the classrooms in which they were expected to practice. For instance, flutes and oboes (Fl and Ob) were allocated the classroom H2-5. The numbers in red ink, written beside each allocated classroom, denote the floor of the classroom. At the bottom centre-right, in the red text box, the text says that the senior second graders' lunch location is in room H2-6 (The clarinets – Cl – whose practice was in H2-6, would leave the room during lunch). Photo taken by author.

From the figure above, we could see that this practice not only communicated information to club members, but also reinforced the seniors' right to a reserved and privileged territory. In the music room, the special right of senior first graders to use almost a third of the total available space, and their right to use chairs, also facilitated the materialisation of hierarchical relations. Both these practices reinforced the status division and difference in roles among group members.

In addition, the "after hours" following formal club activity represent yet another (informal) social situation in which senior second year students of Tokyo Daiichi Girls' Orchestra had exclusive rights to use spaces and objects. Though not always strictly enforced, school rules stipulated that junior high students should conclude their club activities and leave no later than 17:30, and senior high students no later than 18:00.[110] Throughout my fieldwork, a common scene was that, at 18:00, when the debriefing session for senior high members was nearing its end, the senior second graders would add a formulaic expression *mou rokuji nanode hayaku kaettekudasai* (it's already six o'clock, please go home soon) to conclude the debriefing session and urge the senior first graders to leave. The senior second graders, on their part, did not leave immediately, as on any day during "after hours" following club activity, a group of at least several senior second grade members could be seen hanging around for another half an hour or so. This represented another instance of the exclusive rights of the senior second years in the orchestra to make use of the club space as and when they desired, even during non-club hours. Together with the use of the music room, the seniors' exclusive right to use the whiteboard was also made clear to juniors constantly. Often, while juniors were cleaning up the music room after practice, senior second graders would use the whiteboard not only for club-related matters, but also to display their artistic talents and for fun. For an illustration, see Figure 6.2 below.

The Figure 6.2 below shows that, on the left, they celebrated one of their peers' (nicknamed Nacchan) birthday, in the centre they displayed their drawings, and on the right side there was serious business: rehearsal procedures for their annual concert. Because the senior second graders had the right as well as the time to use the whiteboard while students of other grades performed their cleaning tasks (or were urged to go home), this particular image of the whiteboard in Figure 6.2 communicates a clear consequence of *jouge kankei*.

During conversations I had with junior club members in Tokyo Daiichi Orchestra, although most admitted that they would also have loved a specially allocated space, or more freedom to use the music room, or the opportunity to draw on the whiteboard after practice, they did not mind their current situation with limited rights. This was because, so long as they could stay together as a cohort and not be mixed with people more senior to them during informal events, they could truly relax, be themselves, and enjoy their breaks. It turned out that a major reason attributed to this "unwanted stress" was that, in the presence of seniors, juniors had to use honorifics, as well as mind their expressions and behaviours (hence not able to "be themselves" and relax).

---

110 Exceptions were granted to senior second and third year students who wished to do quiet self-study in preparation for university entrance examinations. In that case, they were allowed to stay in school until 19:00 daily, but had to remain in a special study room under the supervision of a teacher on duty.

Figure 6.2: The whiteboard in Tokyo Daiichi Girls' Orchestra's music room, with senior second graders' drawings and messages. Photo taken by author.

6.3 Encoding, experiencing, and appropriating meanings in space in daily behaviour

In this section, I show what kinds of meanings are encoded in organisational space, how they are encoded, as well as how actors experience and appropriate them. I focus on both seniors' and (new) junior members' perspectives.

6.3.1 Entering and leaving the music room

Recent scholarship on club activities in Japanese schools has established that, in sports clubs, members are expected to respect and be thankful to the "place" where they practice their activities (for example, a baseball court or an arena for martial arts). This is seen as part of the moral and spiritual education students receive through participation in sports club activities, and manifested above all in the form of greetings (*aisatsu*) to such places and/or objects (Blackwood 2016;

Cave 2004). This is, however, not peculiar to sports clubs. Consider the following regulations stated in Tokyo Daini Boys' Orchestra's booklet on code of conduct (refer to appendix 2 for a full translation of the booklet):
- When you enter the music room, be sure to say "*chiwa*" (truncated form of *konnichiwa*, which means "good day") loudly. In addition, say "*chiwa*" loudly to seniors, alumni, club supporters, external instructors, and teachers in charge whenever you meet them.
- When you leave at the end of a practice session, be sure to say "*sausu*" (formulaic utterance used expressly by orchestra members when bidding farewell). Above all, be sure to say "*sausu*" when seniors, alumni, external instructors or teachers in charge leave.

As I have pointed out in chapter three, such booklets are distributed to all incoming new members and they are given several months' time to read, understand, and ultimately follow the codes of conduct. In it, we see explicit instances of meaning-encoding to specific spaces of which the club makes use. In this case, the music room and people of higher authority in the club (seniors, teachers, etc.) are conflated in the same section. Junior members are told that they should treat both in the same manner, that is, to greet and acknowledge both respectfully (even when the music room is empty or when seniors are not aware of the juniors' presence) when they start and end their day in the club. In this way, the higher status of a senior is also assigned to the music room space, and the discursive practice that constitutes such hierarchy is instilled in junior members.

6.3.2 Reserved territories for seniors

Similar to senior second year members in Tokyo Daiichi Girls' Orchestra, seniors in Tokyo Daini Boys' Orchestra also had their reserved territory. This was known as the *rokuonshitsu* (literally recording room, but it was actually a storeroom for musical notes, plus some tables and chairs). The existence of such a special space and its exclusive nature was made known to incoming members from the outset of their club stint, as stated in the booklet:
- If you want to enter the recording room and it is empty, be sure to enter with an accompanying person who is at least of senior high second grade.
- Before entering the recording studio or the music teachers' room, first check that you are in proper attire (all buttons buttoned up, school badge in place, nothing in your pocket). Then, knock the door and say "*shitsureishimasu*" (excuse me) before walking in. Before walking out, be sure to say "*shitsureishimashita*" (excuse me, after having done an action).

Club regulations stipulated that juniors were not allowed to enter this reserved space alone when it was empty, and could only do so accompanied by a senior member (at least senior high second grade). In addition, if they felt the need to enter this space, they were required to be in proper attire, and the appropriate discursive formulae were to accompany their act of "intruding" into this reserved territory.

The afore-mentioned two instances illustrated the ways in which meanings were encoded in spaces and how particular spaces were assigned to a group of people (seniors) in Tokyo Daini Boys' Orchestra, irrespective of the social situation. They also demonstrated how expectations were cast upon each batch of new incoming members as to how they were to live in the spaces, accompanied by the proper discursive practices.

6.3.3 Learning process of juniors

In this sub-section, I examine the learning process of new junior members, in particular, how those who just joined the club experienced and appropriated meanings in the organisational space of their club, through corrections by seniors. I illustrate this by showing juniors' experiences in the specific daily social situation of *hanseikai* (debriefing session),[111] conducted at the end of the practice session before members were dismissed:

Vignette 6.2: New members' first debriefing session in the beginning of the school year 2016

The new school building that Tokyo Daini Boys' Junior and Senior High School had been building before I started my fieldwork was completed on time for the new school year of 2016. On my way to school today, I saw that the new building was already in use by classes and clubs. Accordingly, from now on, all activities by the orchestra will also be held here (either in the main music room for the combined rehearsals or in separate classrooms for sectional practices). This also holds true for the daily debriefing sessions. While the orchestra has received a much more spacious store room for instruments and equipment, the actual music room is smaller, and to make things "worse", there is now only one room for both the strings and winds sections, whereas previously in the old building they had

---

111 The literal translation of *hanseikai* is "evaluation meeting". However, I use the term "debriefing session", just as I use it for the orchestra and choir in Tokyo Daiichi Girls' School (known here as *kaeri no kai*), because albeit the formality the name *hanseikai* suggests, the debriefing sessions all comprise of activities of a very similar nature.

separate rehearsal rooms which made it look as though they were two separate clubs. The new arrangement means that they now have to do things such as the debriefing together (it was always done separately prior to this).

The debriefing session started punctually at 17:30. According to the custom at Tokyo Daini Orchestra, senior second and third year members lead debriefing sessions by taking attendance, making administrative announcements, and occasionally prompting junior club members to reflect on their daily performance. To perform their duties, senior second and third graders are allowed to stand, walk around, and even talk among themselves during the debriefing. Club members from junior first to senior first grades are expected to sit at attention, close their eyes, lower their heads, clench their fists and listen attentively to their seniors.[112] As this was the first time a debriefing session was held in the (smaller) new music room for the entire orchestra, there was a bit of commotion at the beginning as to finding one's right place to sit. The senior first graders took up the first two rows, followed by the junior third year members behind them. By the time the junior second graders took up all their seats, the seniors had already started talking while the three new junior first year members (more new members joined about two weeks later) were still wondering where to sit. Being already late, they took three chairs and sat at the far corner where I was standing, and quickly settled down and lumped their schoolbags in a pile in front of them. During the debriefing, the three new members did not know exactly how they should behave themselves during seniors' "lectures", which was normal as this was their first day. They were looking around, and one of them even holding on to his bag. Halfway into the debriefing session, one of the senior second graders walked all the way from the other corner diagonally across to come and whisper to these new members on how they should behave and the right posture to maintain. Also, he reminded them to stay silent and instructed them to move their chairs further away from each other, as well as taught them to arrange their bags neatly under their chairs. Before leaving, this senior told the new members to concentrate, not move around, and reply promptly and loudly to seniors' calls, because failure to do so would be caught by other seniors walking around.[113]

In this situation, new members first experienced the use of available space and objects in a passive way: being "pushed" to the back by more senior students right before the debriefing session, then being corrected on their behaviour by an approaching senior. Together with the appropriate formulaic discourses of

---

[112] There exist codes of conduct regulating minute details of members' comportment during debriefing sessions. Refer to appendix 2.
[113] Observed in Tokyo Daini Orchestra on 29.04.2016.

acknowledging and replying to seniors, they were also told the right way to make use of the space around them: not to sit too close to each other, and where to put their bags so as to create a neat and tidy space around them. Furthermore, they also learned that, during the social situation of a debriefing session, the same space (music room) was used by different people (according to hierarchy) in different ways: while they were expected to remain seated and maintain all the right postures, seniors were entitled to talk freely and walk around. Lastly, they were reminded of the importance of *kotobazukai* (way of speaking) as well as honorific rituals that complemented their bodily movements. The appropriate ways of using this designated space as conceived by seniors also implied that, in order to preserve the mobility of seniors walking around during the debriefing (and to a lesser degree, the aesthetics of the room), juniors had to arrange their belongings neatly and carefully.

6.4 Language and spatial segregation based on grades

Club members' actions and use of space in groups according to grades (except during rehearsal and practice sessions) were also complemented by another factor – that of language use. The code of conduct of Tokyo Daini Boys' Orchestra stated that:
– You must absolutely use honorific language to seniors, alumni, external instructors, and school teachers.

However, based on my fieldwork findings, junior members of the orchestra, especially those from the junior first grade, revealed that they were not confident in using honorific language because they had not yet received proper training to use it in an active way. Indeed, according to the junior high school curriculum guidelines, students were expected to know the functions of honorifics by the end of junior high second grade, and use it in appropriate interactional contexts by their junior high third grade. However, the discrepancy between teaching agenda in the classroom and the actual social life of *jouge kankei* students faced in clubs discouraged inter-grade interactions, at least on the part of junior members, who were reluctant to engage or mingle with seniors due in part to a lack of proficiency and confidence in the use of honorifics.

This was also not peculiar to Tokyo Daini Boys' Orchestra. During my time with the Tokyo Daiichi Girls' Orchestra's saxophone section, junior members, especially junior first and second grade members, very often shied away from their seniors even if their seniors took the initiative to try and get them to join in the group conversation. More often than not, however, even when senior second grade members approached one of the groups of junior high saxophone members during break time in an attempt to chat, the juniors showed a reluctance to engage in extended conversations by providing only single-word, perfunctory responses[114] to their seniors' prompts.

A general behaviour observed across all three clubs in both schools during my fieldwork was that actors of the same grade would congregate and associate among themselves, and that the most senior grade present would get the most spacious and comfortable spots/rooms. The senior second grade acting president of the Tokyo Daiichi Girls' Choir explained such segregations and special uses of spaces by grades as such:

> We are a big choir, we have around 160 members, so even this big music room is a bit of a squeeze. We have a separate piano room behind, it used to be a storeroom for our pianos, but now the pianos are permanently located in the music room, the piano room became an office for our senior third year members. It is as big as a normal classroom, but usually only a handful of the senior third years come for practice, due to examination preparations. But even when there is no third year seniors present, the rest of the choir cannot enter and use it, because you never know when some of the seniors could drop by. We the senior second years are quite well-off, the smaller storeroom is just for us. We get to keep our belongings there and during lunch breaks or after practice we have kind of a private space too, unlike the rest of the choir. Though having privacy is good, we as seniors don't mind talking to juniors and mixing around with them. But maybe they do, because they have to use polite language [*teineigo*] to us, maybe they mind because they wouldn't be able to relax.

From the extract above, we see not only parallels in terms of the assignment of space based on seniority across different schools and clubs, but also in terms of the expectations of seniors as to the appropriate (linguistic) behaviour their juniors should adopt in inter-grade (informal and extensive) interactions. Throughout my fieldwork, such interactions rarely took place. As we have seen in earlier chapters, honorifics and the conventions on language use and behaviour are not a mere issue of language alone. This is because they play a broader constitutive role in enacting power relations, obligations, rights, as well as in- and out-group (juniors vs. seniors) membership and identity in the social order of *jouge kankei*. Discursive practices in the hierarchical structure of club activities thus have an effect on *spatial segregation* and *social distancing* among members situated at different ends of the hierarchy.

---

114 Instances like this suggest that the pervasive nature of *jouge kankei* and its constitutive discursive practices dictate the behaviour of actors implicated in it more so than the personalities of specific individuals (for example, relatively open-minded and friendly seniors).

6.5 The use of signs and symbols as discursive practice: The case of school uniforms

As mentioned in chapter one, I adopt a double-pronged approach of analysing both macro-level "Discourse" and micro-level "discourse", comprising not only (linguistic) speech and text, but also (extra-linguistic) features such as space, objects, signs and symbols (Gee 2014). From a sociology of knowledge and social constructionist point of view, this means that discourse is "performed by actors following social instructions"[115] (Keller 2011: 48). Therefore, discursive practices (of which linguistic practices are a part) are social practices that constitute *jouge kankei*. Thus far, I have examined, through this perspective, the concrete and material nature of discourse in the forms of text, speech, as well as the use of space and objects. In this final empirical section, I turn the focus to signs and symbols (as part of macro-level Discourses).

In Japanese school settings, the single most prevalent source of signs and symbols related to an individual is the school uniform, not least because almost all junior high schools and most senior high schools in Japan require students to wear uniforms (Brasor and Tsubuku 2016). Far from being merely uniform clothes, school uniforms fulfil important functions in school settings since their inception in the late 19th century. As part of the country's modernisation programme, Western-style school uniforms for boys were introduced in Japanese schools in the middle of the Meiji era, during which the Prussian-inspired style of black jackets with golden buttons and a tight stand-up collar began to spread (BAMF 2006). This remains to this day the dominant style of school uniforms for boys, especially in junior and senior high schools (Andoh 1997; BAMF 2006). As for girls, the dominant styles of their uniforms changed several times throughout the Meiji and Taisho epochs: from the continued use and adaptation of Kimono-based uniforms in the late 19th and early 20th centuries to the final adoption of the sailor suit style uniform in 1921, which remains the main style today (Andoh 1997; BAMF 2006). Very little research has been dedicated to studying school uniforms and their social functions in and out of school. Out of the few existing studies exclusively dedicated to school uniforms, attention has been on the synchronisation of the changing styles of girls' uniforms and the country's modernisation process as regards the role of girls and women (Andoh 1997), and the ways in which wearing school uniforms could influence order and delinquency rates among adolescents

---

[115] Insofar as this research topic is concerned, the social instructions are notably manifested in the language socialisation process in clubs. These include guidance sessions and seniors' teachings and reprimands, which are also efforts to constitute, legitimise, and objectivise institutional hierarchy.

(Tanioka and Glaser 1991). In his ethnographic study on educational roles of club activities in Japanese schools, Cave (2004) mentions in passing that (sports) clubs he observed had club uniforms that not only facilitated the building of a sense of belonging to the clubs, but also that the uniforms were "often slightly different for each year, moreover, so that the age-status hierarchy is clearly demarcated" (Cave 2004: 410). Cave's (2004) observation offers an important clue to analysing *jouge kankei* in schools, but also highlights several shortcomings in extant literature. Firstly, club uniforms of this sort are less ubiquitous than school uniforms, because not even all the sports clubs have them. Secondly, and more importantly, the question of '*how* do uniforms demarcate age-status hierarchy?' is left unanswered. To date, no study has looked at the school uniforms in the constitution of hierarchy from a discursive perspective, that is, focussing on the signs and symbols of the uniforms and the ideas, concepts, and meanings they communicate and enact. Hence, in the ensuing sub-sections, I show the ways in which signs and symbols, as part of discursive practice, mark and facilitate the reinforcement of institutional hierarchy in school club settings.

6.5.1 Tokyo Daiichi Girls' Junior and Senior High School uniform: Marked from head to toe

In both schools where I conducted my fieldwork, a six-year programme from junior first grade to senior third grade was offered (refer to chapter two). Hence, in both schools, two main styles of uniform, designed for junior high and senior high students respectively, could be observed.[116] In Tokyo Daiichi Girls' School, junior high students wore a sailor suit uniform, whereas senior high students wore shirts plus blazers and ties, typical for girls in most schools in Japan. The Figures 6.3 and 6.4 below give an overview:

At first sight, these two figures show some very general features of girls' uniforms in Japan. It appears that junior high students wear a white sailor outfit in summer and navy blue sailor outfit in winter, coupled with white socks. Senior high students wear a short-sleeved white shirt with a beige colour tank top in summer, and a long-sleeved shirt with a tie and a navy-blue jumper in winter, coupled with blue socks.[117] However, the very fact that junior and senior high students have different uniforms already marks status differences. Besides

---

[116] Each style has a corresponding summer and winter version.
[117] As I conducted the main phase of fieldwork in the two schools from October to May, most students wore the winter version throughout, but distinctions were the same, as I will show.

166 — 6 Space, signs, symbols, and objects used in conjunction with discourse

Figure 6.3: Illustrative example of junior high students' sailor suit uniform. The winter version is shown in the centre, whereas the sides show the summer version. Image taken from the school's website with permission to reuse.

Figure 6.4: Illustrative example of senior high students' uniform. The summer uniform is shown on the left, and the winter uniform on the right. Image taken from the school's website with permission to reuse.

this main difference, the abundance of signs and symbols that demarcate age-status hierarchy (as Cave 2004 noticed, but did not illustrate on club uniforms) becomes even more apparent upon closer inspection. There is a *colour-coding* divided into three categories: green, pink, and blue. These three colours correspond to the three grades in both junior and senior high sections: green for junior and senior first grade, pink for junior and senior second grade, and blue for junior and senior third grade.[118] Irrespective of the grade and season, one can find these colours on the students' uniforms. For instance, Tokyo Daiichi's school initials were sewn onto the left sleeve of students' sailor outfit or shirt, in one of these three colours. The initials of the name of an individual student were also sewn onto either the sailor suit or the tank top/jumper, again in one of the three colours. Another important element of Japanese school uniforms that is not shown in the figures is indoor shoes (*uwabaki*).[119] At Tokyo Daiichi, everyone wore the same type of shoes: white and resembling gymnastics shoes. The only difference was that, according to one's grade, one's indoor shoes had colour stripes in one of the three colours. In addition, a common practice was that each student wrote her name on her indoor shoes for easy identification. Combining all these, one could tell with one glance exactly which grade a particular individual was in, for example, a person wearing indoor shoes with green stripes and a sailor outfit would be junior first year, whereas a person wearing indoor shoes with pink stripes and white shirt plus jumper with pink school and name initials would be senior second year.

6.5.2 Tokyo Daini Boys' Junior and Senior High School uniform: More subtle and less-nuanced markings

Tokyo Daini Boys' Junior and Senior High School followed the same standard logic of dividing the types of uniform according to junior and senior high sections, albeit with less extensive distinctions, as shown in Figures 6.5, 6.6, and 6.7.

From these three figures, it is apparent that everyone wears the black jacket with golden buttons and a tight stand-up collar in winter. However, when indoors, and especially during club activities, students usually wear only the

---

[118] These were the colour codes observed at the beginning of my fieldwork. When students from a particular grade are promoted at the beginning of a new academic year, they retain their colour code.

[119] Indoor shoes are commonly worn in Japanese schools for cleanliness purposes. Each student has a designated shoe box where outside shoes and indoor shoes can be changed. Both are part of the school uniform.

Figure 6.5: Illustrative example of boys' winter uniform. Image taken from the school's website with permission to reuse.

Figure 6.6: Illustrative example of boys' summer uniform. Image taken from the school's website with permission to reuse.

white long-sleeved shirt. It is during this time that signs of different grades become evident: the Tokyo Daini's school crest was sewn onto the shirt in two colours: red for junior high students and blue for senior high students. Unlike Tokyo Daiichi Girls' School, there was no further distinction according to specific grades, and everyone also wore the same type and colour of jumper in winter and tank top in summer. As regards footwear, junior high students wore black sneakers while senior high students wore leather shoes. The only distinction that was as fine-grained as that of Tokyo Daiichi was the sports footwear in Tokyo Daini (not in shown in the figures above). Also functioning as indoor shoes, the sports shoes had three colour codes as well to denote each of the three

Figure 6.7: Illustrative example of boys' shoes. The pair of sneakers on the left is for junior high students, whereas the pair on the right is for senior high students. Image taken from the school's website with permission to reuse.

grades in junior and senior high sections. However, during the entirety of my fieldwork, such footwear was not worn as indoor shoes because the on-going renovation works in their school compound meant that everyone (students, teachers, and construction workers) wore their normal footwear on campus.

6.5.3 Implications of such signs, symbols and objects

School uniforms with such an elaborate coding-system made identities and statuses of students instantly recognisable by downplaying any differences in physical appearance (for instance, some junior members were taller and looked more mature relative to their peers). On my first visit to each of the two schools, one of the first things that seniors and teachers in charge explained to me was how to recognise the different types of uniforms and colour codes. From a senior's perspective, the signs and symbols on uniforms provided a means of easy identification at a glance, during practice sessions. As the acting president of Tokyo Daiichi Girls' Choir explained, it proved useful in ensuring that the division of labour in the choir was observed and maintained by the members in the respective grades (refer to chapter three), as it was easy to identify juniors amidst the large groups present in the music room, and to monitor their performance (or omission) of greetings and other responsibilities. My interactions with students from different grades showed that beyond serving as a "monitoring tool" for seniors, the signs and symbols on uniforms also helped junior members to identify seniors via the relevant signs and symbols denoting their year and grade. This proved to be easier than memorising all the seniors' names and faces. Especially in the first few months after joining a club, these signs often guided junior new members in making sense of their new social life in the institutional hierarchy in clubs. For instance, as new junior first graders officially began their club activities at Tokyo Daiichi Girls' Orchestra, the club teacher in charge, Shimura, repeatedly urged them to greet all seniors eagerly, even if they did not remember their seniors' faces or names. Therefore, such signs and symbols were adopted, utilised, and accepted by both junior and senior club members of different backgrounds and statuses, as part of their social lives in clubs.

The afore-mentioned means of using signs, symbols and objects in the hierarchy of school clubs were by no means peculiar to the two schools I observed. As early as in the first stage of my fieldwork in autumn 2015, the interviewees mentioned similar types and styles of uniforms used for different grades in their experience. For instance, an interviewee who had completed her junior high education in a public school in Kyoto and was a member of the school's soft tennis club recalled the following as regards the use of tennis bags (both as an object and a part of the officially recognised school uniform for tennis club members):

> Here's another weird rule. You know those tennis bags that are shaped like a racquet? So all the tennis club members would have one of those bags, we would take it to school and put our books in there too. So the freshmen couldn't use those bags when they first joined the club, even though the bags were widely available in any major store and parents usually bought it soon after their children joined the tennis club. But freshmen couldn't carry them to school and had to wait for at least half a year. It wasn't a written rule, but a tradition on when freshmen were allowed to use it, like a status thing. Isn't it weird?[120]

Just like not every member was entitled to use chairs during lunch breaks or the whiteboard in Tokyo Daiichi Girls' Orchestra, not every member had the right to use the tennis bag in this soft tennis club in Kyoto. Objects such as chairs and tennis bags, as are signs on uniforms, become status symbols in Japanese school club activities.[121] In this regard, the ability of these signs and objects to ascribe meaning to their wearers or users and "transform" physical to social facts (that is, an individual wearing particular signs is transformed into a *senpai/kouhai*) resembles the working mechanisms of language use, which represent what people say (and by extension, do and be) and *communicate* concepts and ideas (Hall et al. 1997). These extra-linguistic elements, together with language use, play complementary roles in the broad social behaviour responsible for the discursive construction of hierarchy in Japanese school clubs.

---

120 Interview conducted on 24.10.2015.
121 Though students also wear their uniforms and use objects during non-club hours, the *communicative function* of these is absent in, say, classroom interactions without the age-based hierarchy of *jouge kankei*.

6.6 Summary of chapter

In this chapter, I first examined the relationship between discursive practice (specifically, of using honorific language to seniors and *kotobazukai*) and the spatial segregation among members of different grades. This might portray a rather strict demarcation of organisational space according to the hierarchical structure in club activities. That organisational space is hierarchical and facilitates the production and maintenance of power relations is not unfamiliar in studies focussing on such phenomena in the adult world (such as in office settings, refer to Dale and Burrell 2008; Zhang and Spicer 2014). However, specially designated and privileged spaces in Japanese school clubs are not just accessible to a select few and inaccessible to the vast majority in a strict longitudinal sense, because there will come a day when juniors become seniors and can therefore access such spaces. In addition, I have thus far illustrated in this chapter the different types and colour codes on uniforms, as well as the ways in which they facilitate the recognition of statuses along the *jouge kankei*. Such practices, together with the use of available objects to complement the manifestation of hierarchical order, are not confined to specific types of clubs or schools. These extra-linguistic features, or Discourses, form the broader framework of the discursive constitution of hierarchy because they function in conjunction with speeches and texts (discourse) to help actors of different ranks to talk the talk while walking the walk. New data presented and analysed in this chapter attest that the enactment, maintenance, and reification of *jouge kankei* in secondary school clubs involve a whole package of Discursive-discursive practices.

In the next and final chapter, I sum up key characteristics of *jouge kankei* based on my findings. To highlight some of its unique features, I also argue that, despite its hierarchical nature as we have seen, *jouge kankei* does encompass egalitarian elements. It is important for us to recognise this, lest we reject *jouge kankei* outright as completely undesirable. Lastly, I reiterate limitations of the present study and propose areas for future research in language and socialisation.

7 *Jouge kankei*: Discursive construction, characteristics, implications and future outlook

In this final and concluding chapter, I first summarise the key findings of this volume to highlight the main characteristics of *jouge kankei*, and how results of this study have answered my research questions raised in chapter one. Next, I show that, despite how *jouge kankei* could change its degree of manifestation depending on certain variables and contexts, its nature and underlying ideology remain rather consistent. On this basis, and comparing my data with existing studies, I draw parallels between *jouge kankei* in school clubs and in adult corporate contexts. Lastly, I discuss reasons for and the implications of the enduring nature of *jouge kankei* in Japanese social life, limitations of my current study, as well as future research outlook.

7.1 Summary of findings and answers to research questions

Thus far, chapters in the present book have presented and analysed the ways in which language (micro-level discourse) and para-linguistic features (macro-level Discourse) enact and constitute *jouge kankei*. The ways in which new secondary school *bukatsudou* members go through the socialisation process in order to speak and act competently in such a hierarchical order have also been examined. Therefore, the main questions I raised in chapter one can now be answered: what constitutes *jouge kankei*; when, where, and how do individuals growing up in Japan first come into contact with *jouge kankei* and learn to function in it on a large, collective scale?

Firstly, discursive practices constitute *jouge kankei* and individuals growing up in Japan are first socialised into this hierarchical inter-personal order on a collective scale from junior high school onwards, in the milieu of *bukatsudou*. To be sure, individuals are also exposed to hierarchy before this stage (see chapter one). However, the crux of the issue of language socialisation and hierarchy at the secondary school stage is that sanctions and punishments are systematically enforced by seniors on juniors who do not conform to established conventions. As this present volume has shown, the constitutive Discourse/discourse and the hierarchical order interact in complementary ways. On the one hand, discursive practices are used to enact and maintain hierarchical identities and relationships between younger and older student club members; and on the other hand, once in place, the very hierarchical structure constrains actors' (discursive) behaviour through the development of conventions and behavioural norms (chapter three). Such orientation guidelines and "ways of thinking" (Gee 2014: 222) about the social world, in the form of club rules (macro-level Discourse), are interpreted by club seniors and teachers in charge and taught to each cohort of junior new members upon gaining entry into a junior high school club. This helps the latter make sense of the new social environment and adjust their comportment. As a result, although *jouge kankei* is discursively constituted in interactions, it remains stable and enduring, for it constrains and regulates actors' interactional behaviour, and is transmitted from one generation to the next.

In everyday club life, seniors and juniors use a variety of macro- and micro-level Discourse/discourse in different ways to constitute the hierarchy. For instance, my findings reveal that, while juniors have the obligation to use honorifics and designated address terms to address their seniors, seniors are at liberty to use any style of talk they wish, and enjoy exclusive privileges such as priority access to space, objects, as well as the use of signs and symbols by virtue of their *senpai* status. In addition, while there have been attempts by actors to change the behavioural norms of *jouge kankei* through modifying the discursive rules, these have been unsuccessful, with those who initiated such a change being collectively reprimanded by the club leadership for breaking the club atmosphere. Furthermore, the extent to which ToA conventions in school clubs remained rigid and were upheld without exception deterred even siblings from joining the same club, out of the uneasiness of having to address and talk to one's own elder sibling in strictly regimented manners. This stands in stark contrast to Western ToA and social practices where the degree of familiarity among interlocutors would facilitate a shift from formal to informal address terms (chapter four). From this, we can not only witness the endurance of the discursively constructed *jouge kankei* in social life in secondary school clubs, but also its rigidity and the impossibility of a transition once discursive norms are established.

The research findings underscore that individuals' knowledge of conventions and norms of *jouge kankei* is not innate, meaning that one must be socialised to fit in; there has to be moments in one's life where one is exposed to it and acquires sufficient knowledge to function competently in it. Further data presented in chapters five and six suggest that, in secondary school extra-curricular clubs, students get exposed to and are linguistically and discursively (forms of talk, word choices, using signs and symbols) socialised into *jouge kankei* on a large, collective scale. This is reinforced by the fact that, prior to junior high school, interactions between two people of different age status do not assume the same consequences, nor are they bound by the behavioural norms and regulations as outlined in this volume. This explains why club experiences in junior and senior high schools are qualitatively different from those in primary schools.

Hence, the core of this language socialisation process is to impart an objectivised common-sense knowledge that a difference in age cohort has implications in everyday interpersonal relations. New members are expected to acquire, in as timely a fashion as possible, a series of discursive practices (both linguistic and paralinguistic; i.e. "Discourse" and "discourse") necessary to speak and act as competent actors in the club *jouge kankei*. In addition, so long as an individual has not yet reached the apex of power, that is, the most senior grade in her/his club, s/he can be reprimanded by club seniors should her/his comportment deviate from established norms. The repeated use of discursive practices (specialised ToA vocabulary, forms of talk, and extra-linguistic features) to enact *jouge kankei* and to transmit it to each generation of new incoming junior club members further legitimises and strengthens its structure. Learning to be a part of this hierarchical order is in turn seen by an overwhelming majority of students, teachers, parents, and even employers as legitimate and a necessary step in an individual's educational path towards competent adulthood. Hence, secondary school club members' experience in *jouge kankei* accompany them well beyond the confines of their school clubs and into the adult (corporate) world (Lee-Cunin 2004). This also reaffirms my claim at the beginning of this volume that secondary school club activities are anything but "extra", since it represents an important milieu where individuals are socialised into the *jouge kankei* style of communication and behaviour prevalent in the adult world.

7.2 Implications across time and space in secondary school *bukatsudou*

What do the afore-mentioned findings imply? Are there factors that affect how *jouge kankei* manifests itself across time and space? Based on my research findings, we could consider the extent to which time and space factors affect the degree of *jouge kankei* manifestation in group dynamics. Varying degrees of manifestation here refer to both: (i) variation from one club to another (space), and (ii) changes within a single club such as when a new cohort of leading *senpai* reaches the highest grade (time). This represents a summary of observations and findings from the three school clubs where I conducted my data collection (for details see chapter four section 4.3.1.). Evidence from these three clubs should, of course, not be used to over-generalise on *jouge kankei*. However, I contend in the following section that certain aspects of the nature of *jouge kankei* do seem to be largely present in most urban school settings, as corroborated by existing quantitative survey results.

First and foremost, informants recognised that the relative strictness (*kibishisa*) of hierarchical interpersonal relations could depend on what a club sets out to achieve, that is, its ambitions (for instance, the desire to be in the national finals every year). As the main teacher in charge in Tokyo Daiichi Choir explained, there was a constant need to maintain the strictest of rules and clearly demarcated roles, duties and expectations on behaviour in her club because "our club gets into the national finals every year and we aim to be Japan's top school choir" (refer to chapter four, section 4.2). In the eyes of the teachers and senior club members in Tokyo Daiichi Choir, the goal of maintaining the club's prestige and competitiveness on a national level translated into the strictest possible observance of the codes of discursive conduct (ToA, honorifics, the use of space and objects) on the part of juniors. This is to ensure that they maintain a clear understanding of the different statuses and duties. During my fieldwork, it was apparent that juniors were constantly reminded of their assigned roles and duties (by seniors), which they could then fulfil without confusion or complacency. It should be noted, however, that this is not peculiar to *jouge kankei* in Japan. It has been acknowledged in management and organisational studies in non-Japanese contexts that there exists a functional and efficiency aspect to hierarchy, since clearly defined roles and responsibilities allow people to focus on carrying out their required tasks and assigned duties (Diefenbach 2013).

The second factor held to influence the degree of *jouge kankei* was the leadership style, or desire, of senior club leaders. As evidenced in the data, secondary school club leadership changes every year with the automatic promotion of an entire cohort to the most senior grade, upon the graduation of their immediate seniors. My data have demonstrated that, more often than not, newly promoted senior club leaders did not have the exact same vision as their predecessors concerning what would constitute an ideal *funiki* (ambience) as regards *senpai-kouhai* relations in their clubs. Therefore, new leaders occasionally attempted, within a rather limited framework for manoeuvre, to "tighten" or "loosen up" the hierarchical order and ways of doing things as established by the outgoing cohort of seniors (refer to chapter four, section 4.3).

Thirdly, gender plays a role as well. In effect, because of the dearth of scholarship on this topic and the lack of attention to questions of gender as regards *jouge kankei* in school settings, my only clue prior to my fieldwork was the NINJAL survey in 2002. As my discussions of the NINJAL (2002) survey results in chapter two revealed, it is thought that girls might be more careful in their speech, and behave in a more respectful manner in secondary school *bukatsudou*. Reflecting upon my fieldwork experience and data gathered, differences across general gender lines indeed emerged, and were based on language use and the use of paralinguistic signs and symbols. It transpired that girls' groups usually tend to have a finer hierarchical order which makes more status distinctions and more complex interpersonal relations across age cohorts. Contrary to the situation in Tokyo Daiini Boys' Orchestra, in girls' groups of Tokyo Daiichi, a difference in *every* grade matters, with appropriate behavioural norms strictly in place. The data show that girls were more creative and employed a much wider range of ToA (refer to chapter four). Such a distinction has also been corroborated by data in this volume. Compared to Tokyo Daini Boys' Orchestra, the two clubs in Tokyo Daiichi Girls' Junior and Senior High school's more complex ToA practices and the more fine-grained distinction in the use of symbols, signs, and space presented new junior members with not only an hierarchical order that is at least as strict as that in Tokyo Daini Boys' Orchestra, but one that was also in many ways organisationally more sophisticated.

Having made the afore-mentioned observations notwithstanding, there is a need to recognise that such discursive differences in girls' and boys' groups have not been found to fundamentally differ in *nature*, insofar as using them to enact hierarchy in secondary school clubs is concerned. Moreover, there are also differences within the gender group. For instance, members of the clarinet section in Tokyo Daini Boys' Orchestra employed a wider range of ToA than other sections (refer to chapter five). Hence, while more research is needed to come to a comprehensive conclusion with regard to the importance of gender, it would also seem more appropriate to consider specific group dynamics and contexts in addition to macro categories such as gender.

According to the informants and my participant observations, all these factors enumerated above could slightly alter the extent to which *jouge kankei* is manifested in a club, for instance, in the case where seniors preferred to enforce some rules less strictly to create a more "relaxed" environment. The aim of this book is not to over-generalise on the phenomenon of *jouge kankei* in *bukatsudou*, because *jouge kankei* could well work differently in different school and club settings as outlined above. However, extant survey results on language use, hierarchy and inter-personal relations, such as the comprehensive and nation-wide NINJAL 2002 survey (see chapter two), do suggest that the basic mechanisms of *jouge kankei* (power and hierarchy between *senpai* and *kouhai*) and their discursive constitution via honorifics exist in most types of schools and clubs across the country. Therefore, the focus of this volume is rather to show the relatively common *nature* of *jouge kankei* as constituted, maintained, and transmitted by discursive practices. As an interviewee succinctly revealed, upon becoming the most senior grade in her club, even when her cohort wanted to reduce the extent of hierarchy to the flattest possible level, there still had to be some "bottom line principles" such as appropriate ToA, language use to seniors, greetings and salutations (refer to chapter four). These, as it transpires, are the central tenets of the discursive practices that constitute and sustain the very *jouge kankei*, and this nature remains constant in both time and space, viz. largely unaffected by the handover of power or individual schools/cities. Hence, although *jouge kankei* works differently in different school and club contexts (due to size, ambition, urban-rural location, leadership change), the difference pertains more to a question of degree than nature.

7.2.1 Further implications on the connection of *jouge kankei* between secondary school and adult contexts

A further question is: what do the above-mentioned findings of my research on *jouge kankei* mean beyond the confines of secondary school clubs? Based on my fieldwork data and existing research on language socialisation and hierarchy in the adult world, I contend that a clear connection between *jouge kankei* in secondary school *bukatsudou* and in adult life exists. This is manifested in two ways, (i) how secondary school *bukatsudou* alumni remain implicated in their club *jouge kankei* years or decades after graduation, and (ii) the similar nature of language socialisation for new company recruits in corporate Japan.

As regards how secondary school alumni continue to be involved in their club *jouge kankei*, Shimura, one of the teachers in charge of Tokyo Daiichi Orchestra, recounted his very own experience:

> I am very active in music-making. So not only do I enjoy my supervision duties here at Tokyo Daiichi Orchestra, I also go back regularly to my former senior high school orchestra to play and help out. An instance I still fondly remember happened a few years ago when I was at the summer camp, training my *kouhai* for their competition. One evening I received a call from home, my grandfather just passed away. I really wanted to go back home on that day, but we were in a rather remote place and there was no longer bus service to the nearest train station. Well, even if there were any, I would have to first catch a train back to Tokyo and then see how I could go from there. So a *senpai* of mine who used to coach me in high school, and who was also there at the camp, offered to drive me home. He ended up driving several hundred kilometres from our camp location to my home and then back again. At that moment I felt he was truly a *senpai* on which I could rely and count, and was so grateful we had met in this orchestra during our school days.[122]

In the case of Mr Shimura, it shows that the *jouge kankei* forged during secondary school club years continues to adult life, even decades after graduation.

---

[122] Interview conducted on 20.02.2018.

7.2 Implications across time and space in secondary school *bukatsudou* — 179

Since this particular senior used to be Shimura's *senpai* during their school days, he continued to see himself as such. Hence, when his junior, Shimura, was in need of help, he offered a helping hand as a senior. This resembles what I observed in Tokyo Daini Orchestra, where one alumnus who was already in university went back to Tokyo Daini Orchestra not only to coach his juniors, but also to organise for and bring them to a round of *yakiniku*[123] in an outside restaurant, in the capacity of their *senpai* and an adult (refer to vignette 4.1 in chapter four).

In effect, this is also the case in all clubs where I conducted my fieldwork. In all cases, alumni members regularly returned to their secondary school *bukatsudou* to continue to perform their function as a "*dai senpai*" (big *senpai*). These came in the forms of coaching juniors during annual summer training camps, running errands during annual concerts (when all active student members were busy performing on stage), or even training new junior high first graders in both etiquette and music-making. As a result, current club members treat these *dai senpai* with utmost respect in terms of Discursive-discursive behaviour. In the process, people who are socialised into their secondary school club *jouge kankei* and who remain implicated in it years after graduation cultivate a sense of duty and character that are sought after by potential employers. The following section will show similarities between *jouge kankei* experience in secondary school clubs and socialisation training in the adult corporate world. In a way, the nature of *jouge kankei* and socialisation processes continue into adult life.

Secondly, comparing my data with existing research findings on language socialisation and hierarchy in adult society, we could discern the similar nature of *jouge kankei* socialisation and ideology. It is widely acknowledged that in corporate Japan, new employees are expected to master business manners, etiquettes, as well as rules and conventions governing corporate social interactions. A common channel through which new recruits familiarise themselves with these is training seminars/orientation workshops, either organised and conducted by firms themselves, or outsourced to specialised workforce development training companies who conduct such seminars (Cook 2018; Dunn 2011). In effect, as one emeritus professor of education, who is currently a career guidance counsellor in a university in Western Japan, put it, "it is natural for medium-sized and large companies to provide on-the-job orientations so that new recruits master the etiquettes, know their place in their team, and cultivate loyalty to the company, the companies have this *duty* to complement graduates' education in this way" (emphases added).[124] Teaching contents in

---

123 Japanese grilled meat, see chapter four section 4.1.
124 Interview (supplementary) conducted on 26.11.2018.

these seminars/orientation sessions may vary from one case to another, but several key topics in business manners are common to all: honorifics, language skills (*kotobazukai*), bodily postures and movements in diverse situations, as well as personal attire and appearance (Dunn 2011; Wetzel and Inoue 1999). Just like in secondary school *bukatsudou*, the significance of this type of training lies as much on the ideological level (of what the social world of corporate relations should be) as it is on the technical level (of personal skills and behaviours). For instance, Dunn (2011) observed that, in such seminars:

> [S]pecific forms of linguistic behavior are constructed as normative ideals. Honorific language is presented in the training courses as part of a larger semiotic system of polite behaviors including both extra-linguistic forms, such as dress and posture [what I classified in this book as Discourse], and many of the verbal politeness strategies [what I classified in this book as discourse] [. . .] [V]erbal strategies as well as honorific use are presented in the training as a matter of conformity to the social conventions of the business world. (Dunn 2011: 3644)

In effect, what new employees are learning is to first and foremost be able to recognise indexical (and hierarchical) relations in and through language use and paralinguistic elements. From the perspective of language socialisation, extant research posits that there is a significant "break" between school and work life in Japan. This reflects the change of status for an individual who turns from a *gakusei* (student) to a *shakaijin* (literally "society/social person", i.e. full member of society) following graduation and entrance into the workforce. For example, Dunn (2011) claims that:

> In Japan, the shift from being a student to entering full-time employment is seen as a major life transition in which young adults take on new roles as *shakaijin*, contributing, adult 'members of society.' A major part of this transition involves shifts in their self-presentation and language use, particularly in developing their skills in the more formal, honorific registers of Japanese. (Dunn 2011: 3644)

However, data of this present study highlight that, insofar as the importance of self-representations, language use, honorifics, and formal speech in groups where unequal (power) dynamics are at play are concerned, similarities abound between secondary school *bukatsudou* and corporate world contexts. While such company trainings are no doubt occasions to help individuals refine their skills in honorifics and language use, secondary school graduates who have gone through *jouge kankei* socialisation in *bukatsudou* would have already been exposed to this hierarchy. A comparison of actual teaching contents of secondary school clubs' training of new club members and firms' new recruit training reveals significant parallels. The following comparisons between language socialisation trainings in secondary school *bukatsudou* and in adult corporate settings are made on two levels: (i) macro-level rhetoric on the importance and goals of such socialisation trainings, and (ii) typical training contents. Data concerning language and discursive socialisations in secondary school club contexts originate from my own fieldwork. As regards the situation in the adult corporate society, the main source of reference is Dunn's (2011) comprehensive and detailed study.

Table 7.1 below illustrates the macro-level rhetoric on the importance and goals of language socialisation trainings in both school clubs and adult company settings:

Table 7.1: Trainers' perspectives on teaching contents and goals in language and discursive socialisation.

Trainers' goals and perspectives	Secondary school clubs*	Companies+
Importance of (verbal) manners (regardless of the nature of activity)	– "[A]s a human being, because we are in an extra-curricular club activity, we have to learn some basic social manners. In a club, everything starts with manners." (Tokyo Daiichi Orchestra's teacher in charge Shimura)	– "Instructors in the courses emphasized that their goal was to teach *kihon no manā* which may be translated as either 'basic manners' or 'standard manners'." (Dunn 2011: 3651)
Importance of extra-linguistic skills and feelings to complement communication	– Show consideration for interlocutors, put yourself in their shoes, show sincerity and honesty (*sunaosa*) in communications (Tokyo Daini Orchestra Manners Guidebook)	– "One instructor said . . . 'even if you make mistakes in honorific use, if you speak very cheerfully and um clearly and precisely, speaking kindly and showing consideration for the listener, then that is more likely to make people like you.'" (Dunn 2011: 3646)

*Data gathered during my fieldwork.
+Cited from Dunn (2011).

From Table 7.1, we clearly see that the underlying rhetoric in both secondary school and company training sessions, irrespective of the nature of work concerned, are essentially the same: the *importance of basic manners*, as well as the necessity to *transmit sincere feelings and honesty in bright and cheerful ways* to interlocutors during communication processes. If the emphasis on basic, standard manners are ubiquitous, what, then, constitute such manners in school clubs and corporate settings respectively? Table 7.2 below offers important clues:

Table 7.2: Typical teaching contents in school clubs and companies. *Data gathered during my fieldwork.

	Secondary school clubs*	Companies+
Focal areas of training	– Personal appearance/how to wear uniform – Vocal expression – Bodily movement – Honorifics and *kotobazukai* – Seating priority (as part of the rules of using space)	– Personal appearance/body etiquette/business attire – Facial and vocal expression – Bodily movement – Honorifics and *kotobazukai* – Seating priority – Telephone manners – Exchanging business cards
Specific examples	– When you refer to yourself, use the first-person pronoun of "*watakushi*" – When apologising, do not use "*gomennasai/gomenkudasai*", but "*sumimasen*" – Greetings (*aisatsu*) and responses (*henji*) to seniors have to be clear, loud, and bright (*akarui*) – School uniform should be ironed, tucked in to trousers, coats buttoned all the way in the presence of seniors, hair must be properly trimmed – Training in bowing posture and timing in front of seniors – Training in how to stand and sit properly when seniors talk – Training in the use of space according to seniority: who stands where during debriefing, or who sits where during lunch/meetings when different cohorts are present	– For self-reference, "*watakushi*" is the desirable form and "*watashi*" the undesirable form – "*Moshiwake gozaimasen*" is the preferred form of apology rather than "*gomenkudasai/sumimasen*" – Recruits are trained to use higher than normal pitch for greetings and to respond with loud and prompt "*hai!*" when called by superiors – Body etiquettes as regards properly trimmed hair, ironed clothes, polished shoes – Training in bowing posture, timing, and correct angle – Training in determining correct seating order in conference room, taxi, etc

+Cited from Dunn (2011).

We could clearly see overwhelming similarities and overlaps in terms of the *nature* of language socialisation and focus areas in both school clubs and the corporate world. In some cases, the corporate context represents a step up and also more comprehensive in terms of coverage. This is manifested, for example, by the fact that while in school clubs the term "*sumimasen*" would have sufficed when making an apology to seniors and/or in formal situations, in the corporate context new recruits were taught that "*moshiwakegozaimasen*" would be preferred to "*sumimasen*". In addition, while each new cohort of junior club members learn the seating and standing priority and arrangements according to status in school clubs, new company recruits not only learn this, but also how to identify correct seating order "outside", that is, in taxis, conferences, and so on. Such a more refined and comprehensive training approach is only natural, given the fuller range of activities in which adults in the corporate world are expected to partake, as compared to secondary school students in *bukatsudou*. However, when it comes to the crucial point of language socialisation and the ideologies behind honorifics, *kotobazukai*, and extra-linguistic elements (such as the ideology of subordination and discernment to superiors and group cohesion), the vast majority of individuals who have accumulated club experiences would have already been exposed to the same *rationale* of such socialisation. To put it differently, students who have been in a *bukatsudou* in secondary schools have been exposed to the very same logics of basic manners and etiquette training in companies during their school club stint. *Jouge kankei* socialisation in school clubs, in this sense, provides a socialisation link between school and work.

Moreover, the nature and characteristics of language socialisation and the discursive construction of *jouge kankei* in secondary school *bukatsudou* are not confined to the three clubs where I conducted my fieldwork. As I mentioned in chapter two, results of the large-scale national survey on *Honorifics in Junior and Senior High Schools* (NINJAL 2002) study show that social norms and expectations on club members (from as young as junior high first grade) as regards a calibrated speech (*kotobazukai*) and the use of honorifics are indeed common across the country. Therefore, what I highlighted here with regard to the *nature* of language socialisation and discursive constitution of *jouge kankei* and its related ideology is not confined to the three clubs I observed, but rather applicable nation-wide. Comparing existing quantitative data on the use of honorifics in secondary schools and the findings in this book, there seems to be little variation in the past 25 or so years, at least insofar as secondary school club students' speech styles are concerned: the importance to speak well and the mastery of honorifics. Since secondary schools train competent adults for the society, we could in turn assume that society's general expectations on how a competent adult should speak and behave (and by extension, recognise hierarchy and fit her/himself in) have largely remained constant. Indeed, numerous studies on company-based new *shakaijin* trainings (Cook 2018; Dunn 2011; Shire 1999) attest to the fact that the discursively constituted *jouge kankei* in secondary school *bukatsudou* as presented in this book exist by and large in a basically similar nature in the adult corporate world in Japan.

This volume therefore complements extant research on language socialisation and hierarchy in Japan by filling in the gap on what happens in secondary school *bukatsudou*, a hitherto less researched milieu, as well as revealing the seamless flow of language socialisation from adolescent to adult years.

7.3 Limitations, suggestions, and outlook

This book has sought to shed light on the language socialisation process of secondary school students into the *jouge kankei* hierarchy in Japan, as well as the constitutive elements of such a hierarchy (both Discourse and discourse elements). I have hence filled a lacuna in Japanese language socialisation research on how educational contexts in schools mould adolescents into competent "social adults" (*shakaijin*) (Cook 2008). In this final section of the book, I discuss limitations of the present study and suggestions for future research, the enduring nature of *jouge kankei* in Japanese social life, as well as its outlook in Japanese social dynamics.

In my attempt to address the questions laid out in chapter one as best as possible, decisions were made along the way, especially before and during my fieldwork, which meant certain things must be forgone. This brought about limitations. In particular, my choice of single-sex club settings meant the impossibility to observe mixed gender interactions within the framework of club hierarchy.[125] However, as this book represents the first study that examines the nature of the discursive constitution of *jouge kankei* and secondary school club students' socialisation process into it, it is more important to find a conducive environment to analyse the nature and characteristics of *jouge kankei*. As I explicated in chapter two and showed throughout this work, such research goals could be best achieved in a six-year club environment. Since six-year club settings are usually only found in single-sex schools, I opted for such a choice. Having answered the research questions, my main research goal has been

---

125 Note, however, that conducting research in a co-educational school club does not automatically and necessarily guarantee a balanced gender mix. Refer to Blackwood (2016) and Hebert (2012) for an overview of how the choice of clubs are clearly divided along gender lines in co-educational schools.

achieved. This in turn demonstrates that, as long as it is a six-year environment, the benefits of studying single-sex club settings outweigh those of mixed club settings inasmuch as this topic of inquiry is concerned. On this foundation, future research could explore similarities and differences in the degree of manifestation or discursive constitution of *jouge kankei* in single-sex and mixed school club settings. In addition, comparative studies of the discursive socialisation of students into *jouge kankei* in *bukatsudou* in urban and rural schools would also be a welcomed addition to the current research agenda.

As we have witnessed from numerous empirical examples and analyses throughout this book, the discursively enacted *jouge kankei* hierarchical order entails power asymmetries, as well as the concomitant and extensive rights and entitlements of superiors (*senpai*) over subordinates (*kouhai*). In fact, in the club context, seniors' rights and powers to enforce rules and regulations, often codified in guidebooks, are so extensive that they create the risk of abuse of power. For instance, the teacher in charge of Tokyo Daiichi Orchestra, Shimura, once showed me anonymised school and club evaluation surveys by parents. Understandably, one sees parents of junior high first and second graders (that is, those occupying the lowest ranks along the age-based hierarchical structure) expressing the opinion that *jouge kankei* in the school's clubs was "strict and feudal", as well as the fact that their children were often deprived of time to consume their *bento* lunch during club activities. This was in addition to the ways in which senior club members could reprimand and physically punish juniors at will for any failure to comply with regulations. We cannot but ask, how can such a social structure proliferate across time and space? Why is it that this kind of power asymmetry represents such an enduring feature of Japanese social life from the very early stages of primary socialisation to adulthood? To have a better grasp of this, we have to examine the other side of the hierarchical coin: that juniors have rights and entitlements and seniors have obligations and responsibilities, too. Indeed, despite being occasionally feudalistic in a sense, *jouge kankei* in itself is not about repression and exploitation on the part of seniors, but rather creating and maintaining a harmonised and predictable social order, in which the "less powerful" actors can be progressively empowered. In this sense, what is built in is the *risk* of abuse of power, but not actual abuse itself. Furthermore, for juniors, being implicated in *jouge kankei* does not only constrain behaviour by requiring obedience to seniors and respecting the numerous linguistic codes of conduct, but also serves to enable them in various ways. This is most clearly and concretely manifested in the system of supervision in club activities, whereby it is a *senpai*'s responsibility to teach her/his *kouhai* both the activity in question (e.g. playing an instrument or type of sport) and etiquettes that would transform the *kouhai* into a more competent and accepted member of the social group.

Besides having the right and being able to achieve social growth, juniors who are implicated in *jouge kankei* know that as one ages, one's rank, status, opportunities and life chances increase as well, in tandem with the status transition from subordinate to superior. Under this system, there is no "selection process" in which only the "very few" would become the ultimate seniors of a group. This is because, once a particular age cohort reaches the top, its members will collectively assume the *senpai* status,[126] hence shoulder responsibilities, enjoy privileges and prerogatives as a group, as I have illustrated throughout this book. In other words, in secondary school clubs, everyone involved in *jouge kankei* can, and will, arrive at the top of the hierarchical ladder. Hence, contrary to what it may ostensibly seem to be at first sight, *jouge kankei* is predicated upon the *principle of egalitarianism*,[127] where every person has her/his chance to advance, if we consider an individual's entire tenure in the club. This renders one's future prospects certain and allows one to know what prerogatives one could expect with certainty, as one moves up the pecking order with age. For a large majority of individuals hence socialised, it would seem more bearable, and indeed attractive, to remain in this hierarchical order even when one's position is low, hence the durability of *jouge kankei*. In other words, *jouge kankei* is about risk aversion, if we understand risk as uncertainties.

This highlights an important implication of the consequences of continued language socialisation of secondary school students into the *jouge kankei* ideology and practice. In recent years in corporate Japan, there have been attempts to do away (at least partially and incrementally) with *jouge kankei*. In the most concrete sense, companies have aimed to emphasise more on employees' performance, rather than experience (tied to the length of service – seniority in the firm), in promotion and wage determination. At the core of the issue is the challenge to the long-held rationale that age equals experience and corresponding entitlements/rewards as predicated by principles of *jouge kankei*. A relatively

---

126 Bearing in mind that the *senpai* status is all that matters as regards prerogatives and how juniors should treat them. Administrative roles (such as president, student conductor, etc) have little, if any impact on a *senpai*'s prerogatives, nor on the discursive constitution of hierarchy between a junior and a senior. Refer to chapter two.

127 With Japan ranked 115 out of 153 countries on "economic participation and opportunity" for women in the 2020 Global Gender Gap Report (World Economic Forum 2020), it could be argued that the egalitarian element of *jouge kankei* in adult corporate Japan extends mainly to men. This is also of concern for future social research.

new phenomenon in the past decade without much traction, there has correspondingly not been extensive empirical research in the sociology of organisations and management studies on the trends and actual practices of attempts to move from seniority to performance-based remuneration and promotion. There have been, however, some initial exploratory surveys conducted, which revealed that most companies were either lukewarm towards this change or found it difficult to implement in a sustainable way (Firkola 2006). From the perspective of this book, we could argue that such reforms aimed to change the quintessence of the very social world into which each generation of school graduates have been discursively and culturally socialised. The consequence in the corporate world is similar to that in a secondary school *bukatsudou* (whose main aim is to prepare students for adult life): predictability of actions, social and group coherence, and a fit in the conventional *Weltanschauung* of finding one's place in group hierarchy and behaving according to unwritten rules. For instance, with seniority firmly in place, firms do not have to worry about losing human capital and extra spending to retrain new recruits. Employees, in turn, do not have to worry about "unnecessary" competition with colleagues for pay rise/promotion (Firkola 2006: 121). The purpose of this book is not to evaluate the benefits and disadvantages of seniority-based and performance-based systems in corporate Japan. However, if reforms to the deep-rooted seniority-based system in the corporate society were to achieve meaningful results, it would perhaps be wiser to start the reform in the education sector; more precisely, in the ways in which students in secondary school clubs, or in even earlier stages, are socialised to make sense of a seniority-based social order. Furthermore, it is beyond the scope of this study to examine and compare how do students without *bukatsudou* experience deal with *jouge kankei* and its discursive constitution (both linguistic and extra-linguistic) in interpersonal relations in adult life. Do these people find it more difficult adjusting in the workplace? Where do they acquire social knowledge and where do they get the *jouge kankei* socialisation from? How do they acquire such social capital? The present volume has highlighted how secondary school *bukatsudou* acts as one of the important factors contributing to the socialisation of Japanese students who are club members into *jouge kankei*. Future research could also examine how non-club members acquire such social skills and knowledge, especially during the critical adolescent years of growing up.

 A thorough understanding of how individuals are socialised into this hierarchical order, as well as what elements constitute it, would be essential in comprehending how these very individuals think and behave in the adult world. In addition, besides examining the enculturation process of Japanese youths through such discursive socialisation, future scholarship should also put adequate emphasis on the *acculturation* process into the words and deeds of *jouge kankei* of people from non-Japanese language and cultural backgrounds. Namely, the challenges and unique circumstances and social dynamics in which migrants and their offspring learn to speak the language of *jouge kankei*, be a competent member, and make sense in this hierarchical social order both in school and at work. This would be of continued topical interest, especially given the changing demographic and social fabric of an increasingly diverse Japanese society.

Appendix 1: Junior High School Curriculum Guidelines, Published by the Ministry of Education, Culture, Sports, Science and Technology (MEXT)

Translated sections of the relevant guidelines cited in this book can be found below (emphases added):

Subject	Grade	Section	Guidelines
Japanese	2	Traditional aspects and special characteristics of the national language	– On matters related to rules and characteristics of the language – Students should *understand* the difference between spoken and written language, the roles fulfilled by the common language and dialects, and *the functions of honorifics*
	3	Teaching contents	– On nurturing students' speaking and listening abilities – To use honorifics appropriately according to interaction situations and the state of interlocutors
		Traditional aspects and special characteristics of the national language	– On matters related to rules and characteristics of the language – Together with the understanding of diachronic changes of language and the differences across generations, *students should appropriately use honorifics in their social life*

(continued)

Subject	Grade	Section	Guidelines
Health and Physical Education	1 and 2	Sports theory	– On the ability to understand the importance and effects of sports – Through exercising and doing sports, students can expect effects that raise their social abilities, such as reaching mutual agreements on rules and manners, as well as building appropriate interpersonal relations
Social Studies	1, 2 and 3	Goals of civic education	– To raise students' awareness necessary for the carrying out of the sovereignty of the people as citizens, such as the importance of respecting individual dignity and human rights
Moral Education	1, 2 and 3	Teaching contents	– On matters related to relations with others – Students should understand the importance of manners, and use appropriate words and deeds (*gendou*) that correspond to cases and occasions

The guidelines can be consulted and downloaded here: http://www.mext.go.jp/a_menu/shotou/new-cs/youryou/chu/ (Last accessed on 21.05.2019)

Appendix 2: Guidelines for codes of conduct in extra-curricular club

As mentioned in this volume, guidebooks outlining the codes of conduct expected of members constitute a common practice in secondary school clubs in Japan, and they existed in all the three clubs where I conducted my fieldwork. Two of the clubs, Tokyo Daiichi Girls' Orchestra and Tokyo Daini Boys' Orchestra, agreed to my publishing the contents of their guidebooks for research purposes. To the best of my knowledge, this is the first instance where a researcher examining language use, hierarchy and socialisation in Japanese schools analysed and presented such materials. I believe these materials will benefit future research and I offer their translated and modified versions here. Important terms in Japanese – those that connect to the discussion in this volume – are given in parenthesis. Slight modifications had to be made so that information that could reveal the schools' real identities is removed. In addition, as these are lengthy documents covering a wide range of issues, only sections pertaining to codes of conduct guiding behaviour in *jouge kankei* are presented. All sections in bold represent original emphasis. All translations are mine.

Guidebook 1: Tokyo Daiichi Girls' Orchestra (2016): Guide to the Orchestra – Rules and regulations (*busoku to kokoroe*)

Club regulations [Section 1 omitted]

Section 2. Everything starts with manners
To produce good music and performance, manners are of utmost importance. One must be clearly aware of the interpersonal relations. **The initiation of interpersonal relations begins with manners, the first step of which is greetings** (*aisatsu*). **If you greet and reply in a clear way, just like when you perform in a clear way, you will be able to express yourself better and get your message across to your interlocutors**. As a performer and as a person, try to reflect on your normal behaviour and put more importance on manners:
– Am I capable of greeting teachers and seniors clearly?
– Are my greetings becoming hollow, without emotions?

- Other than seniors and teachers of my club, am I capable of greeting others such as visitors?
- Am I capable of replying (*henji*)?

A positive club atmosphere is built by your everyday measures, especially manners like greetings. If your greetings are cheerful and bright, so will the club atmosphere. **Please remember that you are responsible for the right atmosphere in your club.**

Section 3. The value and importance of obedience

Please accept advice from teachers and seniors without objecting. Please strive to become capable of apologising immediately by saying "*gomennasai*" and "*sumimasen*" when you think you are at fault. **People with such gentle and obedient characters not only become good players of music, but are also trustworthy.**

Section 4. Thinking about others' standpoint

If you are not capable of thinking about your partners' standpoint, you cannot do it the right way in building interpersonal relations or in performing. To think that it is alright to do what you like just because of your status as a senior or teacher or having superior musical skills is absolutely not accepted.

Guidebook 2: Tokyo Daini Boys' Orchestra: Four etiquettes of the music club

[Note: here we can see that even in sections not directly related to speech behaviour, the regulations touch upon how members should behave and outline normative expectations of language use (to guide members to "talk the talk while walking the walk")

Section 1. Instruments, music scores, and music stands are the treasures of the club

- When carrying instruments and music stands, carry them properly and be sure not to throw them around.

- Always keep your music scores organised in such a way that, whenever you are told "take out the music score for . . . (title of music)", you could immediately find it and take it out.
- Before you leave your seat, remove your music score from the music stand. If you are using a foldable music stand, fold up the top part of the stand before leaving your seat.

Section 2. Regarding the saying of "shitsureishimasu" (excuse me) while walking past seniors
- When walking past seniors, alumni, external instructors, and teachers in charge, give a slight bow and say "*shitsureishimasu*".

Section 3. Proper ways of sitting
- Place your shoes 45 degrees in front of you to your right, clench your fists with the four fingers wrapping your two thumbs on each hand, and place your hands on your thighs.
- Do not sit with your knee drawn up.
- When a senior says "*kuzushitemoiiyo*" (you may empty saliva from your instrument), reply with "*shitsureishimasu*", empty any waste from your instrument quickly, and return to the original sitting position.
- The proper way of sitting also means that you must lower your head and close your eyes while seated.

Section 4. Proper ways to raise your hand
- When raising your hand, raise your right arm, be sure to straighten your elbow and raise your right arm straight up behind your right ear.
- Do not lower your arm before a senior tells you to do so.

[Note: the title and the content page of the guidebook imply that there are only four sections as mentioned above, but the list of regulations continues from here. In fact, the rules above represent only two and a half out of 11 pages of rules in total]

Miscellaneous matters
- When you enter the music room, be sure to say "*chiwa*" (truncated form of konnichiwa, which means "good day") loudly. In addition, say "*chiwa*"

loudly to seniors, alumni, club supporters, external instructors, and teachers in charge whenever you meet them.
- When you leave at the end of a practice session, be sure to say *"sausu"* (this term has no particular meaning). Above all, be sure to say *"sausu"* when seniors, alumni, external instructors or teachers in charge leave.
- When seniors, alumni, external instructors or teachers in charge come to direct a practice session, be sure to button your shirt and coat all the way, and say *"renshuuonegaishimasu"* (roughly translated as "we would like to start the practice"). At the end of the session, say *"renshuuarigatougozaimashita"* (thank you for the practice).
- When seniors, alumni, external instructors or teachers in charge ask you to do something, be sure to stop whatever you are doing at the moment immediately, and proceed to do what has been instructed to you.
- When seniors, alumni, external instructors or teachers in charge are carrying things, be sure to approach them, say *"kawarimasu"* (I shall take over) and take over whatever they are carrying.
- When seniors, alumni, external instructors or teachers in charge called for you, be sure to approach them quickly.
- Before entering the recording studio or the music teachers' room, first check that you are in proper attire (all buttons buttoned up, school badge in place, nothing in your pocket). Then, knock the door and say *"shitsureishimasu"* (excuse me) before walking in. Before walking out, be sure to say *"shitsureishimashita"*.
- When you turn up late for practice, be sure to communicate your presence. If it is during a combined rehearsal, report to the conductor. If not, report to the club president, the in-charge for attendance, or your section's leader.
- If you were absent for or left the practice early, be sure to report it during your next practice. When you name is called during attendance taking, answer with *"hai"*, get up from the chair, stand straight, and put your hands behind your back, and say *"kinou wa . . . no tame kurabukenseki/chikokushimashita. Doumo sumimasendeshita"* (Because of . . . (reason), I was absent/left early yesterday. Please excuse me).
- If you were late for the day's practice, report it during attendance taking before the daily debriefing session. Follow the above-mentioned procedures (what to say and how to say it).
- In addition, if you were absent the previous day and late for practice during the actual day, be sure to give the reasons separately for the two occasions, using the above-mentioned formula. If you had been away for longer periods, be sure to mention the exact period during which you were away.

- When entering the music room, enter through the front door. You may only enter through the back door when a practice session in going on.
- When replying, be loud, clear, and bright.
- Be sure to concentrate fully during practice.
- When you refer to yourself, use the first-person pronoun of "*watakushi*". [Note: In the guidebook, the character 私 was first written, then a pronunciation guide on top of the character showed that instead of pronouncing the usual "*watashi*", it should be read "watakushi"]
- When someone talks to you, listen with the right attitude, and look at the person.
- You must always button up your uniform in school. You must button up all buttons when wearing the winter uniform, and all but the top button when wearing the summer uniform.
- If you are absent, leave early or report late for a session, be sure to submit the official notification of absence/early leave/lateness with your parents' seal.
- If you are absent, leave early or report late for a session, be sure to notify the club president, the in-charge for attendance, and your section's leader.
- You must absolutely use honorific language to seniors, alumni, external instructors, and school teachers.
- Besides club teachers, be sure to greet also school teachers.

[Note: the rules concerning attendance/absence/lateness and politeness/*kotobazukai* and dress code, all reflect to a strikingly large extent the kind of etiquette companies and society hold dear. This highlights the main function of clubs in socialising students into the *jouge kankei* system early and preparing them to be competent adults.]
- If you want to enter the recording room and it is empty, be sure to enter with an accompanying person who is at least of senior high second grade.
- If you borrow keys to the music staffroom, recording cum store room, etc, be sure to return immediately after use and do not keep the keys.

On cleaning
- Tidy up your instruments, scores and music stands immediately after your practice. You will also hear the following from your seniors " . . . *(fun) made souji, madoakete*" (you have until . . . (timing in hour and minutes) to clean up, also open the windows). Upon hearing this, reply loudly with "*hai*", open all windows, and start cleaning.

- Once you finished cleaning, you will hear the following from your seniors "*madoshimete*" (close the windows). Upon hearing this, reply loudly with "hai", close all windows and curtains, tidy up your attire, and get ready for debriefing.

On debriefing
- If you are expected to be seated, sit on chairs, if you are expected to be standing, face the whiteboard and arrange yourselves according to descending orders of height from the right, put your hands at the back and make sure your attire is proper. If you have violated the attire rules (missing buttons and/or badge), go and report to the committee members. After this, when senior first graders shout out "*mokusou*" (meditate, contemplate), close your eyes.
- During debriefing, committee members, senior third graders, and alumni will say [honorific verb: *ossharu*] "*kyou wa doumo gokurousamadeshita*" (loose translation: it has been a hard day), be sure to reply with "*sausu*" and bow.
- When seniors talk during the debriefing, there will be occasions where your reply is needed, be sure to reply loudly.
- At the end, the club president will say [honorific verb: *ossharu*] "*kyou wa korede owarimasu*" (we shall call it a day here). If you are seated, open your eyes, and upon hearing the president's next words "*kyou wa doumo gokurousamadeshita*", reply with "*sausu*" and bow.

On annual training camps
- To build harmony: to strengthen vertical and horizontal relations – relations with seniors and those in the same grade.
- To improve personal playing skills: come to the training camp with goals, do not waste time during the camp and keep your focus.
- To pay attention to health management: take good care of your physical condition.
- To clearly distinguish proper etiquette: to achieve a level of politeness and display better manners than usual towards teachers in charge, parents, and external instructors.
- When you board the bus before departure, be sure to say loudly "*yoroshiku onegaishimasu*". When you alight, be sure to thank loudly "*arigatou gozaimashita*".
- When alumni arrive at the camp site, be sure to greet them loudly "*chiwa*" (truncated form of *konnichiwa* good morning), approach them and take

over their baggage while saying "*kawarimasu*" (I will take over), and guide them to their rooms.
- Be sure to arrange all indoor sandals neatly (not just those in your own room, but also those in the rooms of alumni, senior third graders, and committee members, as well as in front of toilets). Also, be sure to check them during breaks to make sure they are in order.
- Be swift in moving instruments and preparing for practice sessions.
- When you get up in the morning, the president will come [honorific verb: *irassharu*] in to your room. Before his arrival, be sure to sit properly. When he comes [honorific verb: *irassharu*] in, say "*ohayou gozaimasu*" (good morning) and bow. After this, be sure to listen to his instructions.
- When you enter the rooms of alumni, senior third graders, or the committee members, be sure to knock on the door first. Upon hearing a reply, enter and say "*shitsureishimasu*" (excuse me).
- If it is your turn to do kitchen duty, be sure to be present at the canteen 15 minutes prior to meal time.
- When you enter the canteen, be sure to greet "*ohayou gozaimasu*". When you leave after your meal, be sure to say "*gochisousamadeshita*" (loose translation: thank you for the feast).
- Be aware that you are expected to remain seated properly during debriefing sessions. Be sure to avoid wearing jeans or clothes that make you feel uncomfortable.
- At the end of debriefing, the president will say [honorific verb: *ossharu*] "*oyasuminasai*" (good night). Upon hearing this, reply "*oyasuminasai*" and bow.
- When lights are out, bear in mind that you have to be ready for the next day's practice, be sure to sleep immediately.
- During breaks, do not play around, rest.
- Be sure to bear in mind the goals of the annual training camp.
- Be sure to bear in mind that you should always be ready 10 minutes before the stipulated times.

Do not bring to the camp things not mentioned. If it should become necessary for you to bring such things, report to every member of the committee at least two to three days prior to the training camp and ask for their permission.

Appendix 3: On the Romanisation of Japanese

Throughout this work, I adopt the "modified Hepburn" system when transliterating Japanese into the Latin alphabet. For an overview of different systems of transliteration and their usage, refer to the article on "Japanese Romanization" prepared by the University of Hawai'i at Manoa Libraries at the following link: http://www.hawaii.edu/asiaref/japan/online/rom_hist.htm.

Under this system, long vowels are traditionally rendered with either a macron or with a circumflex accent. For example, ō or ô for long vowels of o + o or o + u. For convenience, I use long vowels (for example, oo for o+ o, and ou for o + u) in this book instead.

Appendix 4: Glossary of Japanese Terms

Bukatsudou	Extra-curricular club activities
Hanseikai	Debriefing session at the end of a club session
Jouge kankei	Higher-lower relations of hierarchy between superiors and subordinates
Kouhai	Subordinate in *jouge kankei*
Senpai	Superior in *jouge kankei*

Appendix 5: List of Standard Abbreviations used according to the Leipzig Glossing Rules

COND	Conditional
OBJ	Object
POSS	Possessive
PRF	Perfect
PRS	Present
Q	Question particle/marker
SBJ	Subject

References

Ackroyd, Stephen. 'Utopia or Ideology: Karl Mannheim and the Place of Theory'. *The Sociological Review* 50, no. 1_suppl (2002): 40–58.
Adger, Carolyn, and Laura Wright. 'Discourse in Educational Settings'. In *The Handbook of Discourse Analysis*, edited by Deborah Schiffrin, Deborah Tannen, and Heidi Hamilton, 503–17. Malden: Blackwell, 2005.
Agency for Cultural Affairs. '"Bunkachou 'Kokugo Ni Kansuru Yoronchousa' Ni Miru Keigo Ishiki" (Honorifics Consciousness as Seen from the Opinion Poll on the National Language)'. Tokyo: Agency for Cultural Affairs, 2005.
Agha, Asif. *Language and Social Relations*. Studies in the Social and Cultural Foundations of Language, no. 24. Cambridge; New York: Cambridge University Press, 2007.
Alcadipani, Rafael, Robert Westwood, and Alexandre Rosa. 'The Politics of Identity in Organizational Ethnographic Research: Ethnicity and Tropicalist Intrusions'. *Human Relations* 68, no. 1 (2014): 79–106.
Allan, Kenneth. *Contemporary Social and Sociological Theory: Visualizing Social Worlds*. Thousand Oaks, Calif: Pine Forge Press, 2006.
Andoh, Yoshinori. 'For the "Politics" of Body in Modern Japan: Focusing on the Clothes of Girls' Secondary Schools in the Meiji and Taisho Eras'. *The Journal of Educational Sociology* 60 (1997): 99–116.
Austin, J. L. *How to Do Things with Words*. 2d ed. The William James Lectures 1955. Oxford [Eng.]: Clarendon Press, 1975.
BAMF. 'School Uniform in Germany: Documentation of the Current Debate with Special Regard to Questions of Integration'. Federal Agency for Migration and Refugees (BAMF), 2006. https://www.bamf.de/SharedDocs/Anlagen/DE/Publikationen/WorkingPapers/wp07-einheitliche-schulkleidung.pdf?__blob=publicationFile.
Baur, Nina, Linda Hering, Anna Laura Raschke, and Cornelia Thierbach. 'Theory and Methods in Spatial Analysis: Towards Integrating Qualitative, Quantitative and Cartographic Approaches in the Social Sciences and Humanities', Vol.39: S.7. GESIS – Leibniz-Institut für Sozialwissenschaften, 2014. https://www.wiso-net.de/docPreview/primo/SOLI__9D93D49C90977EE336837D2B4EFDFD01?ZG_PORTAL=portal_exlibris.
Bayer, Klaus. 'Die Anredepronomina Du Und Sie: Thesen Zu Einem Semantischen Konflikt Im Hochschulbereich (Addressing Pronouns "Du" and "Sie": Theses on Semantics Conflicts in the Domain of Higher Education)'. *Deutsche Sprache* 3 (1979): 212–19.
Bayley, Robert, and Sandra R. Schecter, eds. *Language Socialization in Bilingual and Multilingual Societies: Edited by Robert Bayley and Sandra R. Schecter*. Bilingual Education and Bilingualism 39. Clevedon; Buffalo: Multilingual Matters, 2003.
BENESSE. 'Houkago No Seikatsu Jikan Chousa: Kodomotachi No Jikan No Tsukaikata (Ishiki to Jittai)" (Children's Time Management and Life after School: How Children Use Time (Consciousness and Actual Situation)'. Benesse Educational Research and Development Center, 2008. http://berd.benesse.jp/shotouchutou/research/detail1.php?id=3209.
Berger, Peter L., and Thomas Luckmann. *The Social Construction of Reality: A Treatise in the Sociology of Knowledge*. Harmondsworth: Penguin, 1966.
Bestor, Theodore C. *Neighborhood Tokyo*. Studies of the East Asian Institute. Stanford: Stanford Univ. Press, 1989.

Bhappu, Anita. 'The Japanese Family: An Institutional Logic for Japanese Corporate Networks and Japanese Management'. *The Academy of Management Review* 25, no. 2 (2000): 409–15.

Blackwood, Thomas. 'Homo Athleticus: The Educational Roles of Extracurricular Clubs in Japanese Schools'. In *Nonformal Education and Civil Society in Japan*, edited by Kaori Okano, 71–91. London: Routledge, 2016.

Blackwood, Thomas, and Douglas C. Friedman. 'Join the Club: Effects of Club Membership on Japanese High School Students' Self-Concept'. *Japan Forum* 27, no. 2 (3 April 2015): 257–75.

Blommaert, Jan. *Language Ideological Debates*. Berlin [u.a.]: Mouton de Gruyter, 1999.

Bourdieu, Pierre, and John Thompson. *Language and Symbolic Power*. Cambridge: Polity, 1991.

Brasor, Philip, and Tsubuku Masako. 'The Changing Values behind School Uniforms'. The Japan Times, 23 April 2016. http://www.japantimes.co.jp/news/2016/04/23/business/changing-values-behind-school-uniforms/#.WQiZXvnyi00.

Braun, Friederike. *Terms of Address: Problems of Patterns and Usage in Various Languages and Cultures*. Contributions to the Sociology of Language 50. Berlin: Mouton de Gruyter, 1988.

Breeze, Ruth. 'Critical Discourse Analysis and Its Critics'. *Pragmatics: Quarterly Publication of the International Pragmatics Association* 21, no. 4 (2011): 493–525.

Brown, Penelope, and Stephen C. Levinson. *Politeness: Some Universals in Language Usage*. Reissued with corretions, new Introduction and new bibliography. Cambridge: Cambridge University Press, 1987.

Brown, Roger, and Albert Gilman. 'The Pronouns of Power and Solidarity'. In *Style in Language*, edited by Thomas Sebeok, 253–76. Boston: MIT Press, 1960.

Burdelski, Matthew. 'Socializing Politeness Routines: Action, Other-Orientation, and Embodiment in a Japanese Preschool'. *Journal of Pragmatics* 42, no. 6 (June 2010): 1606–21.

Burdelski, Matthew. 'Socializing Children to Honorifics in Japanese: Identity and Stance in Interaction'. *Multilingua* 32, no. 2 (2013): 247–73.

Cave, Peter. '"Bukatsudō": The Educational Role of Japanese School Clubs'. *Journal of Japanese Studies* 30, no. 2 (2004): 383–415.

Cave, Peter. *Schooling Selves: Autonomy, Interdependence, and Reform in Japanese Junior High Education*. Chicago; London: University of Chicago Press, 2016.

Clyne, Michael G., Catrin Norrby, and Jane Warren. *Language and Human Relations: Styles of Address in Contemporary Language*. Cambridge, UK; New York: Cambridge University Press, 2009.

Coffey, Amanda. *The Ethnographic Self: Fieldwork and the Representation of Identity*. London; Thousand Oaks, Calif: SAGE Publications, 1999.

Collins, Randall. *Interaction Ritual Chains*. Princeton: Princeton University Press, 2005.

Comrie, Bernard. *Aspect: An Introduction to the Study of Verbal Aspect and Related Problems*. Cambridge: Cambridge University. Press, 1976.

Cook, Haruko Minegishi. 'Japanese Language Socialization: Indexing the Modes of Self'. *Discourse Processes* 22, no. 2 (September 1996): 171–97.

Cook, Haruko Minegishi. 'Situational Meanings of Japanese Social Deixis: The Mixed Use of the Masu and Plain Forms'. *Journal of Linguistic Anthropology* 8, no. 1 (1998): 87–110.

Cook, Haruko Minegishi. 'Language Socialization in Japanese Elementary Schools: Attentive Listening and Reaction Turns'. *Journal of Pragmatics* 31, no. 11 (November 1999): 1443–65.
Cook, Haruko Minegishi. 'Japanese Politeness as an Interactional Achievement: Academic Consultation Sessions in Japanese Universities'. *Multilingua: Journal of Cross-Cultural and Interlanguage Communication* 25, no. 3 (2006): 269–91.
Cook, Haruko Minegishi. 'Language Socialization in Japanese'. In *Language Socialization*, edited by Duff, Patricia A and Hornberger, Nancy H. Encyclopedia of Language and Education, 313–26. New York: Springer Science, 2008.
Cook, Haruko Minegishi. 'Are Honorifics Polite? Uses of Referent Honorifics in a Japanese Committee Meeting'. *Journal of Pragmatics* 43, no. 15 (2011): 3655–3672.
Cook, Haruko Minegishi. 'Socialization to Acting, Feeling, and Thinking as Shakaijin: New Employee Orientations in a Japanese Company'. In *Japanese at Work: Politeness, Power, and Personae in Japanese Workplace Discourse*, 37–64. London: Palgrave Macmillan, 2018.
Cook, Haruko Minegishi, and Janet S Shibamoto-Smith. *Japanese at Work: Politeness, Power, and Personae in Japanese Workplace Discourse*, 2018.
Dale, Karen, and Gibson Burrell. *The Spaces of Organisation and the Organisation of Space: Power, Identity and Materiality at Work*. Basingstoke: Palgrave Macmillan, 2008.
Davies, Charlotte Aull. *Reflexive Ethnography: A Guide to Researching Selves and Others*. London; New York: Routledge, 1999.
Deacon, Roger. 'An Analytics of Power Relations: Foucault on the History of Discipline'. *History of the Human Sciences* 15, no. 1 (February 2002): 89–117.
Dedoussis, Vagelis. 'Simply a Question of Cultural Barriers? The Search for New Perspectives in the Transfer of Japanese Management Practices'. *Journal of Management Studies* 32, no. 6 (November 1995): 731–45.
Deutsche Industrie- und Handelskammer in Japan. 'Educational System', 2017. http://japan.ahk.de/en/japan-info/customs-culture/education-system.
DeWalt, Kathleen Musante, and Billie R. DeWalt. *Participant Observation: A Guide for Fieldworkers*. Walnut Creek, CA: AltaMira Press, 2002.
Diefenbach, Thomas. *Hierarchy and Organisation: Toward a General Theory of Hierarchical Social Systems*. London: Routledge, 2013.
Dierkes, Julian. 'Privatschulen und privatwirtschaftliche Zusatzschulen in Japan: Bildungspolitische Lückenbüßer und Marktlücke (Private schools and additional schools organised as private industries: makeshifts and market gaps in education policy)'. *Zeitschrift für Pädagogik* 55, no. 5 (2009): 732–46.
Dijk, Teun A. van. *Ideology: A Multidisciplinary Approach*. London [u.a.]: Sage Publ, 1998.
Duff, Patricia A. 'An Ethnography of Communication in Immersion Classrooms in Hungary'. *TESOL Quarterly* 29, no. 3 (1995): 505.
Duff, Patricia A, and Hornberger, Nancy H, eds. 'Language Socialization in Japanese'. In *Language Socialization*, 313–26. New York: Springer, 2008.
Dunn, Cynthia Dickel. 'Formal Forms or Verbal Strategies? Politeness Theory and Japanese Business Etiquette Training'. *Journal of Pragmatics* 43, no. 15 (December 2011): 3643–54.
Dunn, Cynthia Dickel. 'Speaking Politely, Kindly, and Beautifully: Ideologies of Politeness in Japanese Business Etiquette Training'. *Multilingua* 32, no. 2 (18 January 2013): 225–45.
Duranti, Alessandro. 'Language in Context and Language as Context: The Samoan Respect Vocabulary'. In *Rethinking Context: Language as an Interactive Phenomenon*, edited by

Alessandro Duranti and Charles Goodwin, 79–99. Cambridge: Cambridge University Press, 1992.

Durkheim, Emile. *The Elementary Forms of the Religious Life: (K.E. Fields, Trans)*. New York: The Free Press, 1912.

Enyo, Yumiko. 'Exploring Senpai-Koohai Relationships in Club Meetings in a Japanese University'. University of Hawai'i at Manoa, 2013.

Enyo, Yumiko. 'Contexts and Meanings of Japanese Speech Styles: A Case of Hierarchical Identity Construction among Japanese College Students'. *Pragmatics* 25, no. 3 (2015): 345–67.

Ervin-Tripp, Susan M. *Language Acquisition and Communicative Choice*. Language Science and National Development. Stanford, Calif: Stanford University Press, 1973.

Fairclough, Norman. *Language and Power*. 2nd ed. Language in Social Life Series. New York: Longman, 1989.

Fairclough, Norman. *Analysing Discourse: Textual Analysis for Social Research*. London; New York: Routledge, 2003.

Firkola, Peter. 'Japanese Management Practices Past and Present'. *Economic Journal of Hokkaido University* 35 (2006): 115–30.

Freeden, Michael. *Ideology: A Very Short Introduction*. Oxford [u.a.]: Oxford UnivPress, 2003.

Fukada, Atsushi, and Noriko Asato. 'Universal Politeness Theory: Application to the Use of Japanese Honorifics'. *Journal of Pragmatics: An Interdisciplinary Journal of Language Studies* 36, no. 11 (2004): 1991–2002.

Fukuzawa, Rebecca Erwin, and Gerald K. LeTendre. *Intense Years: How Japanese Adolescents Balance School, Family, and Friends*. New York: Routledge Falmer Press, 2001.

Gee, James Paul. *An Introduction to Discourse Analysis: Theory and Method*. Fourth edition. New York: Routledge, 2014.

Geertz, Clifford. *The Interpretation of Cultures: Selected Essays*. New York: Basic Books, 1973.

Geyer, Naomi. 'Interpersonal Functions of Style Shift: The Use of Plain and Masu Forms in Faculty Meetings'. In *Style Shifting in Japanese*, edited by Jones Kimberley and Tsuyoshi Ono, 39–70. Amsterdam: John Benjamins Pub, 2008.

Gottlieb, Nanette. *Kanji Politics: Language Policy Oand Japanese Script*. Japanese Studies. London; New York: Distributed by Columbia University Press: Kegan Paul International; 1995, 1996.

Guardado, Martin. *Discourse, Ideology and Heritage Language Socialization: Micro and Macro Perspectives*. Contributions to the Sociology of Language Volume 104. Boston Berlin: De Gruyter Mouton, 2018.

Hall, Christopher J., Patrick H. Smith, and Rachel Wicaksono. *Mapping Applied Linguistics: A Guide for Students and Practitioners*. Milton Park, Abingdon, Oxon; New York, NY: Routledge, 2011.

Hall, Edward T. *The Silent Language*. New York: Anchor Books, 1973.

Hall, Stuart, Jessica Evans, and Sean Nixon, eds. *Representation: Cultural Representations and Signifying Practices*. London: SAGE, 1997.

Harris, Nigel. *Die Ideologien in der Gesellschaft: eine Untersuchung über Entstehung, Wesen und Wirkung (The ideologies in society: an examination on formation, nature, and effect)*. München: Beck, 1970.

Heath, Shirley Brice. *Ways with Words: Language, Life, and Work in Communities and Classrooms*. Cambridge [Cambridgeshire]; New York: Cambridge University Press, 1983.

Hebert, David G. *Wind Bands and Cultural Identity in Japanese Schools*. Dordrecht: Springer, 2012.
Heinrich, Patrick, and Galan, Christian, eds. *Being Young in Super-Aging Japan: Formative Events and Cultural Reactions, 1st Edition (Hardback)* – London: Routledge, 2018.
Held, Gudrun. 'Submission Strategies as an Expression of the Ideology of Politeness: Reflections on the Verbalisation of Social Power Relations'. *Pragmatics: Quarterly Publication of the International Pragmatics Association* 9, no. 1 (1999): 21–36.
Hendry, Joy. *Understanding Japanese Society*. 2nd ed. Nissan Institute/Routledge Japanese Studies Series. London; New York: Routledge, 1995.
Heritage, John. 'Conversation Analysis as Social Theory'. In *The New Blackwell Companion to Social Theory*, edited by Bryan Turner, 300–320. Oxford: Wiley-Blackwell, 2008.
Heritage, John. 'Language and Social Institutions: The Conversation Analytic View'. *Journal of Foreign Languages* 36, no. 4 (2013): 2–27.
Holtgraves, Thomas. 'Politeness'. In *The New Handbook of Language and Social Psychology*, edited by Peter Robinson and Howard Giles, 341–55. Chichester: J. Wiley, 2001.
Hudson, Mitsuko Endo. 'Riyuu "Reason" for Nai Desu and Other Semi-Polite Forms'. In *Style Shifting in Japanese*, edited by Kimberly Jones and Tsuyoshi Ono, 131–59. Amsterdam: John Benjamins Publishing Company, 2008.
Hudson, Mutsuko Endo. 'Student Honorifics Usage in Conversations with Professors'. *Journal of Pragmatics: An Interdisciplinary Journal of Language Studies* 43, no. 15 (2011): 3689–3706.
Ide, Sachiko. 'Japanese Sociolinguistics: Politeness and Women's Language'. *Lingua: International Review of General Linguistics* 57, no. 2–4 (1982): 357–85.
Ide, Sachiko. 'Sociolinguistics: Honorifics and Gender Differences'. In *The Handbook of Japanese Linguistics*, edited by Natsuko Tsujimura, 444–80. Malden: Blackwell Publishers, 1999.
Inoue, Fumio. *Nihongo Wocchingu: Japanese Language Watching*. Tokyo: Iwanami Shoten, 1998.
Iwama, Hiroshi. 'Japan's Group Orientation in Secondary Schools'. In *Japanese Schooling: Patterns of Socialization, Equality, and Political Control*, edited by James Shields, 73–84. Pennsylvania: The Pennsylvania State University Press, 1995.
Jørgensen, Marianne, and Louise Phillips. *Discourse Analysis as Theory and Method*. London; Thousand Oaks, Calif: Sage Publications, 2002.
Keating, Elizabeth. 'Moments of Hierarchy: Constructing Social Stratification by Means of Language, Food, Space, and the Body in Pohnpei, Micronesia'. *American Anthropologist* 102, no. 2 (2000): 303–320.
Keller, Reiner. 'The Sociology of Knowledge Approach to Discourse (SKAD)'. *Human Studies: A Journal for Philosophy and the Social Sciences* 34, no. 1 (2011): 43–65.
Keltner, Dacher, Deborah H. Gruenfeld, and Cameron Anderson. 'Power, Approach, and Inhibition'. *Psychological Review* 110, no. 2 (April 2003): 265–84.
Kevenhörster, Paul, Werner Pascha, and Karen Shire, eds. *Japan: Wirtschaft – Gesellschaft – Politik*. 2., aktualisierte Aufl. Wiesbaden: VS, Verl. für Sozialwiss, 2010.
Kienpointner, Manfred. 'Ideologies of Politeness: Foreword'. *Pragmatics, Pragmatics. Quarterly Publication of the International Pragmatics Association (IPrA)* 9, no. 1 (1999): 1–4.
Kumaravadivelu, B. 'Critical Classroom Discourse Analysis'. *TESOL Quarterly* 33, no. 3 (1999): 453–84.
Lee-Cunin, Marina. *Student Views in Japan: A Study of Japanese Students' Perceptions of Their First Years at University*. Rochdale: Fieldwork, 2004.

Leech, Geoffrey. 'The Distribution and Function of Vocatives in American and British Conversation'. In *Out of Corpora: Studies in Honour of Stig Johansson*, edited by Johansson Stig, Hilde Hasselggard, and Signe Oksefjell, 107–18. Amsterdam: Rodopi, 1999.
Lefebvre, Henri. *The Production of Space*. Oxford, UK [u.a.]: Blackwell, 1991.
LeTendre, Gerald K. *Learning to Be Adolescent: Growing up in U.S. and Japanese Middle Schools*. New Haven: Yale University Press, 2000.
Levinson, Stephen. 'Pragmatics and Social Deixis: Reclaiming the Notion of Conventional Implicature'. *Proceedings of the Fifth Annual Meeting of the Berkeley Linguistics Society*, 1979, 206–23.
Liebscher, Grit, and Jennifer Dailey-O'Cain. *Language, Space and Identity in Migration*. Houndmills, Basingstoke, Hampshire; New York: Palgrave Macmillan, 2013.
Light, Richard. 'Learning Masculinities in a Japanese High School Rugby Club'. *Sport, Education and Society* 13, no. 2 (1 May 2008): 163–79.
Lukes, Steven. *Power: A Radical View*. 2. ed. Basingstoke [u.a.]: Palgrave Macmillan, 2004.
Macgilchrist, Felicitas, and Tom Van Hout. 'Ethnographic Discourse Analysis and Social Science'. *Forum Qualitative Sozialforschung / Forum: Qualitative Social Research* 12, no. 1 (30 January 2011).
Magee, Joe C., and Adam D. Galinsky. 'Social Hierarchy: The Self-Reinforcing Nature of Power and Status'. *Academy of Management Annals* 2, no. 1 (1 January 2008): 351–98.
Mannheim, Karl. *Ideology and Utopia: An Introduction to the Sociology of Knowledge*. New ed. London [u.a.]: Routledge, 1991.
Manzenreiter, Wolfram. 'No Pain, No Gain: Embodied Masculinities and Lifestyle Sport in Japan'. *Journal of the German Institute for Japanese Studies Tokyo* 25, no. 2 (2013): 215–236.
Martin, Samuel E. *A Reference Grammar of Japanese*. Honolulu: University of Hawai'i Press, 1964.
Matsumoto, Yoshiko. 'Reexamination of the Universality of Face: Politeness Phenomena in Japanese'. *JPrag* 12, no. 4 (1988): 403–26.
McDonald, Brent, and Chris Hallinan. 'Seishin Habitus: Spiritual Capital and Japanese Rowing'. *International Review for the Sociology of Sport* 40, no. 2 (2005): 187–200.
McVeigh, Brian. 'Aisatsu: Ritualized Politeness as Sociopolitical and Economic Management in Japan'. In *Exploring Japaneseness: On Japanese Enactments of Culture and Consciousness*, edited by Ray Donahue, 121–36. Westport: Ablex, 2002.
Meek, Christopher B. 'The Dark Side of Japanese Management in the 1990s: Karoshi and Ijime in the Japanese Workplace'. *Journal of Managerial Psychology* 19, no. 3 (2004): 312–31.
Mendenhall, Mark E., and Gary Oddou. 'The Cognitive, Psychological and Social Contexts of Japanese Management'. *Asia Pacific Journal of Management* 4, no. 1 (1 September 1986): 24–37.
Meyer, Heinz-Dieter, and Brian Rowan, eds. *The New Institutionalism in Education*. Albany: State University of New York Press, 2006.
Ministry of Education, Culture, Sports, Science and Technology (MEXT). '"Chuugakkou Gakushuu Shidou Youryou" (Curriculum Guidelines for Junior High Schools)', 2008. http://www.mext.go.jp/a_menu/shotou/new-cs/youryou/chu/.
Miwa, Masashi. *Ninshoushi to Keigo: Gengo Rinrigakuteki Kousatsu (Personal Pronouns and Honorific Language: A Language Ethics Study)*. Kyoto: Jinbun Shoin, 2000.
Morita, Emi. 'Children's Use of Address and Reference Terms: Language Socialization in a Japanese-English Bilingual Environment'. *Multilingua: Journal of Cross-Cultural and Interlanguage Communication* 22, no. 4 (2003): 367–95.

Mühlhäusler, Peter, and Rom Harré. *Pronouns and People: The Linguistic Construction of Social and Personal Identity*. Language in Society. Cambridge, Mass., USA: B. Blackwell, 1990.
Nakane, Chie. *Japanese Society*. Berkeley, Calif.: Univ. of California Press, 1970.
Nakane, Chie. 'Review Work(s): Japanese Society by Chie Nakane'. *Current Anthropology* 13, no. 5 (1972): 575–82.
Niedzielski, Nancy A., and Dennis R. Preston. *Folk Linguistics*. [Paperback ed.]. Berlin [u.a.]: Mouton de Gruyter, 2003.
NINJAL. 'Honorifics in Japanese Schools I: Results from Questionnaires'. Tokyo: National Institute for Japanese Language and Linguistics (NINJAL), 2002.
Nishiyama, Kazuo. 'Interpersonal Persuasion in a Vertical Society-the Case of Japan'. *Speech Monographs* 38, no. 2 (2009): 148–54.
Niyekawa, Agnes M. *Minimum Essential Politeness: A Guide to the Japanese Honorific Language*. 1. ed., 1. [Dr.]. Tokyo [u.a.]: Kodansha Internat, 1991.
Norbeck, Edward, and Harumi Befu. 'Informal Fictive Kinship in Japan'. *American Anthropologist* 60, no. 1 (1958): 102–17.
Ochs, Elinor. *Culture and Language Development: Language Acquisition and Language Socialization in a Samoan Village*. Studies in the Social and Cultural Foundations of Language, no. 6. Cambridge; New York: Cambridge University Press, 1988.
Ochs, Elinor, and Carolyn Taylor. 'The "Father Knows Best" Dynamic in Dinnertime Narratives'. In *Linguistic Anthropology*, edited by Alessandro Duranti, 435–51. Oxford: Wiley-Blackwell, 1995.
OECD. 'PISA Country Report for Japan'. Organization for Economic Cooperation and Development (OECD), 2015. http://www.compareyourcountry.org/pisa/country/jpn?lg=en.
Ommen, Mattias van. 'Extracurricular Paths into Job Markets in Contemporary Japan: The Way of Both Pen and Soccer Ball'. *Japanese Studies* 35, no. 1 (2 January 2015): 85–102.
Ono, Yuta, and Ichiko Shoji. 'Senior-Junior (Senpai-Kohai) Relationships in Secondary School Activities'. *Japanese Journal of Educational Psychology* 63, no. 4 (2015): 438–52.
Pennycook, A. 'Incommensurable Discourses?' *Applied Linguistics* 15, no. 2 (1 June 1994): 115–38.
Perez-Agote, Jose Maria. 'Los retos del proceso de socialización en los sistemas educativos de las sociedades modernas avanzadas | Política y Sociedad (The challenges of the socialization function of school in advanced societies)'. *Politica y Sociedad* 47, no. 2 (2010): 27–45.
Pizziconi, Barbara. 'Honorifics: The Cultural Specificity of a Universal Mechanism in Japanese'. In *Politeness in East Asia*, edited by Daniel Z. Kadar and Sara Mills, 45–70. Cambridge: Cambridge University Press, 2011.
Reisigl, Martin. 'Critical Discourse Analysis'. In *The Oxford Handbook of Sociolinguistics*, edited by Bayley, Robert, Cameron, Richard, and Lucas, Ceil, 67–90. Oxford: Oxford University Press, 2013.
Roberts, Andrew. *Hitler and Churchill: Secrets of Leadership*. London: Weidenfeld & Nicolson, 2003.
Roberts, Celia. 'Language Socialization in the Workplace'. *Annual Review of Applied Linguistics* 30 (March 2010): 211–27.
Rogers, Rebecca, ed. *An Introduction to Critical Discourse Analysis in Education*. Second Edition. New York: Routledge, Taylor & Francis Group, 2011.
Rohlen, Thomas P. *Japan's High Schools*. Berkeley: University of California Press, 1983.

Schieffelin, Bambi B. *The Give and Take of Everyday Life: Language Socialization of Kaluli Children*. Studies in the Social and Cultural Foundations of Language, no. 9. Cambridge; New York: Cambridge University Press, 1990.

Schieffelin, Bambi, Ochs, Elinor. 'Language Socialization'. *Annual Review of Anthropology*, no. 15 (1986): 163–91.

Searle, John R. *Making the Social World: The Structure of Human Civilization*. Oxford [u.a.]: Oxford UnivPress, 2010.

Shibamoto-Smith, Janet, and Haruko Cook. 'Negotiating Linguistic Politeness in Japanese Interaction: A Critical Examination of Honorifics [Special Section]'. *Journal of Pragmatics: An Interdisciplinary Journal of Language Studies* 43, no. 15 (2011): 3639–42.

Shire, Karen A. 'Socialization and Work in Japan: The Meaning of Adulthood of Men and Women in a Business Context'. *International Journal of Japanese Sociology* 8, no. 1 (November 1999): 77–92.

Spradley, James P. *Participant Observation*. New York: Holt, Rinehart and Winston, 1980.

Sturtzsreetharan, Cindi. 'Ore and Omae: Japanese Men's Uses of First- and Second-Person Pronouns'. *Pragmatics* 19, no. 2 (2009): 253–278.

Sugimoto, Yoshio. *An Introduction to Japanese Society*. 3. ed. Cambridge: Cambridge Univ. Press, 2010.

Sugimoto, Yoshino. 'Japanese Society: Inside out and Outside In'. *International Sociology* 29, no. 3 (1 May 2014): 191–208.

Tanioka, Ichiro, and Daniel Glaser. 'School Uniforms, Routine Activities, and the Social Control of Delinquency in Japan'. *Youth & Society* 23, no. 1 (1991): 50–75.

Turner, Bryan S, ed. 'Conversation Analysis as Social Theory'. In *The New Blackwell Companion to Social Theory*. Oxford: Wiley-Blackwell, 2008.

Turner, John C. 'Explaining the Nature of Power: A Three-process Theory'. *European Journal of Social Psychology* 35, no. 1 (2005): 1–22.

Watts, Richard. 'Linguistic Politeness and Politic Verbal Behaviour: Reconsidering Claims for Universality'. In *Politeness in Language*, edited by Richard Watts, Sachiko Ide, and Konrad Ehlich, 43–70. Berlin/New York: De Gruyter Mouton, 2005.

Webb, Jen, Tony Schirato, and Geoff Danaher. *Understanding Bourdieu*. London; Thousand Oaks, Calif.: SAGE Publications, 2002. http://public.eblib.com/choice/publicfullrecord.aspx?p=689552.

Wetzel, Patricia J., and Miyako Inoue. 'Vernacular Theories of Japanese Honorifics'. *The Journal of the Association of Teachers of Japanese* 33, no. 1 (1999): 68–101.

White, Merry Isaacs. 'Taking Note of Teen Culture in Japan: Dear Diary, Dear Fieldworker'. In *Doing Fieldwork in Japan*, edited by Theodore C. Bestor, Patricia Steinhoff, and Victoria Lyon-Bestor, 21–35. Honolulu: University of Hawai'i Press, 2003.

Woolard, Kathryn. 'Language Ideology: Issues and Approaches'. *Pragmatics* 2, no. 3 (1992): 235–249.

World Bank. 'Human Capital Index 2018'. World Bank, 2018. http://www.worldbank.org/en/publication/human-capital.

World Economic Forum. 'Global Gender Gap Report 2020'. Cologny/Geneva: World Economic Forum, 2020.

Zhang, Zhongyuan, and Andre Spicer. '"Leader, You First": The Everyday Production of Hierarchical Space in a Chinese Bureaucracy'. *Human Relations* 67, no. 6 (2014): 739–762.

Index

Agency for Cultural Affairs 37, 42, 93, 148
Aisatsu 65, 66, 68, 69, 113, 158, 182, 191

Bukatsudou 8, 12–14, 17, 18, 21, 27, 29–31, 34, 36, 42, 55, 60, 71, 72, 85, 102, 123, 151, 153, 173, 176–180, 183–185, 187, 201
–musical groups 43, 44

Common-sense knowledge 16, 77, 80, 108, 112, 113, 116, 117, 137, 175
Critical discourse analysis 15, 113, 116, 138
–two-pronged approach 16

Ethnography 9, 18, 19, 22, 43
–participant observation 12, 20, 21–23, 25, 27, 54, 82, 93, 139, 145, 149, 177
–reflexive 22, 25, 26
–researcher identity 22, 23, 25
Etiquette 1, 6, 19, 27, 36, 38, 43, 64, 65, 71, 73, 79, 126, 131, 145, 179, 182, 183, 186, 192, 195, 196
–books 27
–guidance sessions 69–72, 79, 84, 116, 164
–guide 64
–training 183

Gender 25, 26, 34, 94, 101, 102, 137, 176, 177, 184, 186

Hierarchy 2–5, 8, 10, 12, 13, 15, 16, 19, 20, 26–30, 34, 39, 44, 48, 49, 51, 52, 55, 57, 60–65, 69–71, 73, 78, 81, 83–85, 88, 92–94, 98, 100, 102, 103, 105, 108, 109, 113, 114, 116, 118, 122, 127, 134, 139, 143, 145, 149, 151, 153, 154, 159, 162–165, 167, 169–171, 173, 174, 176–180, 184, 186, 187, 191, 201
–enduring nature 4, 28, 94, 173, 184
–seniority-based 3, 8, 29, 30, 33, 72, 74, 84, 99, 187

Kotobazukai 36, 65, 68, 69, 81, 124, 149, 162, 171, 180, 182

Language-ideology-power nexus 108, 111, 114, 116, 117, 122, 137, 138, 140, 147
Language socialisation 2, 5, 9–13, 18, 28–30, 32–34, 38, 39, 43, 45, 55, 60, 61, 72, 139, 164, 173, 175, 178–181, 183, 184, 186

MEXT (Ministry of Education, Culture, Sports, Sciences and Technology) 38, 39, 189
–curriculum guidelines 31, 38, 39, 162, 189

Paralinguistic features 15, 16, 20
Power 7, 12, 18, 20, 51, 53, 73, 81, 87, 89, 90, 93, 108, 111, 113–116, 118, 120–122, 127, 132–134, 137–140, 147, 149, 152, 153, 163, 171, 175, 177, 178, 180, 185
–abuse of 185
–behind discourse 111, 117
–epistemic order 17, 140, 142, 143, 145, 146
–in discourse 111, 117, 138
–semantic 87, 89, 97, 111, 116

School uniform 28, 151, 164, 165, 167, 169
–colour codes 167–169, 171
Secondary education 12, 24, 29, 32, 36, 55
–adolescents 10, 12, 26, 30, 34, 48, 137, 164, 184
Secondary educational 11, 31
Social constructionism 18, 60, 122
Social institution 25, 63, 70, 84, 90, 114, 117
Sociology of knowledge 14–16, 164
–legitimisation 15, 78
Supervision 55, 62, 63, 157, 178, 185
–reprimand 61, 80, 84, 164, 185
–reprimanded 67, 78, 82, 106, 174, 175
–reprimanding 20, 27, 80, 81